how to survive
and prosper as
an artist

Dear Ve,
I hope this book
is helpful; I find it
quite valuable.
It is great sharing
the world of ART with you.
God bless us as we
strive to be the best
we can be.
With Love
S Sierra W

July 1994

how to survive and prosper as an artist

Third Edition

Selling Yourself Without
Selling Your Soul

. . .

caroll michels

An Owl Book
Henry Holt and Company • New York

Published by Henry Holt and Company, Inc.,
115 West 18th Street, New York, New York 10011.
Published in Canada by Fitzhenry & Whiteside Limited,
91 Granton Drive, Richmond Hill, Ontario L4B 2N5.

Library of Congress Cataloging-in-Publication Data
Michels, Caroll.
How to survive and prosper as an artist :
selling yourself without selling your soul / Caroll Michels.—3rd ed.
p.   cm.
"An Owl book."
Includes bibliographical references and index.
1. Art—United States—Vocational guidance.   2. Art—United
States—Marketing.   I. Title.
N6505.M46   1992   91-43638
706'.8—dc20   CIP
ISBN 0-8050-1953-7 (An Owl Book: pbk.)

Henry Holt books are available at special discounts
for bulk purchases for sales promotions, premiums,
fund-raising, or educational use. Special editions
or book excerpts can also be created to specification.
For details contact:
Special Sales Director, Henry Holt and Company, Inc.,
115 West 18th Street, New York, New York 10011.

Third Edition—1992

Designed by Paula R. Szafranski

Printed in the United States of America
Recognizing the importance of preserving the written word,
Henry Holt and Company, Inc., by policy, prints all of its
first editions on acid free paper. ∞

1   3   5   7   9   10   8   6   4   2

This book is dedicated to the memory of Marlene Finney.

Contents

Acknowledgments

A very special thanks to the Alden B. Dow Creativity Center, Midland, Michigan, for providing an opportunity to research and prepare material for this new edition under the most ideal circumstances.

Preface to the New Edition

T he new edition of this book includes expanded information, many new topics, and new chapters. For example, a new chapter entitled "Presentation Tools and Packages" has been added; it contains suggestions for preparing visually effective and cost-effective alternatives to traditional slide packages. It also provides examples of artist statements, a guide to writing cover letters, and ideas for streamlining arts-related paperwork. Also added is a chapter entitled "Pricing Your Work: How Much Is It Worth?" In addition to discussing the general issue of pricing, it covers gallery discounts and studio sales.

The chapter "Exhibition and Sales Opportunities: Using Those That Exist and Creating Your Own" contains expanded information on the corporate market and public art programs, as well as a new section on making national and international connections. And "Dealing with Dealers and Psyching Them Out" provides many new insights into the art world.

The Appendix of Resources has been completely revamped and includes more than 450 new entries, including such new categories as "Artists' Housing," "Artwork Care and Maintenance," "Disabled Artists," "International Connections," "Organizing Paperwork," "Prints and Printmaking," and "Public Relations/Press Relations."

Introduction

In 1978 I began counseling visual and performing artists and writers on career management and development. I set up my own business and called myself an "artists' consultant."

Ranging in age from twenty-one to more than seventy, my clients have included painters; sculptors; graphic artists; poets; playwrights; novelists; cartoonists; journalists; photographers; craft artists; theater and film directors; film and video artists; performing artists; choreographers; dancers; classical, jazz, and pop musicians and composers; and opera singers. They have included well-known artists, unknown artists, emerging artists, midlife career changers, artists fresh out of schoool, and college dropouts. My clients have also included groups of artists, artist couples, arts administrators, curators, gallery dealers, art consultants, critics, arts service organizations, and theater and dance companies. I have assisted a rabbi, a retired executive of Macy's department store, a retired host of a television variety show, a gossip columnist, ex-offenders, corporate executives, architects, psychologists, lawyers, and editors.

Although the majority of my clients live in the New York City area, I have helped artists nationwide, as well as some living in Canada and in Europe.

I have advised and assisted artists in developing such basic career tools as résumés; exhibition, performance, and employment contacts and opportunities; grant applications; proposals; public relations and publicity; fund-raising; and presentations. I have also counseled on complex and seemingly less tangible career problems such as developing and focusing on goals; handling rejection as well as success; cultivating and maintaining art dealer, curator, and critic relationships; and learning to see oneself in relation to the world at large and as a participant in the specific world of art and its various components.

However, the most significant aspect of my work is helping artists find self-motivation and the ability to take control of their careers.

Calling myself an artists' consultant and "hanging out a shingle" was not an easy task. For valid and comprehensible reasons, deep-rooted skepticism is intrinsic to all arts communities. Initially, it was difficult to reach artists and convince them that what I had to say and offer was worthwhile.

I jumped this major hurdle when a writer from the *Village Voice* wrote an article about me and why my services were needed and necessary. It was only one journalist's opinion, but the endorsement was set in type, and I was deemed legitimate!

Literally an hour after the *Voice* article hit the newsstands my life changed drastically. I was swamped with phone calls from artists eager to set up appointments.

Nevertheless, after fourteen years of counseling artists, I still find it is not uncommon to be questioned about why I am qualified to give artists advice. Some of my specific accomplishments are sprinkled throughout this book, cited to make or emphasize a point or convey an experience. I've always been proud that I have been able to live solely off my earnings as an artist. I have exhibited at museums and cultural institutions throughout the United States and in Europe. I have a solid track record for winning grants and corporate contributions. I developed and implemented all of my own public relations and publicity. And I have been regularly published in newspapers and periodicals.

Managing my own career was something that *no one person* taught me. I learned from several individuals, positive and negative encounters, trial-and-error experiences, and personal intuition. This book contains information and advice derived from these experiences and encounters, as well as those of my clients. I've attempted to offer perceptions, observations, and advice that would have been invaluable to me when I first started to make a career as an artist.

What artists need most is objective advice, but what they usually receive is reinforcement of a myth of what it is like to be an artist. All too often artists are characterized as underdogs, and accordingly this image is reinforced throughout their careers. I can't promise that all of my advice is objective, since my personal experiences come into play, but the incentive to write this book came from realizing how much underdog philosophy was being published under the guise of "nuts and bolts" career management. Much of the reading material flatly states that the way the art world operates will always remain the same and it is naive to try to change it. Other publications are more subtle, but the tone is patronizing: "Yes, artists, you might be creative, talented, and have a lot to give to the world, but there are 'others' who *really* know what is going on, *others who know best.*"

This book addresses artists' roles in advancing and bettering their lot, taking control of their careers, learning to market their work, learning to exercise self-motivation, and approaching and managing their careers as other professionals deal with theirs. In other words, artists should apply many of the same techniques that other self-employed professionals use to make their careers work.

You will rarely find the word *talent* used in the forthcoming pages. The belief that an artist has talent is a subjective judgment, and there is no guarantee that a talented artist will be successful or that a successful artist is talented. When I use the words *success* and *successful* I am referring to the relative level of achievement within a specific category, not the inherent talent of an artist.

Measuring my success as an artists' consultant is very similar to measuring my success as an artist. In both professions I have achieved immediate success, long-range success, and no success. I have received direct feedback, indirect feedback, and no feedback. I have felt successful in my work when my clients have followed up and used the leads, information, and advice that has enabled some of them to win grants from foundations and government agencies, fellowships to artist-in-residence programs in the United States and abroad, and invitations to exhibit and perform. Clients have received press coverage and have had their work published. In some instances I have been successful in providing information and advice that was put to immediate use, and in other cases it has taken up to four years to see any new development.

Although many of the examples and anecdotes I use to illustrate or make a point involve visual artists, performing artists and writers will also be able to identify with many of the situations. All artists in all disciplines will get something out of this book.

This book will not provide all of the answers an artist is seeking, nor does it contain everything an artist needs to know about the art world. However, it fills in the gaps that have been omitted, overlooked, or ignored in other publications; it elaborates on subjects that have been inadequately covered and challenges some basic notions about what being an artist is all about. It contains advice, opinions, and impressions that will not be particularly palatable to members of the art world—*including artists*, the media, funding agencies, patrons, art dealers, administrators, curators, and critics—because it also explores the ills and injustices of the art world and sheds some light on who is to blame.

The art world is in dire need of reforms and structural changes. These changes will not happen overnight, but they *will* happen if more and more artists take control of their careers, reject the image of artists as sufferers, and refrain from practicing a dog-eat-dog philosophy when it comes to competing with other artists.

Some time ago I gave this same lecture to a client who has been seeing me since I began counseling artists. He had been represented by a dealer for more than three years, during which time his work substantially increased in sales and in value.

From the beginning of their relationship, much against my judgment, the artist refused to have a written contract with the dealer drawn up. However, the artist accepted and acted upon my advice to learn to market his work, independent of the annual one-person show he received at the gallery. Eventually, he became highly skilled in initiating new contacts and following up on old ones. Both initiatives resulted in many sales.

When the dealer saw what was happening, she added some new stipulations to their oral agreement, which originally set forth a specified commission on all work sold through the gallery. She began charging "special commissions" for special circumstances, circumstances in which she was not directly involved either in initiating a sale or in doing the legwork or paperwork to make it happen. The artist, who was afraid to challenge the dealer because he felt that it would jeopardize their relationship, acceded to her demands.

I pointed out to the artist that, apart from money, a principle was at stake, and that each time an artist compromises a principle, his or her career and the status of artists in general, now and in the future, are set back another notch.

I advised the artist to confront the dealer with a proposal that was more equitable. If the artist must give the dealer a commission on every work sold, even if the sale did not originate with the gallery, the dealer should give the artist something in return, such as a monthly advance against future sales. I pointed out that if the artist had a written contract, chances are the dealer would never have tried to impose an arbitrary commission formula. I also pointed out that the artist had adequately proved his market value and selling power to the dealer, who was deriving steady revenue from the sale of the artist's work, a situation that the dealer would not want to give up easily. *It had not occurred to the artist that he had bargaining power.*

Such occurrences are common in the art world—unnecessary dilemmas and frustrations created by middlepeople who have usurped power from artists and by artists who allow their power to be usurped.

Artists, by the fact they are artists, have power. *Artists provide thousands of nonartists with jobs!* Examples of nonartists who depend on artists for jobs include dealers; gallery staffs; curators; museum staffs; arts administrators; critics and journalists; corporate art consultants and advisors; federal, state, and municipal employees; teachers; framers; accountants; lawyers; and art suppliers.

Yet more nonartists than artists make a living from art, and nonartists make *more* money from art than artists! This inequity exists, as do many others, because artists, the "employers," individually and collectively have not yet recognized their power.

Another problem among artists is a diffusion of power. Although there are more artists than ever before, as the community of artists multiplies it simultaneously divides into different factions, movements, self-interest groups, and trends. There are artists who segregate themselves into pockets of racial, sexual, and ethnic identity. Everyone is vying for the same bone; no one wants to share it.

On the other hand, some aspects of the artistic community are in good shape and are getting better all the time, particularly the headway that has been made in art law, legislation, artists' rights, the opening up of more exhibition and performance opportunities, and the proliferation of general and specialized periodicals, publications, and newsletters on subjects of interest and importance to artists and their careers.

If I didn't believe that there is a lot of room in the art world for many artists to make a decent living, I certainly never would have started a consulting service or written a book about art-career management. There is ample opportunity for artists, even within the still imperfect art world.

The structural changes in the art world will come about only through artist pressure, artist initiative, and artist participation. While the prospects of radically changing the art world might seem overwhelming to any one artist, one of the most important contributions that any artist can make is to *restructure and take control of his or her own career.* The following chapters will elaborate on why this is important and provide options, suggestions, and advice on how to make it happen.

The addresses of organizations, programs, and publications mentioned in the text are listed in the Appendix of Resources at the back of the book. I have also included my address in the Appendix section "Career Management, Business, and Marketing" in response to the numerous readers who complained that they had a difficult time contacting me, and for future readers who might need some help and advice.

how to survive and prosper as an artist

1

Launching or Relaunching Your Career

If you walk, just walk, if you sit, just sit, but
whatever you do, don't wobble.

—*Zen Master Unmon*

Overcoming Career Blocks

As an artist you have experienced the exuberance of creating something you like, which might be the culmination of a direction in your work or might articulate something new. It felt good. The goodness screamed out. You mastered and controlled. The power felt good. Your expectations were rewarded.

However, producing something you like and believe in does not resolve the question of how to use your creation to survive and prosper. For artists, the question is particularly complex because of the difference between survival and prosperity as defined by artists and those in other professions. For an artist, *survival* often means bare-bones existence; *prosperity* may be keeping your head above water. In other professions, *survival* is keeping your head above water; *prosperity* is success.

Being an artist means believing you are an artist; making a living as an artist requires mastering many of the skills and professional attitudes shared by successful self-employed persons engaged in other occupations. Equally important, it is necessary to overcome the career blocks that are particular and indigenous to the fine arts field.

Rejecting the Myth of the Artist

Over many years our society has created a myth about what it means to be an artist. Perpetuated consciously and subconsciously by artists and nonartists, this myth is based on trading off many of the things that other people value for the right to be an artist.

For example, the myth tells us that struggle, complexity, and suffering are necessary components of creativity, and without these key elements an artist will stagnate. The myth tells us that the desire for comfortable lives and financial success will ultimately poison and distort art, that a true artist is concerned *only* with art and anyone else is a dilettante. The myth tells us that *real* artists do not discover themselves. Other people do, preferably when the artist is dead!

The myth warns us about *selling out*, although the majority of artists who are concerned about this issue are not in a position to sell out, nor are they quite sure what it means.

The myth says that artists are expected to be flamboyant, provocative, moody, weird, or antisocial. Writer and social critic Tom Wolfe suggests that this stereotyped image of the artist was formed in the nineteenth century, based on the style and behavior of writer and art critic Théophile Gautier. Wolfe writes:

> With Gautier's own red vests, black scarves, crazy hats, outrageous pronouncements, huge thirsts, and ravenous groin . . . the modern picture of The Artist began to form: the poor but free spirit, plebeian but aspiring only to be classless, to cut himself forever free from the bonds of the greedy and hypocritical bourgeoisie, to be whatever the fat burghers feared most, to cross the line wherever they drew it, to look at the world in a way they couldn't see, to be high, live low, stay young forever—in short, to be the bohemian.[1]

Many of the basic problems of artists trying to enter the art world and sustain a career there are created by their own low self-esteem and feelings of helplessness. There is a direct correlation between how artists see themselves and where art-world power is currently centered. For example, the term *stable of artists* is commonly and casually used by both artists and dealers alike. It refers to the artists who are represented by a gallery, but it implies much more, and, unfortunately, as a metaphor it works well. It suggests that artists are like herds of animals that need to be contained in an environment where their master can control their lives.

Artists for a Better Image, better known as the ArtFBI, is a not-for-profit organization concerned with the stereotypes of artists in contemporary society. As a national information-gathering and advocacy group, the ArtFBI collects and monitors examples of stereotypes of artists as portrayed in literature and in the media. The organization has compiled a videotape of artist stereotyping, entitled *TV Bloopers and Practical Jokes: Media Representations of Artists*, extracted from popular television shows. The address of the ArtFBI is listed in the Appendix section "Arts Legislation and Artists' Advocacy."

Perceiving "Fine Artist" as a Valid Profession

In our society, there is a myth that suggests that to be antibourgeois, a free spirit, and classless, one should not have an occupation. The myth implies that being an artist is a state of mind, and casts great doubts on whether being an artist is a valid profession.

Seeds of doubt suggesting that fine art is not a valid occupation are planted and reinforced, for example, by educators who, under the guise of providing career advice, emphasize *alternatives to fine art* and steer students into applied arts fields. Medical and fashion illustration, set design, graphic design, industrial design, and commercial photography are viewed as viable alternatives to painting, sculpture, and fine art photography. Students in art school are encouraged to take a lot of education courses to have something to fall back on. If we were educated to believe that being a fine artist is a valid profession, there would be fewer artists needing an occupational backup. Has a law student ever been advised to take a lot of education courses to have something to fall back on?

Even a book offering career advice to fine artists warns, "It is unrealistic, wishful thinking on the part of any fine artist to believe that he is going to earn his living by works of art. Should it happen in the course of time, it would be a great bonanza—but don't count on it."[2] The implication is that an artist can seriously dabble in art but shouldn't take it seriously as a profession!

Although the cautious advice given to artists comes from people who are trying to be helpful, it is advice based on other people's experiences, as well as on hearsay and myths. Other people's reality should not be your reality, nor can it be.

Believing in other people's perceptions is a disastrous trap. However, artists sometimes find it attractive, hoping that it can be a shortcut on the road to success or shield them from confrontations. Ralph Charell, author of *How to Make Things Go Your Way*, observes:

If you filter the perceptions you receive through mediators, you deprive yourself of a direct encounter with the event itself. The more you come to depend on the perceptions and opinions of others, the less of yourself you are able to put into the equations of various experiences of your own life. Soon, if the process continues, your life becomes dim and pale and you are eventually at sea, tossed and buffeted, alone under a starless sky, without an internal compass of your own.[3]

Dual Careers and Low Income Expectations

Art educator Ronald H. Silverman clearly sees the correlation between how artists are viewed as low-income producers and the low priority art is assigned in school curriculums. Pointing out that substantial evidence indicates that more than 90 percent of school-age children do not connect art with a means of acquiring money or earning a living,[4] Silverman goes on to say:

While these figures may reflect pervasive cultural attitudes which stereotype artists as starving Bohemians, they may also be the consequence of current art education practices. Teachers are either ignoring the economic impact of the arts or they are telling their students that an interest in art has little if any economic career implications. Although these approaches may be the honest view of well-intended teachers, they do not square with the facts. They may also be the key deterrent to art becoming a part of the basic school curriculum.[5]

Low expectations of artists' earning power have given rise to the practice of dual careers. While few question its symbolic implications, the concept of dual careers for artists is a widely accepted norm that is readily encouraged and propagated. For example, the academic dean of an art college condones the practice of dual careers:

We are teaching [artists] that having a dual career does not necessarily mean that you make less art. After all, what's the point of having all your time free to make art if you have no money for materials and supplies? This no longer means that artists have to wait on tables. There are many more opportunities and diverse choices for the artist today than ever before. They may go into arts administration or arts-related services.[6]

The phrase *dual career* is a euphemism for *holding two jobs*, and under the Judeo-Christian work ethic it is emblematic of fortitude, stamina, dedication, and responsibility. But in reality, anyone engaged in a dual career for any length of time understands that it creates a life-style of frustration, confusion, stress, chaos, exhaustion, and guilt.

Insufficient Training of
Fine Artists

Even when students persevere and select fine arts against all odds, they may enter their careers questioning the propriety of earning a living as a fine artist. Moreover, they usually haven't the foggiest notion of how to begin.

A few years ago, the College Art Association held its annual conference in New York City. Responding to an open call for panel discussion topics, I submitted a proposal suggesting that the conference include a panel focusing on the importance of including career management courses in fine art college and university curriculums. Although the response to the idea was less than enthusiastic, I did not receive a total bum's rush, and was given fifteen minutes to state my case at a session called "Special Projects," a potpourri of topics not valued enough to warrant panel discussions.

Five of the fifteen minutes had to be used to establish my credentials to this particularly credential-conscious audience. With a limited time allotment I managed to make the point that hundreds of students are being graduated each year ill equipped to handle the realities of life after art school or navigate the maze of confusion surrounding the art world.

There was polite clapping, and a few members of the audience later told me they were in agreement with my position. But it was apparent that career courses for fine artists were not on most educators' list of priorities.

In many schools even the mention of "career" and "life after school" is discouraged—or, as one recent graduate of an art school in an Ivy League university complained, "My teachers made me feel guilty when I asked questions that were in any way related to the business aspect of art or how to go about finding a gallery. I was chastised for admitting that I was concerned about making a living from photography."

Some academics who discourage career advice at the college level believe that students should be sheltered from real-life survival issues while in school. But many fine arts faculty members are opposed to career development courses for selfish and self-serving reasons: they are aware that today's student artists will become tomorrow's practicing artists, and eventually artists with whom they will compete for gallery, museum, and press attention, so there is much resistance to imparting any sort of information that could possibly give these future peers a career edge or jeopardize their own pecking order in the art world.

Career development information is not only opposed by academia for self-serving reasons, but it has also been used as a scapegoat to explain the ills of the art world. For example, the book *Has Modernism Failed?* by Suzi Gablik contains a reprint of a brochure announcing a series of workshops called "The Business of Art and the Artist," sponsored by the Maryland Summer Institute for the Creative and Performing Arts, the University of Maryland, and the U.S. Small Business Administration. Gablik concludes that the workshop was

> another telling example of how much career progress, even in art, now depends on making organizational values an intrinsic part of one's life. . . . The assumption is that success in the higher corporate world of art requires training in the techniques of business administration, and it leaves no doubt that the principles and practices of corporate management now produce the psychological model shaping even the lives of artists.[7]

The development of a program on survival skills for artists—one that covers such topics as health hazards, contracts, copyright, estate planning, insurance, and record keeping—is hardly an indication that artists are motivated by corporate institutional and organizational values. But Gablik is not the only misguided individual who believes in the myth that it is far nobler for artists to drive a cab to support their art than to derive a living from creating art!

To launch or relaunch a career that is earmarked for success, artists must emphatically reject the myth of the artist. The myth, like racial and religious prejudice, is subtle and sneaks up without warning. Do not underestimate the extent to which aspects of the myth can affect, influence, and limit an artist's career.

If artists go along with the myth, they must accept the consequences of leaving their careers in the hands of others. If artists do not develop and expand meaningful goals and act on these goals, their careers will be formed, manipulated, and eventually absorbed by people who have goals that are meaningful only to them. Artists become a means to the ends of others.

Entering the Marketplace

An artist who wants to sell work must enter the marketplace, a highly structured world made up of many networks. There are two ways to enter—haphazardly or with a plan. Unfortunately, most artists enter haphazardly, which means short stays and unhappy endings.

Entering the marketplace with a plan means that your tools are lined up (see the next section) and your psyche is tuned up. How well you tune up your psyche depends on how thoroughly you have rejected the myth of the artist, have developed personal goals, and have been willing to act on these goals and get yourself moving. A good plan also includes having a well-thought-out philosophy about money: how much you want to earn as an artist, and how much you are willing to spend in order to earn it.

How much is my work worth? How much am I worth? How much do I need this year, this month, this week? What can I afford? How much should I be earning? Thoughts of money are ever present and, depending on one's situation, the thoughts are in the forefront of one's mind or are nestled in the subconscious.

There are artists who have identified with poverty for so long that when money finally comes their way they are consumed with enormous guilt, a theme that dominates their existence. There are artists who become Little Johnny One-Notes, churning out whatever made money in the past, in fear that venturing in new directions will bring them back to Poverty City. And there are artists who attach so many stigmas to the concept of prosperity that they undervalue their work, riding the train to martyrdom.

The most common money-related mistake artists make is a reluctance to invest in their own careers. Although artists are willing to spend relatively large amounts of money on work materials and equipment, they are miserly and skimpy when it comes to other important aspects of career development, such as travel, presentations, and publicity, and such preventive medicine as using contracts, hiring lawyers and accountants, and enrolling in career development courses. Subsequent chapters discuss why these expenditures are important. It simply boils down to this: *If you are not willing to invest in your career, who is?*

Homework: Down to Basics

The following homework includes basic investments necessary to launch, relaunch, and sustain an artist's career. Some investments require money, some require time, and some require both.

Read, Note, File, and Retrieve

During the last twenty years the art trade publications field has expanded and diversified, with each of the art disciplines having at least two or three newspapers, tabloids, and magazines that focus on *real art news* rather than reviews and critical essays. These publications contain valuable information on numerous aspects of the business of art and the business of being an artist, including grant, exhibition, and employment opportunities, legal and accounting advice, health hazards related to the arts, and arts-related legislation.

There are publications with a regional focus, such as *Artweek*, devoted to artists living in the Northwest, Southwest, Alaska, and Hawaii; *Art New England*, geared to artists in the Northeast; *Art Papers*, for artists in the Southeast; and *Chicago Artists' News* for artists in the Midwest. There are also publications of national interest, such as *ArtCalendar*. The *CARO Bulletin* and *Agenda* are two of the publications that serve Canadian artists. In addition, there are periodicals that specialize in various disciplines, such as *The Crafts Report, Sculpture*, and *Afterimage*. The addresses of these publications can be found in the Appendix sections "Career Management, Business, and Marketing," and "Periodicals."

Become aware of the numerous local, regional, national, and international arts service organizations, and take advantage of their various programs, services, and publications. Throughout the Appendix, many service organizations are listed that have a regional, national, or international focus.

For example, the *National Association of Artists' Organizations Directory* lists many of the organizations that offer assistance to visual and performing artists, writers, and filmmakers, with detailed information on services, publications, programs, and facilities. In addition, *Artlines 1991–1992: An Annotated Guide to Organizations and Publications Essential to Artists* provides information on arts organizations lending support to artists. Both publications, as well as other useful references, are listed in the Appendix (see "Arts Service Organizations").

The Arts Resource Consortium Library in New York City is a national information and referral service for artists and arts managers. The library sponsors the Visual Artist Information Hotline, a toll-free service that provides information on a variety of subjects including funding sources, health insurance, legal issues, arts service organizations, and technical assistance. Arts service organizations have also been organized to serve the needs of special-interest groups. Examples include the Asian American Arts Alliance, Inc.; the Association of Hispanic Arts, Inc.; the Interfaith Forum on Religion, Art and Architecture; the National Center on Arts and the Aging; the Disabled Artists' Network; and Deaf Artists of America. The addresses of these and other arts service organizations are listed in the Appendix sections "Arts Service Organizations" and "Disabled Artists."

With the plethora of information available, there is no excuse for artists not to be well versed in what is going on in their own profession.

Read, note, file, and retrieve—or practice what authors Judith

Appelbaum and Nancy Evans refer to as the "pack-rat system."[8] Set up a file and contact system that is imaginative and considers the present and the future. Contacts and information that might not necessarily be of interest or apply to your career now could be important and relevant in the future.

Review the files on a regular basis. Unless you have a photographic memory, you will forget a lot of information that has been clipped and stored away.

Set up files for various categories, those that make sense and have meaning to you. My file system includes the following categories: grants (visual arts, general arts, performing arts, music, film/video, and writing); artist-in-residence programs; art colonies; international connections; alternative space galleries; museums; art consultants and art advisors; curators; collectors; professional art organizations; management organizations; loan resources; consulting services; legal, accounting, and insurance information; employment opportunities; mailing lists; public art programs; and slide registries.

I spend an average of three hours a month in the library updating and adding to the files. Developing the system and organizing and deciphering cryptic notes and messages that I had written over the years took about three weeks of work. It was a mere three-week investment, but it has paid off in many ways. For example, much of the material contained in my files was used to write this book.

Mailing Lists—The Usual and Esoteric

Starting and developing a good mailing list requires a lot of time and energy, but it is well worth the effort. Like a file/contact system, a mailing list can and should be used over and over again. It should be updated on a regular basis to reflect the changes you are making in your career (new contacts) and the ever-changing scene in the art world (the names usually stay the same, but the institutions and organizations might fluctuate). A good list implies quality more than quantity, meaning that your list should include the names and addresses of people who can do something for your career—directly or indirectly—now or in the future.

Do not wait until you need to use a mailing list to put one together. Develop a list when "nothing's happening" so that when something happens it will not become one of the thousand other chores you have to do in connection with exhibition/performance planning.

It is common practice for artists to buy mailing lists from arts organizations and galleries. I have screened many such lists and find that they are rarely (if at all) updated and contain many duplications. In addition, gallery lists tend to include everyone who has signed the gallery guest book, which does not necessarily mean that all the people are of interest to you. Other artists' lists include other artists' contacts, contacts that, again, might be of no use to you. Particularly in view of the rising cost of postage, a mailing list should be well screened.

In the long run it is best to start a list from scratch because you will then have total control of the contents. Start off with the following categories:

FANS AND COLLECTORS. Include anyone who has purchased or expressed interest in purchasing your work.

GALLERIES AND ALTERNATIVE SPACES. Be selective. Many galleries specialize in certain styles, periods, and disciplines (as well as by ethnic group, gender, etc.). Include the galleries that are relevant to you.

MUSEUMS. Include the names of curators who are associated with your particular discipline (e.g., photography, sculpture, drawing, painting). Their names, addresses, and areas of expertise are listed in the *American Art Directory* and *The Official Museum Directory* (see "General Arts References" in the Appendix).

DOMESTIC AND INTERNATIONAL ART PUBLICATIONS. Include the names of editors and associate editors. Also note the names of contributing editors, but send material to their home addresses or to the publications where they spend the most time. For example, if a contributing editor writes for daily, weekly, and monthly publications, chances are that he or she spends more time at the office of the daily or the weekly (see "Periodicals" in the Appendix).

INTERIOR DESIGN AND ARCHITECTURE PUBLICATIONS. Again, include the names of editors and associate editors. Also note the names of contributing editors, but send material to their home addresses or to the publications where they spend the most time (see "Interior Design and Architecture" in the Appendix).

TRADE PUBLICATIONS. This is one of the most underexplored areas of artists' mailing lists. Trade publications often include articles about new and unusual uses of the materials that they promote. For example, if you are a sculptor working with glass, include the names of trade publications in the glass industry. The names of trade publications can be obtained from *The Encyclopedia of Associations, Writer's Market*, and *Internal Publications Directory* (see "Public Relations/Press Relations" in the Appendix). It is highly conceivable that articles in trade publications can lead to corporate commissions, acquisitions, and sponsorships.

NEWSPAPERS. Include the names of feature and news editors and journalists who write about the arts.

CRITICS. Include, if possible, a critic's home address or the address of the publication for which the critic most frequently writes. That is, if a critic writes for a daily newspaper and a monthly art journal, include the name of the daily newspaper.

CORPORATE CONSULTANTS/ADVISORS AND CURATORS. (See "The Corporate Art Market" in Chapter 5.) The names of corporate consultants and advisors can be found in the index of the *Art in America Annual Guide to Galleries, Museums and Artists* and the *Directory of Fine Art Representatives and Corporations Collecting Art* (see "Corporate Art" in the Appendix). The names of corporate curators can be obtained in the *International*

Directory of Corporate Art Collections (see "Corporate Art" in the Appendix).

INTERIOR DESIGNERS AND ARCHITECTS. Include the names of interior designers and architects you personally know, and use your list of interior design and architecture publications to reach this group. In addition, the names of architects and interior designers in your area can be obtained through local chapters of the American Institute of Architects and the American Society of Interior Designers (see "Corporate Art" in the Appendix).

TELEVISION AND RADIO STATIONS. Include the names of news reporters who cover cultural events, and hosts of talk shows that cover cultural issues. Good resources for obtaining information on radio and television contacts can be found in the *Talk Show Directory for Radio and Television*, the *Talk Show Guest Directory*, and the *National Radio Publicity Directory* (see "Public Relations/Press Relations" in the Appendix).

HOMETOWN NEWSPAPERS. If you are living in a place other than where you were born or raised, include the names of newspapers in your hometown. (Write a cover letter to accompany any material that is sent, pointing out that you are a native of the area.)

ALUMNI PUBLICATIONS. Include the names of alumni/alumnae publications issued by the college or university you attended. (Send a cover letter with any material you send them, pointing out that you are an alumnus or alumna.)

FOUNDATIONS AND ARTS COUNCILS. Include the names of officers and directors of foundations where you have applied for grants or are planning to apply. Include the names of key personnel in your discipline in local and state art councils.

FREE LISTINGS. Include the names of publications that offer free listings to announce an exhibition, performance, or cultural event.

Buying Mailing Lists

Under certain circumstances you might want to purchase a mailing list to reach specific markets. For example, Compuname sells labels with all the names and addresses that appear in the *Art in America Annual Guide to Galleries, Museums and Artists*, which lists galleries, museums, private dealers, art consultants, publishers, alternative spaces, and university galleries. The Arts Information Exchange, a service of the Mid Atlantic Arts Foundation, offers a computerized list of arts-related organizations and individuals in the Mid-Atlantic region. The ArtNetwork sells mailing lists of art consultants and critics. The addresses of these companies and other resources are listed in the Appendix section "Mailing Lists." If you are using mailing lists to write *cover letters* (see page 39), make sure the lists that you plan to purchase *include the names of specific individuals*, and not just generic titles such as "gallery director" or "curator."

Know the Law

Twenty-five years ago a friend of mine lost approximately 150 paintings in court. He gave his work to a Washington, D.C., gallery owner on consignment without a receipt or any form of written agreement.

After six months he asked to "borrow" some of his paintings in order to enter a juried show. The dealer said that she didn't have his paintings and didn't know what he was talking about.

The artist hired a lawyer. It took another six months for the case to go to court. On the day of the trial, the dealer brought a majority of the lost paintings to the courtroom. She had a simple explanation: she told the judge that the artist had given her all of the paintings as a *birthday present*. The judge believed her. She was free to keep the paintings and do with them what she wished. Case dismissed.

With new legislation and changes in laws that protect artists from being victimized, much has changed in twenty-five years. But undoubtedly a day does not pass that some artist is ripped off by an opportunist or discovers a hitch in what seemed a straightforward deal. *The majority of new legislation will not do an artist any good unless he or she bones up on the legal rights of artists and understands how these rights affect or may affect an artist's work and career.*

"Artists should never feel intimidated, helpless or victimized. Legal and business considerations exist from the moment an artist conceives a work or receives an assignment. While no handbook can solve the unique problems of each artist, the artist's increased awareness of the general legal issues pertaining to art will aid in avoiding risks and gaining benefits that might otherwise pass unnoticed,"[9] writes Tad Crawford in his book *Legal Guide for the Visual Artist*, which should be on the top of your list of books to buy. This book is written in down-to-earth language and covers a comprehensive range of subjects that should be near and dear to an artist's heart, including copyright, wills and estates, sales by galleries and agents, income taxation, studios, and leases. It includes examples of sample contracts and agreements for a vast number of situations that an artist might and probably will encounter.

Revised on a regular basis, each edition of *Legal Guide for the Visual Artist* begins with an update on new laws, pending legislation, and information relating to specific areas of art law, such as international copyright, obscenity and moral rights issues, income taxation, and state consignment laws.

Legal Guide for the Visual Artist is among several publications available that zero in on the nitty-gritty of art law. It would be superfluous for me to paraphrase or try to cover the ground that has already been covered by people far more experienced and knowledgeable on the subject. However, the "Law" section of my Appendix provides a solid list of references, both publications and organizations. Many of these publications and organizations provide sample contracts, as well as advice for numerous arts-related legal situations. If you require additional information before a contract is signed, or if you find yourself in the unfortunate situation of needing legal advice after an agreement has been consummated, or for whatever reasons, there are many excellent places to turn.

Not being able to afford a lawyer specializing in art law is no longer a valid excuse! For example, Volunteer Lawyers for the Arts (VLA) in New York City offers free legal consultation and legal services, at minimal administrative fees, to artists and nonprofit organizations. More than forty Volunteer Lawyers for the Arts programs are located throughout the United States, some of which were created by arts councils, arts organizations, state bar associations, law firms, and law schools. Services offered, eligibility requirements, and administrative fees vary. In addition to offering legal assistance to individuals, many VLA groups offer seminars on various art-law-related topics and publish resource books, such as *An Artist's Guide to Small Claims Court*, which is applicable to artists in New York City, and the *VLA Guide to Copyright for the Visual Arts*. The "Law" section of the Appendix lists Volunteer Lawyers for the Arts groups and publications, including the *VLA National Directory*, which describes VLA programs in the United States and in Canada.

In addition, law clinics are sprouting up all over the country that offer legal advice and services at reasonable fees. The National Resource Center for Consumer Legal Services will supply you with a list of legal clinics in your area (see the Appendix section "Law").

Copyright

Without a copyright, once a work of art enters the public domain, the artist loses all rights to that work. This means that if a work of art is sold or exhibited without a copyright it can be freely published and reproduced. The artist has nothing to say about it and is not eligible for any kind of financial remuneration. Therefore, it is imperative that all work have a copyright.

The 1978 Copyright Act has made copyright procedures very simple. It is not retroactive, so all copyright transactions prior to January 1, 1978, are governed by the old law. But the 1978 law is straightforward and easy to comply with. Simply stated, *any artwork is protected by copyright as soon as it comes into being* as long as an artist places a copyright notice on the work. This consists of "Copyright," "Copr." or "©," the artist's name, and the year conceived. The copyright lasts for the duration of the artist's life plus fifty years.

Copyright protection is available to artists working in every medium, including printing, photography, painting, sculpture, drawing, graphics, models, diagrams, film, tapes, slides, records, and compositions. There are special copyright laws for audiovisual materials.

Although you are not required to formally register your copyright, there are certain advantages that mainly concern your rights if anyone tries to infringe on your copyright.

The ins and outs of copyright and how it affects the visual and performing arts are covered in the *VLA Guide to Copyright for the Visual Arts* and the *VLA Guide to Copyright for the Performing Arts*. In addition, a *Copyright Information Kit* can be obtained free of charge from the Copyright Office (see "Law" in the Appendix). Be sure to specify that you are requesting the kit for visual artists.

Contracts

Most visual artists do not use contracts. Performing artists and writers use contracts as regular parts of their professional lives. Why are visual artists reticent about using contracts?

Some artists are averse to the use of contracts because they naively believe that people who sell, buy, and exhibit art are good, kind, and trustworthy by virtue of their involvement with art. However, most artists who resist using contracts are struggling with the issue of psychological leverage, and erroneously believe that they have not achieved a level of recognition or success that permits them to ask for what they want.

Requiring art dealers, art consultants, exhibition sponsors, and clients to use contracts is not a sign of mistrust. Rather, it shows that you take yourself and your work seriously, and you are demonstrating good faith in wanting to maintain a smooth working relationship by ironing out in advance any possible conflicts or misunderstandings.

If an art dealer, art consultant, exhibition sponsor, or client is opposed to using a contract, it usually indicates either that the individual is extremely naive and unenlightened in professional business practices, or that he or she is engaged in unethical business practices and does not want anything in writing that could be used against him or her in court. Another reason dealers and art consultants resist using contracts is that they prefer to see themselves as mentors rather than as business professionals, and they find the use of contracts is not in keeping with their self-image.

If your dealer dies, is your artwork protected from becoming part of his or her estate? If your dealer files for bankruptcy, is your work protected from being used to pay creditors? Is your work insured while it is in a dealer's possession, and is it insured for the full retail value? Is a dealer entitled to a commission on studio sales under all, some, or no circumstances? Should artists split dealer/client discounts? Is an artist required to pay advertising expenses for an exhibition? If so, how much? A good contract should be comprehensive and farsighted.

Protect yourself and your artwork by using contracts when you deal with galleries, art consultants, collectors, exhibition sponsors, and clients. Specific contracts such as consignment agreements, exhibition agreements, and agreements for commissioned work will be discussed in subsequent chapters. The Appendix section "Law" lists publications that provide sample contracts, including *Legal Guide for the Visual Artist, Business and Legal Forms for Fine Artists, The Artists' Survival Manual*, and a "Minimum Artist-Dealer Agreement" offered to members of the National Artists Equity Association.

Accounting

Closely allied to the subject of law is accounting—your tax status, or lack of status, whichever may be the case.

A few years ago I was invited to speak at a conference dedicated to the business of being an artist, sponsored by a college in an affluent suburb of New York City. The audience comprised artists from the area, and from the tone of questions and concerns I quickly ascertained that this was not a group of full-time artists but rather of "Sunday painters." The college had also invited guest speakers from the visual and performing arts and from the publishing industry. During the discussion period I was surprised to find that the person who received the most questions was the guest accountant, and from the level and content of questions it was easy to tell that this audience was very abreast of tax laws governing artists, particularly those related to deductions.

This situation is quite a contrast to the attitude of the many full-time artists I am in touch with. How often I encounter serious and devoted artists who are living underground as far as the IRS is concerned, afraid to prepare a tax return for fear they will have to pay taxes on meager earnings. It is ironic that the artists who probably have the hardest time proving themselves "professional" versus "hobby" artists in the eyes of the IRS are the ones most up-to-date and knowledgeable on tax issues.

I am not going to expound on the morality or virtues of paying or not paying taxes, but what is of concern is that too many artists are spending too much energy agonizing over taxes, energy that takes them away from being artists.

One of the reasons artists are squeamish about taxes is the deep-seated myth that being an artist is not a valid occupation and the government will tax an artist in an arbitrary way. The fact is that the occupation of artist has been duly recognized by the IRS for a number of years, most specifically in the 1969 Tax Reform Law.

"An artist actively engaged in the business or trade of being an artist—one who pursues art with a profit motive—may deduct all ordinary and necessary business expenses, even if such expenses far exceed income from art activities for the year," writes Tad Crawford in *Legal Guide for the Visual Artist.*[10] "The regulations set forth nine factors used to determine profit motive. Since every artist is capable, in varying degrees, of pursuing art in a manner which will be considered a trade or business, these factors can create an instructive model. The objective factors are considered in their totality, so that all the circumstances surrounding the activity will determine the result in a given case. Although most of the factors are important, no single factor will determine the result of a case."[11] (The nine factors are listed in Crawford's book.)

Federal tax laws frequently change, and many of the changes directly affect artists. The Tax Reform Act of 1987 is having an adverse affect on artists in many ways. For example, income averaging (which was very helpful to artists whose income varied widely from year to year) has been abolished. Under the old law a business had to be profitable two out of five years to avoid being treated as a hobby. Under the new law the business has to be profitable *three out of five years;* and the new law makes it tougher for self-employed artists to take their home-office expenses as a deduction. This deduction cannot exceed an artist's net income from the art business, as opposed to the gross income limit under the old law, and the portion of home space claimed as an office or studio must be used *only* for the art business, and on a regular basis.

Some business-related tax deductions artists should be aware of include insurance premiums; studio and office equipment; telephone bills; telephone answering service (on a separate business line); attorney's and accountant's fees; dues in professional organizations; books and professional journals; admission charges to museums and performances; protective clothing and equipment as well as associated laundry bills; commissions paid to dealers and agents; promotion expenses, including photographs, ads, résumés, and press releases; repairs; training and education expenses and tuition for courses that improve or maintain skills related to the profession; shipping and freight charges; the cost of business meetings (such as meals) with agents, patrons, professional advisors, dealers, et cetera, regardless of whether the relationship is established or prospective; business gifts; and automobile expenses for traveling to an exhibition or performance, delivering or picking up work at a gallery, purchasing supplies, driving to courses and seminars, et cetera.

These are only some of the tax deductions that affect artists. The list certainly is not all-inclusive, and there are special rules and regulations governing the application of many of the deductions listed above. Because of the intricacies involved in knowing tax regulations and tax-law changes, if you personally do not keep abreast of the ins and outs and changes, it is very important to *maintain a relationship with an accountant who specializes in the tax problems of artists.*

"You can, through reading, taking courses, and asking others, operate a business without the aid of an accountant, but you'll be like the man who doctors himself: You'll never be certain you're doing right until you get sick,"[12] writes Richard Hyman in *The Professional Artist's Manual.* This book provides an excellent chapter on bookkeeping, with examples of completed ledger sheets. Hyman writes, "An accountant can analyze your business, organize it properly, and set up a bookkeeping system. He can oversee your affairs at regular intervals, provide ongoing, up-to-date advice, help with your taxes, forestall and assist with audits, show legitimate ways to avoid the unnecessary payment of taxes, and help prevent costly or even disastrous errors."[13]

I had been doing my tax returns for years without the aid of an accountant and I always managed to get some taxes refunded, but it was not until I used an accountant that I received a very sizable refund, based on monies that should have been refunded in three previous years.

Accountants who specialize in the arts often advertise their services in art trade publications, such as the ones listed in the "Periodicals" section of the Appendix. If you are unable to find an accountant through a good recommendation, do not hesitate to ask the accountant you do find for a list of references of artists whom he or she has helped in the past. Check out the references to make sure that the clients have been satisfied customers.

An arts service organization can recommend an accountant or even provide assistance. For example, the Artists Foundation in Boston (through Lawyers and Accountants for the Arts) and Business Volunteers for the Arts in Seattle offer accounting advice for artists. These organizations, as well as others, are listed in the Appendix under "Accounting/Bookkeeping."

Insurance: Insuring Your
Health, Work, and Future

Health Insurance

One of my clients broke his leg. He was in the hospital for three weeks and then was an outpatient for several more weeks. During the first week he was hospitalized he learned that he had won an art competition with a cash award of $5,000. But his jubilation over the award was eclipsed when he also learned that his bare-bones hospitalization policy (a so-called fringe benefit of the college where he was teaching) would pay only meager benefits toward his hospital bills and doctors' fees. Thus, he had to use his entire cash award to pay the bills.

One could elaborate for pages about similar and even worse stories involving artists who do not have health insurance or who are not adequately covered. For many years artists were subjected to exorbitant *individual* rates for health insurance. They were ineligible for *group* rates because of the nature of being a self-employed artist, a unit of one. However, times have changed, and there is no longer an excuse for an artist not being adequately covered by health insurance. Many arts organizations throughout the United States offer group plans. Some of the national organizations that offer group rates to members include the American Craft Council, the American Institute of Graphic Arts, the National Artists Equity Association, the College Art Association of America, and the Chicago Artists' Coalition.

Additionally, the National Home Life Assurance Company of New York offers a supplemental hospital protection plan, which is excellent for self-employed persons. If you are hospitalized, you receive payment in addition to any you might receive from other plans. Payment begins the very first day you are hospitalized for an accident and after three days if you are hospitalized for an illness. The premiums are very reasonable, and the money is sent directly to you.

The addresses of the National Home Life Assurance Company

of New York and other organizations mentioned above are listed under "Insurance and Medical Plans" in the Appendix.

Artists' Health Hazards

Before we leave the topic of health, it is important to raise the subject of health hazards to artists, a relatively new area of study, because it has only recently been recognized that various materials used by artists are directly responsible for a multitude of serious health problems, including cancer, bronchitis, and allergies.

Solvents and acids used by printmakers are responsible for many health problems; dirt and kiln emissions have created problems for potters; resins and dirt in a sculptor's working environment and gases and vapors used in photography are also responsible for various ailments. Toxic chemicals in paints are directly linked to cancer, including pigment preservatives used in acrylic emulsions and additives such as those used to protect acrylic paints during freeze-thaw cycles. In addition, improper ventilation is a common abuse, and its side effects are directly responsible for temporary discomfort as well as permanent damage.

Performing artists are also directly affected. Toxic chemicals are found in concert halls and theaters, on stage, in dressing rooms, in makeup rooms, et cetera. Health problems are created by such things as poor ventilation; certain types of aerosols, acrylics, and plastics used in sets and costumes; photographic chemicals; asbestos; sawdust; gas vapors; dust; and machine oil.

If you are not already aware that the materials you might be using in your studio or work environment are considered taboo, it is time to investigate.

The Art and Craft Materials Institute, Inc., certifies 90 percent of all art materials sold in the United States. The institute provides information on hazardous products and publishes a newsletter. The Center for Safety in the Arts is a national organization that disseminates information on the hazards of arts and crafts materials. The center also publishes a newsletter, *Art Hazard News*, and various *Data Sheets* pertaining to specific materials and work processes. The executive director of the center, Dr. Michael McCann, has written an important book, *Health Hazards Manual for Artists*. Another useful publication, *The Artists Complete Health and Safety Guide* by Monona Rossol, discusses how to use potentially toxic materials safely and ethically.

Additional information about the above-mentioned resources is listed under "Health Hazards" in the Appendix.

Studio and Work Insurance

Until recently, artists who tried to obtain insurance for their studios or work embarked on an exercise of frustration. Information was scarce, and if and when insurance was available the costs of premiums were prohibitive.

However, in 1981, "all-risk" insurance policies were inaugurated, specifically designed for artists and their particular needs. "All-risk" policies include those developed by the National Artists Equity Association and the International Sculpture Center (see "Insurance and Medical Plans" in the Appendix).

The National Artists Equity Association's policy insures artwork created by the insured (paintings, drawings, sculptures, etchings, and similar works) during the course of completion, work that has been completed and is being held for sale, and work that has been sold but not delivered. The policy also covers artists' materials, tools, and supplies. It does not cover studio furniture, an art library, or works of art by others in your possession or care.

The policy insures against risk of direct physical loss or damage to the insured property, with the following exceptions: wear and tear; inherent vice; latent defect; gradual deterioration; insects; vermin; mechanical breakdown; damage sustained because of or resulting from any process or actual work upon the property; breakage of fragile property; extreme temperature; war risks; nuclear radiation; weather exposure; delay or loss of market or use; unexplained loss; mysterious disappearance; inventory shortage; loss or damage from fraudulent, dishonest, or criminal acts; loss or damage occurring in transit by mail, except registered mail; and theft from any unattended vehicle (unless the property is in the custody of a public or common carrier).

The policy covers insured work on your premises, on exhibit, and in transit within and between the United States, its territories or possessions, and Canada. There is a $250 deductible for each claim. The minimum amount of insurance you can purchase is $15,000.

The International Sculpture Center offers insurance that covers artwork and work in progress in your studio, in transit, and on exhibition. It covers your artwork as well as that of others you may have in your possession. Perils covered include fire, windstorm, breakage, theft, collapse, riot, vandalism, explosion, hail, water (including flood), earthquake, and collision. There is a choice of deductibles that applies per loss. Commissioned work is insured at the full commissioned price.

In addition, the company Huntington T. Block insures the work of individual artists, and also offers a business package policy if your studio is in a separate location from your home. Connell Howe Insurors Inc. offers a craft package policy consisting of general liability protection, products and completed operations liability protection, medical payments coverage, and content coverage while work is on display.

The addresses of the above-mentioned organizations and companies are listed under "Insurance and Medical Plans" in the Appendix.

Pension Plans: Insuring Your Future

Not everyone is going to retire. Some of us reject the notion on principle, and others will not have any choice in the matter because they will not have stored up a nest egg. If you are heading for the latter category, or if you fall into the first category and are forgetting that bad health might necessitate a change in your plans, or if you are in neither category and basically haven't thought about retirement because you are just getting started, consider this: artists can now participate in pension plans, a fringe benefit once bestowed only on members of society who were willing to devote most of their lives to working for someone else. Now there are pension plans for self-employed persons that *offer financial security for your future*.

Keogh plans are pension plans for the self-employed. However, even if you are employed by a company with a retirement program, you may maintain a Keogh plan and make an annual contribution of up to 20 percent of your net self-employment income, or $30,000 (whichever is less), to the plan. Your money can be invested in a trust, an annuity contract from an insurance company, a custodial account, a special U.S. Government retirement bond, or one of certain face-amount certificates purchased from investment companies. Money contributed to a Keogh plan is tax deductible and no taxes are levied on the growth of your investment until the funds are withdrawn. There are penalties if you withdraw the money before the age of 59½, unless you are disabled.

Another kind of pension plan, an Individual Retirement Account (IRA), is available to anyone who is not covered by a company retirement plan, or anyone who is covered by a company plan but has an adjusted gross income of less than $25,000 ($40,000 for a married couple). In an IRA you can invest up to 15 percent of your adjusted gross income, with a ceiling of $2,000 per year ($4,000 for a married couple who are both working; or $2,250 for a married person with a nonworking spouse). As in a Keogh plan, the money you place in an IRA is tax deductible. There are penalties if you withdraw the money before the age of 59½ unless you are disabled.

For further information on self-employment retirement plans, write to your local Internal Revenue Service office. The addresses of other pension-plan resources are listed in the Appendix under "Pension Plans and Savings and Loan Programs."

Credit Unions

Credit unions are financial cooperatives that are owned and controlled by their members and offer a range of services. For example, the Artists Community Federal Credit Union (ACFCU) is a federally insured credit union that offers special loans to help artists establish a national credit rating. The ACFCU also provides bridge loans to assist artists who have been awarded grants. If an artist's cash-flow needs are not in sync with the funding sponsor's payment schedule, the ACFCU will advance the needed money, using as collateral grant award letters from established funding agencies. Artists in all disciplines are eligible for ACFCU membership, as are people employed in the arts community.

In addition, The Chicago Artists' Coalition has a credit union for its members that offers regular savings accounts; vehicle, home equity, and student loans; and IRAs. The addresses of both organizations are listed in the Appendix section "Pension Plans and Savings and Loan Programs."

➋

Presentation Tools
and Packages

Many people are intimidated by visual art, including many of those who buy and sell art!

The fear of visual art is perpetuated throughout our schooling, beginning as early as kindergarten, as we are bombarded with conflicting messages about the importance and relevance of visual art in our culture. Visual art is either presented as a "filler" subject—not in the same league, for example, as science, mathematics, or history—or as a discipline that can only be appreciated and understood by someone possessing a high IQ or a substantial background in art history.

Lacking extraordinary intelligence or academic credentials in the study of art history, most people are at a loss to respond to visual art, fearing that their perceptions might not be "right" and they will appear stupid! Consequently, presentation materials such as résumés (see page 30), press clipping or excerpts (see page 35), artist statements (see page 37), and cover letters (see page 39) are important props because they help insecure people determine that it is okay to like your work!

This chapter will present guidelines for preparing presentation materials and suggestions for maximizing their effectiveness.

An Artist's Résumé

The specific purpose of an artist's résumé is to impress gallery dealers, curators, collectors, grant agencies, juries, and anyone else in a position to give an artist's career upward mobility. However, since an artist's résumé has purposes other than employment, it requires its own special structure.

A résumé should reflect your achievements in the arts field. It should not be a thesis about what you hope to achieve or an explanation of the meaning of your work. Keep résumés pure—free of narratives that justify or describe your work's inner meanings.

If your achievements amount to more than can be listed on one sheet of paper, use another sheet. *Who said that our lives have to be limited to one page?* On the other hand, if you have substantial achievements, consider a résumé as a tool that highlights your accomplishments and eliminates minor credits. Use the phrase *exhibition highlights* or *selected exhibitions* to convey that this is only a sampling.

The following are suggestions for structuring a résumé and the order in which categories should be listed:

NAME, ADDRESS, AND PHONE NUMBER.

PLACE OF BIRTH. Places of birth can be good icebreakers. You might share a regional or local background with the reader.

BIRTH YEAR. Artists under twenty-four and over fifty sometimes object to putting their birth year on a résumé in fear of the stigma of being considered too old or too young. If a person is negatively influenced by your age, it is a strong indication that his or her judgment is poor, and you wouldn't want to be associated with that person under any circumstances.

EXHIBITIONS/PERFORMANCES. List the most recent exhibitions/performances first. Include the year, exhibition/performance title, name of the sponsor (gallery, museum, or organization), city, and state. In addition, list the name of the curator and whether it was an invitational or a juried show. (If you won an award, mention it in the "Awards and Honors" category described below.)

If you have had four or more one-person shows, make a special category for "Single Shows" and begin the "Exhibitions/Performances" section of the résumé with this category. Make another category for "Group Exhibitions." If you have had fewer than four one-person shows, include the shows under the general heading "Exhibitions/Performances," but code the one-person shows with an asterisk (*) so they stand out, and note the code on the résumé. For example:

EXHIBITIONS. (*Single Shows)

1992   OBJECTS AND IMAGES, Alternative Space Museum, New York City. Curated by Charlie Critic. Invitational.

    *Smith Wheeler Gallery, Chicago, Illinois.

    SPRING ANNUAL, Hogan Gallery, Detroit, Michigan. Juried by Peggy Panelist and Joe Jurist.

COMMISSIONS. List projects or works for which you have been commissioned, including the name of the project or medium, the sponsor (institution, company, person, etc.), and the date.

COLLECTIONS. List the names of institutions that have purchased your work, as well as corporations and well-known collectors. If you haven't been "collected" by any of the above, omit the category (unless you need to pad the résumé with the names of relatives and friends).

BIBLIOGRAPHY. List all publications in which you have been mentioned or reviewed and any articles that you have written related to art. Include the name of the author, article title, name of the publication, and publication date. If you have been published in an exhibition catalog, include the name of the exhibition and the sponsor. If something was written about you in the catalog, credit the author.

AWARDS AND HONORS. Include grants or fellowships you have received. List any prizes or awards you have won in exhibitions or competitions. Include artist-in-residence programs or any other programs that involved a selection process. If you won an award that was associated with an exhibition, repeat the same information that was listed in the "Exhibitions/Performances" category, but begin with the award. For example:

First Prize. Sculpture. SPRING ANNUAL, Hogan Gallery, Detroit, Michigan. Juried by Peggy Panelist and Joe Jurist, 1992.

LECTURES/PUBLIC-SPEAKING ENGAGEMENTS. Use this category to list any lectures you have given and/or radio and television appearances.

EDUCATION. This should be the *last* category. Many artists make the mistake of listing it first. This suggests that the biggest accomplishment in your life was your formal education!

The following is a sample résumé:

Terry Turner
15 West Main Street
Yourtown, U.S.A. 12000
500-832-4647
Born: Washington, D.C., 1962

SELECTED EXHIBITIONS (*Single Shows)

1992 WINTER INVITATIONAL, Whitehurst Museum, Whitehurst, Illinois. Curated by Midge Allen.

OBJECTS AND IMAGES, Alternative Space Museum, New York City. Curated by Charlie Critic. Invitational.

*Smith Wheeler Gallery, Chicago, Illinois.

SPRING ANNUAL, Hogan Gallery, Detroit, Michigan. Juried by Peggy Panelist and Joe Jurist.

1991 ILLUSIONS, Piper College, Lakeside, Pennsylvania. Curated by Abraham Collins.

1990 *Pfeiffer Gallery, Düsseldorf, Germany.

*Limerick Gallery, San Francisco, California.

TEN SCULPTORS, Kirkwood Park, Denver, Colorado. Sponsored by the Denver Arts Council. Invitational.

1989 PITTSBURGH BIENNIAL, Pittsburgh Cultural Center, Pittsburgh, Pennsylvania. Curated by Mary Clark and Henry North.

HANNAH, WRIGHT, AND TURNER, Covington Gallery, Houston, Texas.

1988 THE DRAWING SHOW, traveling exhibition organized by the Southwestern Arts Center, Tempe, Arizona: Seattle Museum, Seattle, Washington; Minneapolis Museum, Minneapolis, Minnesota; Virginia Museum, Richmond, Virginia; and Miami Museum, Miami, Florida.

COMMISSIONS

Outdoor sculpture, Plymouth Airport, Plymouth, Massachusetts. Sponsored by the Plymouth Chamber of Commerce. 1992.

Mural, Bevington Department Store, New York City. Sponsored by the Bevington Corporation. 1992.

Outdoor sculpture, Hopewell Plaza, Chicago, Illinois. Sponsored by the Downtown Citizens' Committee in conjunction with the Chicago Arts Council. 1991.

PUBLIC COLLECTIONS

Whitehurst Museum, Whitehurst, Illinois.
Pittsburgh Cultural Center, Pittsburgh, Pennsylvania.

CORPORATE COLLECTIONS

Marsh and Webster Corporation, New York City.
Avery Food Corporation, New York City.

BIBLIOGRAPHY (*Reviews)

*Bradley Mead, "Terry Turner Opens at Smith Wheeler Gallery," *Chicago Artist News*, February 1992.

*John Short, "Emerging Artists Featured at Whitehurst Museum," *Whitehurst Daily News*, January 16, 1992.

Nancy Long, "Winter Invitational at Whitehurst Museum," *Museum Quarterly*, Winter 1992.

Midge Allen, *Winter Invitational Catalog*, Whitehurst Museum, Whitehurst, Illinois, 1992.

Beth Ryan, "Ten Sculptors Show at Kirkwood Park," *Sculptor's Monthly*, June 1990.

Mary Clark and Henry North, *Pittsburgh Biennial Catalog*, Pittsburgh Cultural Center, Pittsburgh, Pennsylvania, 1989.

AWARDS AND HONORS

First Prize. Sculpture. SPRING ANNUAL, Hogan Gallery, Detroit, Michigan. Juried by Peggy Panelist and Joe Jurist, 1992.

Fellowship. Denver Arts Council, Denver, Colorado, 1991.

Fellowship. Minerva Hills Artist Colony, Minerva Hills, Montana, 1991.

Second Prize. Sculpture. International Sculptor's Competition, Essex, Ontario, Canada, 1990.

Project Grant, Pittsburgh Cultural Center, Pittsburgh, Pennsylvania. Juried, 1989.

LECTURES/PUBLIC-SPEAKING ENGAGEMENTS

Lecture, Pratt Institute, Brooklyn, New York, 1992.

Lecture, Art Department, University of Colorado, Boulder, Colorado, 1991.

Interview, "Culture Hour," WRST TV, Detroit, Michigan, 1990.

Lecture, Covington Gallery, Houston, Texas, 1989.

Interview, "The Drawing Show Artists," WXYZ Radio, Tempe, Arizona, 1988.

EDUCATION

Art Department, Ross College, Huntington, Iowa. B.F.A., 1985.

Thin Résumés

Few of us can begin careers with heavyweight résumés full of fancy exhibition/performance credits and citing articles and reviews in leading publications. But the anxiety of having a thin résumé should not prevent you from putting a résumé together. I like the reaction of a painter whom I was assisting with a résumé. She studied the various category headings and replied: "How exciting. I can't fill in all of these categories, but look at all of the things I can look forward to."

While it is not advisable to pad résumés with insignificant facts and data, a few things can be done to fill up a page so that a résumé does not look bare. For example, double-space between each entry and triple-space between categories. Use "Collections" to list the names of any well-known people or institutions who have your work, even if they did not purchase it. Include student shows in the "Exhibitions/Performances" category and use "Awards and Honors" to list any scholarships or teaching assistantships you have received in graduate or undergraduate school. If you have teaching experience in the arts, list this experience in a new category, "Career-Related Experience" or "Teaching Experience."

Updating Résumés

The following advice might sound silly, but artists are often very negligent about résumés: as career changes and accomplishments occur, update your résumé. If you have been invited to participate in an exhibition/event in the future, add a new category to the résumé, "Forthcoming Exhibitions." If an article is planned in the future, add a new category, "Forthcoming Articles."

A painless, time- and cost-effective way of updating a résumé is to have it word-processed on a computer. Once the information is stored, a résumé can be updated in a matter of minutes.

Excerpts from Publications

If you have received good reviews, excerpt the most flattering quotes on a separate sheet of paper and attach it to your résumé. Credit the author, article, and publication, and give the date. If you have not been reviewed in a periodical but an exhibition catalog contains prose about your work, include the relevant quotes on a separate sheet of paper, credit the author, and give the exhibition title, sponsor, and date. Although many artists present an entire article, unless the key sentences or thoughts are *underlined*, chances are the article will not be read.

Biographies

A biography is a synopsis, written in prose, of your career accomplishments. It highlights various credits listed on your résumé. In certain instances, a bio is used in lieu of a résumé, such as for a handout at exhibitions and to accompany a press release (see page 62). (The narrative style makes it easy for a writer to include biographical information.) A biography can also be used to accompany a résumé when you are submitting slides to dealers, curators, and corporate art consultants and advisors. Following is an example of a biography, based on the sample résumé on pages 32–34.

Terry Turner was born in Washington, D.C., in 1962. She has had one-person shows at galleries in the United States and in Europe, including the Smith Wheeler Gallery, Chicago; the Limerick Gallery, San Francisco; and the Pfeiffer Gallery, Düsseldorf, Germany.

Ms. Turner's work has been featured in several group shows at museums and cultural centers, including the Whitehurst Museum, Whitehurst, Illinois, and Piper College, Lakeside, Pennsylvania; and in "The Drawing Show," a traveling exhibition that toured major museums throughout the United States organized by the Southwestern Arts Center, Tempe, Arizona. In addition, her work is in public and corporate collections, including those at the Pittsburgh Cultural Center and the Avery Food Corporation in New York City.

Ms. Turner is the recipient of numerous awards and honors. In 1991 she received fellowships from the Denver Arts Council and the Minerva Hills Artist Colony, Minerva Hills, Montana. This year she won first prize in sculpture at the Hogan Gallery's Spring Annual in Detroit, Michigan.

Ms. Turner attended Ross College, Huntington, Iowa, and received a B.F.A. in 1985.

Like a résumé, a biography should not be a thesis that explains the meaning of your work. Save such explanations for an artist statement.

Artist Statements

Many artists assume, somewhat naively, that everyone is automatically going to "get" or comprehend their work on the exact level on which they intend it to be perceived. Although an artist statement can be an effective tool in helping insecure people better understand your work, one does not have to be insecure about visual art to appreciate the aid of an artist statement.

But translating visual concepts into clear prose is an exercise that often meets with much resistance. For several years, I have conducted workshops on a variety of career-related subjects, including developing artist statements. Many workshop participants anticipate preparing an artist statement as eagerly as they might a tooth extraction. And I often find the task of getting artists to describe their own work in a meaningful and interesting way not unlike pulling teeth!

As a warm-up exercise, participants are asked to describe the work of an artist whom they admire. For the most part, passionate adjectives and poetic phrases flow with unrestrained ease. But after the warm-up, when artists are asked to describe their *own* work, dry abstractions and clichés fill the page.

Although artists vehemently criticize the overintellectualized style of writing used in leading art magazines, many believe that their work will not be taken seriously unless they *imitate what they despise.*

An artist statement can be used as a tool to help dealers, art consultants, and advisors sell your work, and as background information in helping writers, critics, and curators prepare articles, reviews, and exhibition catalogs. In addition, an artist statement can be incorporated into a cover letter (see page 39) and into grant applications (see Chapter 7).

An artist statement can focus on one or more topics, such as symbols and metaphors, materials and techniques, or themes or issues underlying or influencing your work.

Avoid using weak phrases that reflect insecurities, confusion, or doubt, such as "I am attempting," "I hope," or "I am trying." The statement should be coherent, direct, and upbeat. For example:

> Art in all of its many forms makes me feel connected to something more grand. Exuberant movement and rotating images imply energy and space beyond the boundaries of the canvas. Shadows of transparent color and heavily textured surfaces speak of nature without evoking landscape.[14]

> Color, texture and shape are the core of my relief paintings. Inspired by the rugged untamed beauty of Malta, my native country, I translate these explosive and mythical images of time and nature with mixed media of paper, wood, coarse sand, and pigments. The surfaces of my paintings are worked to reflect these images.[15]

> My forms have memory. They remind me of things I used to examine as a child. For example, my father's Zippo cigarette lighter was my first experience with sculpture as an enigma: its weight, perfect form, and mysterious inscription on the bottom were sources of fascination. Greek warriors, knives, tongues, industrial air vents, and farm

tools were objects that at one time I must have examined closely. Now they appear as abstracted shapes in my work. These images remind me of something deep down in my memory. They are psychological symbols, like the Virgin Mary. But they have no church to give them structural coherence. This process is a form of visual amnesia on the verge of memory.[16]

Cover Letters

The use of a cover letter is more than a courtesy; it can provide a context to help people view your work. Some people need the context of art-world validation, such as the information provided in a résumé (see page 30). Some people are not concerned with glitz but want to know what your work is all about. Others need a combination of glitz and meat. An effective letter can cover all grounds.

It should include the following:

(1) *An introductory paragraph* stating who you are and the purpose of the letter. For example:
I am a sculptor and am writing to acquaint you with my work.

(2) *A brag paragraph* that plucks from your résumé a few credentials. For example:
I have had one-person exhibitions at the Wallace Gallery, and have been included in group exhibitions at the Contemporary Art Museum and Ridgefield Museum. In addition, my work is in public and corporate collections.

Or:
I have exhibited at museums and galleries, including the Alternative Space Museum, New York City; the Hogan Gallery, Detroit; and the Covington Gallery, Houston. In addition, my work is in various public and corporate collections, including those of the Whitehurst Museum and the Marsh and Webster Corporation.

(3) *A short artist statement.* For example:
Color, texture and shape are the core of my relief paintings. Inspired by the rugged untamed beauty of Malta, my native country, I translate these explosive and mythical images of time and nature with mixed media of paper, wood, coarse sand, and pigments. The surfaces of my paintings are worked to reflect these images.[17]

(4) *A concluding paragraph.* For example:
Enclosed are [slides, photographs, or brochures] featuring recent examples of my work. If you find my work of interest I would be pleased to send additional material.

Or:

Enclosed are [slides, photographs, or brochures] featuring recent examples of my work. If you find my work of interest I would be pleased to arrange a studio visit in the near future.

If applicable, a cover letter can point out that you are including copies of press reviews or essays by curators. For example: "I am enclosing copies of reviews written by Mary Smith, art critic of the *Daily Times*, and John Jones, contributing editor of *Art Monthly*." Or, "I am enclosing a reprint of the introduction to the catalog of the traveling exhibition 'Northwest Artists' written by curator Helen Homes."

And, *if applicable*, include a paragraph listing the reasons you are contacting a particular gallery or curator. For example: "I have visited your gallery on several occasions, and believe my work shares an affinity with the work of the artists featured." Or, "I attended the exhibition 'Modern Dreams' and, judging by the selection of artists featured in the show, I thought that you would be interested in my work."

Depending on your career stage, it might not be possible to include a brag paragraph, reviews, or essays, but an artist statement can be integrated into the letter regardless of whether you have been working as an artist for ten months or ten years.

Writing a cover letter and including any one or all of the elements outlined above is no guarantee that you will get what you want. However, with a well-written cover letter you have a better chance of making an impression and setting yourself apart from the hundreds of artists who send packages to dealers, curators, collectors, and exhibition sponsors with form letters, insipid letters, or no cover letters at all.

Visual Presentations

Since few dealers and curators will view original work at a first meeting, most artists have been stuck with the slide/photograph system. This system was designed for the convenience of dealers, curators, and jurors. It is certainly not in the best interest of artists.

With few exceptions, the person who considers your slides will examine them without a slide projector or hand viewer, and will decide whether they like your artwork within thirty seconds.

Thus, after completing a work, you must create an artificial viewing situation that will present the work advantageously in a slide or photograph. Unless the work happens to *be* a photograph, this is not the way it was intended to be viewed or experienced. (The idiocy of the slide system is further heightened when photographers are requested to present slides of their prints!)

Often, because of the importance placed on good photographs, an artist is guided and influenced during the creation process by how well the work will photograph!

The section "Rethinking Presentation Packages" (see page 43) suggests some new ways of presenting visual materials. But if you are unable to change immediately to a new presentation form, following are some pointers on how the slide/photograph system can work best for you.

Slides and Photographs

Photograph your work yourself *only* if you can really do it justice. The publications *Photographing Your Artwork: A Step-by-Step Guide to Taking High-Quality Slides at an Affordable Price* and

Photographing Your Craftwork: A Hands-On Guide for Craftspeople provide guidelines and tips. These publications are listed in the Appendix under "Career Management, Business, and Marketing." If you are unable to take professional-quality slides and photographs, use a photographer experienced in *art* photography. Decide before the shooting how you want the work to look in a photograph and what features you want emphasized. If the final result falls short of your expectations, reshoot, and, if necessary, continue to reshoot until you have what you want. If your work contains details that get lost when the piece is photographed as a whole, shoot separate photographs of the details you want emphasized or clarified.

Since you are going through the time and expense of a photography session, shoot in color and in black and white. Color slides and prints can be used immediately (for dealers, curators, grant applications, slide registries, etc.). Black-and-whites, as well as color prints, can be used later for public relations and press packages (see page 62 for requirements).

Since slides and photographs are lures to get dealers and curators to see your work in person, if they are unimpressed with the work as it appears in photographs, it is unlikely that they will get to your studio. However, for photographic purposes, do not glamorize a piece of work with special effects that misrepresent what the viewer will actually see in person. Ultimately, the deception will catch up with you.

When I discussed the slide system with a curator, she said that artists tend to submit many more slides than are necessary, and without discrimination. If you have never had your work photographed, shoot all of the work, but reserve the older work for personal documentation and future use. Dealers and curators are interested in your current direction and do not want to see a slide retrospective at the first meeting. It is also important that you *show slides of only one medium*. If you paint and draw, show slides of your paintings or drawings, but not both. This advice sounds strange, and it is, but dealers, curators, and jurists want consistency. Keeping art media separate is part of their definition of consistency! However, you can work around this illogical rule by showing one dealer slides of paintings and another dealer slides of drawings.

What you show to whom depends on your research of galleries, including what kind of work they are showing and what kind of work a particular curator is interested in.

One of the biggest problems with slides is that many people do not really know how to read them. Therefore, a viewer should be spoon-fed. All slides and photographs should be *labeled* with the dimensions of the work, the medium, the title (if any), your name, and the date. Notations should be made on the frame or margin to indicate the direction in which the slides or photographs should be viewed. It is intimidating for a viewer to have to hem and haw over the right way to view work. The viewer's embarrassment can create a negative atmosphere, meaning that your work is not being viewed under the best circumstances, and this can lead to a negative response.

Another effective way of presenting work in photographic form is to enlarge some of the slides to at least 5″ × 7″ color prints or use large transparencies. This helps to eliminate doubt about whether a viewer can read the slides. Transparencies are excellent for this purpose.

Make a minimum of a dozen duplicate sets of the slides. The greater the number of slides in circulation, the greater the chances that something positive will happen.

Unless someone requests a specific number of slides, six to eight images are sufficient for an initial presentation.

Rethinking Presentation Packages

A few years ago I began keeping track of the number of presentation packages my clients annually sent to galleries, art consultants, and curators. I learned that generally it takes *fifty* exposures of the *same body of work* to generate *one* positive response.

This means that on the average, fifty people must see slides, photographs, or other visual representations of the same work in order for an artist to receive an invitation to exhibit or spur interest in establishing a consignment relationship, sale, or commission opportunity. Although artists have sent fewer than fifty packages and received good feedback (in one case three packages led to the sale of three paintings), such experiences are by far the exception rather than the rule.

The *good news* is that the number of packages most artists send—between twelve and fifteen a year—does not even begin to approach an effective market penetration level that justifies any sense of defeat or rejection if the response is unfavorable.

The *bad news* is that preparing fifty packages that contain traditional presentation materials, including slides, a résumé, an artist statement, press clippings, a cover letter, and a self-addressed stamped envelope, can be unwieldy, costly, and time-consuming.

Artists spend an average of $12 to $25 on a typical presentation. The high cost factor coupled with much wasted time (waiting for packages to be returned by uninterested parties or tracing lost material) makes it apparent that *there has to be a better way!*

Brochures

Recently, a client decided to publish a brochure in conjunction with an open studio event (see page 110). She had considered using a brochure for a long time, but was troubled by its negative connotations—unfortunately, some people sneer at brochures as a marketing tool, another one of those groundless taboos that have crept into art-world protocol.

With the guidance of a graphic designer, she designed a six-page, 7½" × 9" brochure that on one side included three four-color reproductions, and on the other side contained a one-page biographical narrative listing exhibition credits, collections, educational background, name, address, and phone number, as well as a two-page essay about her work.

One thousand brochures were printed, one third of which were used to accompany an invitation to her open studio. The brochures were sent to New York area galleries, private dealers, art consultants, curators, friends, and people who had previously expressed interest in or purchased her work. In the months following the open studio she sent brochures to galleries, private dealers, art consultants, and curators nationwide. With each brochure she sent a cover letter in which she offered to send a set of slides if the recipient found her work of interest.

I asked the artist to keep track of the response generated from the brochure for a twelve-month period. Here are the results:

- Brochures were sent to 329 art consultants, private dealers, and galleries. She received 48 responses.
- Out of 48 responses, 12 people requested slides; 7 people retained the slides for future consideration.
- The artist developed consignment relationships with two galleries in California, and one gallery each in New Jersey, Connecticut, and Alabama.
- She was invited to have a one-person exhibition at an alternative space in New York City.
- Two paintings were sold at the open studio event, another painting through the art dealer in New Jersey, and another piece at the one-person show.
- In addition, several copies of the brochure were sent to dealers and art consultants with whom she had previously worked, resulting in the sale of two additional paintings and a corporate commission.

Translating the results into dollars and cents, in one year the artist quadrupled her income from the sale of artwork as a result of using a brochure.

The cost of the brochure, including printing, layout, and design for one thousand copies and envelopes, was $2,392. The artist spent another $533 for the design and printing of a letterhead for cover letters, making the total cost of the project $2,925. The brochures were sent via first-class mail at a postage rate of 52 cents each. Thus, the final cost of each package was $3.44.

If the artist had continued to use traditional slide packages, which cost her $25 each, she would have spent $8,225!

In addition to drastic cost savings, there are other important benefits of using a brochure rather than a slide package:

- A brochure allows work to be reproduced in a larger format. The visual impact is much more effective than the tiny image of a slide.
- The use of a brochure also resolves the problem of having to wait for materials to be returned for recirculation. Often several months pass before material is returned, creating false hope that you have won someone's interest, when in reality the package is accumulating dust, the victim of a forgetful or disorganized dealer.
- Brochures are easier to handle and quicker to assemble, though each brochure must be accompanied by a cover letter (see page 39). It is likely that you will follow up on more leads or contacts and send out more large mailings when your time involvement is minimized.
- Brochures can also serve as sales tools for dealers and consultants.

Videotapes

Using the medium of video to present work is another effective alternative to slides and photographs. It is particularly advantageous to sculptors and other artists who have difficulty showing work in still photographs or slides.

Dick Termes, who paints on spheres, is an artist who had difficulties presenting his work through slides. He resolved the problem by using videotapes, and eventually developed three separate presentations. The shortest tape is seven minutes long and includes an overview of his work, background music, and a narration by the artist, who also appears on camera. The tape also features shots of Termes's home and studio, a geodesic dome he built himself in rural South Dakota. He offers a longer tape to those interested in seeing detail shots of the paintings. A third presentation was developed for the purpose of introducing his work to museums and university galleries.

As a result of the video presentations, Termes was invited to exhibit in museums and university galleries throughout the United States and in Japan. He has sold work to museums and corporations, and various public art programs have commissioned him to do projects.

Generally, it costs $1,000 per minute to produce a videotape, but Termes was able to keep costs at a minimum by recycling leftover footage from television programs in which his work had been featured. In addition to production studio rental costs and editing expenses, each videotape copy cost him $2 plus 92 cents in first-class postage. His package also contains a résumé, a cover letter, and a brochure.

Dick Termes points out that the biggest advantage of using video presentations is that "you can control what the viewer is seeing, including details that might ordinarily be missed in a photograph, and to a certain extent create a mood in which the work is being viewed, through the use of background music."[18]

If you are considering the use of videotape to present your work outside the United States, keep in mind that the videotape must be compatible with foreign systems. For example, if you are contacting galleries and museums in Europe, it is necessary to convert a video formatted for use in the United States to the PAL system (except in France, which uses the SECAM system). Although most countries have facilities to do the conversion, generally it is more economical if you do the conversion in the United States. And, needless to say, it would not make a good impression if you sent a museum or gallery an unsolicited videotape that had to be converted before being screened.

In recent years I have seen videotapes produced by art consultants that show a range of work by artists they represent. No doubt, in the near future, dealers will use videotapes to feature the work of gallery artists. Video presentations will make it possible for dealers to represent more artists without actually keeping artwork on the premises, thus resolving the issue of limited space and reducing insurance costs.

When considering videotapes or brochures as an alternative to slide packages, be prepared for negative criticism from peers as well as others in the art world who suffer from petty jealousies or lack understanding of basic marketing principles. Many artists, as well as dealers, are afraid of making a move outside of the archaic and illogical rules of art-world etiquette. But there are also many people in the art world who are looking for fresh, imaginative, and effective ways to find new audiences.

Streamlining Paperwork

This chapter and the previous chapter, "Launching or Relaunching Your Career," outline various tasks, tools, and homework assignments for career development. One of the surest ways to set yourself up for defeat is to become overwhelmed by administrative work.

You can avoid a state of inundation if you aim to accomplish one goal or task at a time, if you do not attempt to do everything simultaneously, and if you learn to streamline paperwork. This is possible if you use a computer, or hire someone to use a computer for you.

Computers can drastically reduce paperwork and repetitive chores. Résumés, cover letters, mailing lists, and artist statements can be stored on a computer and updated in a matter of minutes. A computer can be used to store a variety of information and perform many services, from storing inventories and price lists to creating invoices and contracts. In addition, most word processing programs are capable of creating slide labels.

For more sophisticated organizational needs, special software programs are available. Although the programs were originally designed for art galleries, many of the services they perform are useful and applicable to artists. For example, SoftArt can be used for inventory control, storing consignment information, and tracing taxable costs and commissions. It also provides packing lists, price labels, and slide labels. A Byte of Art is a program for IBM-compatible computers. It allows you to create mailing lists, perform accounting tasks and inventory control, and make slide and price labels.

Business forms for artists are also good timesaving tools. The book *Business and Legal Forms for Fine Artists* by Tad Crawford offers tear-out forms covering a range of needs, including a contract to create a limited edition, an artist's lecture contract, and a licensing contract to merchandise images. Crawford has also compiled a similar publication for photographers titled *Business and Legal Forms for Photographers*.

And yes, artists can have secretaries! Once a system is developed for getting material out and reaching various markets (see Chapters 4, 5, 6, and 7), an assistant can take over.

A workable system does not require full-time energy. It is something that will take you or an assistant a few hours a week or one day a month to maintain.

For additional information about computer software programs and the other organizational aids and publications cited above, see the Appendix section "Organizing Paperwork."

3

Pricing Your Work:
How Much Is It Worth?

Recently, within the same week, two artists called me for appointments. Marsha was in her forties and had a successful career as a real estate agent, but planned to leave her job to paint full-time. She arranged to have a one-day weekend exhibition at a suburban library located outside of New York. In one afternoon she sold $18,000 worth of work. The highest-priced painting sold for $6,000. Prior to the library show, she had never had an exhibition or sold work.

Katherine was also in her forties, but had worked full-time as an artist for more than twenty years. She had exhibited in many well-known museums, and was represented by galleries on the East and West coasts. She had received fellowships from the National Endowment for the Arts and grants from state agencies and private foundations. Her work had been reviewed in leading American and international arts magazines. Katherine's paintings ranged in price from $5,000 to $7,500.

Why is an artist new to the art world and without art-world recognition able to sell work in the same price range as an established artist whose six-page résumé is filled with impressive credentials?

Marsha brought to her new career the philosophy and concerns she had learned in the business world. She recognized the value of her time and valued her talent. Her goal was clear: to derive a decent income from doing what she liked doing best. It was inconsequential whether her work found a home on the walls of a museum or over a living-room couch. Unlike Katherine, she was naive about the criteria used by the art world in pricing work. In this case, ignorance was definitely bliss!

Conflicting Agendas

Setting a price on a work can be a grueling task. Most artists tend to undervalue their work, in the belief that their careers haven't measured up to the criteria necessary to justify charging higher prices. This tendency is reinforced by dealers and art consultants whose pricing agendas are rarely in an artist's best interests.

A primary concern of many dealers is to move work quickly, and, unfortunately, low prices are correlated with making a fast buck. The pricing policies of the majority of dealers basically reflect the amount of money *they think* their constituencies will spend on art.

Few dealers understand that they could sell more work, and at higher prices, if they took the time to help the public understand an artist's vision and the multilayered process and rigorous discipline involved in creating visual art—from conceptualization to actualization.

Most dealers establish a price range based on the hearsay of other dealers, or fall into the trap of believing the myth that the work of unknown artists has little value. Reluctant to move out of established parameters, few dealers will admit that they are vying for a particular price market. They camouflage the "fast buck" philosophy and adherence to a pricing system based on the status quo by using various gimmicks aimed at undermining an artist's work and/or career. For example, an artist is told that his or her résumé does not have the "right" credentials to justify selling work at a higher price. Or the work is attacked on the basis of size, materials, or subject matter. One of the typical ploys used to weaken an artist's self-confidence is an accusation that the work is derivative.

More often than not, artists heed a dealer's self-serving pricing advice, erroneously believing that dealers know best.

Pragmatic Pricing, Market Values, and Self-confidence

Setting a price on artwork necessitates homework. You need to consider and integrate three factors: *pragmatic pricing,* understanding how much it is really costing you to create a work of art; *market value* considerations; and *confidence* in the price you set. Self-confidence is of paramount importance if you hope to get what you want and negotiate with strength.

You can achieve pragmatic pricing by maintaining careful records and keeping tabs on the amount of time you spend creating work, from conceptualization through development to completion. Pragmatic pricing must also include the cost of overhead and materials, prorated accordingly.

For example, if work-related costs, such as studio rental, utilities, professional fees, transportation, dues and publications, postage, documentation, and materials, total $10,000 per year, and you create an average of fifteen pieces of work each year, the overhead expense per work is approximately $667.

After calculating an overhead cost per piece, assign an hourly or weekly value to your time. For example, if one piece required twenty hours and you want to be paid $20 an hour, assign a labor charge of $400. Total the overhead cost and labor cost. In the examples cited above, the total of the overhead and labor costs is $1,067.

Be sure that the price set for your work includes a 100 percent reimbursement of labor, overhead, and material expenses *in addition to* any obligatory sales commission. In other words, a commission should not be paid on labor, overhead, and materials.

For example, if labor, overhead, and materials total $1,067, and the work is sold at $2,000 *without a dealer*, your profit is $933. However, if the work is sold for $2,000 through a dealer who charges a 50 percent commission, you are losing $67.

In many instances, after determining the costs of time, overhead, and materials and comparing the proceeds of a sale, artists discover they are working for less than a dollar an hour!

A rule of thumb is to set a price that builds in a sales commission and profit margin, regardless of whether you sell with a dealer. The amount of profit is a personal decision.

If fabrication costs (for example, foundry fees) are high, these costs must be deducted *before* a dealer's commission is calculated. This "understanding" should not be left to an oral agreement. It must be stated in a contract (see page 18).

You can determine a seemingly elusive market value by visiting many galleries, finding work that is allied to your own, looking at prices and the artists' résumés, and comparing their career levels to your own. But keep in mind that other artists' price ranges should serve only as guidelines, not as gospel, because many artists make the mistake of letting dealers determine the value of their work.

Knowing the amount of labor, materials, and overhead spent on creating work and becoming familiar with market values can help you build confidence for establishing prices. But, of course, the process of gaining self-confidence is quickly accelerated when work is sold at the price you want.

On several occasions I have assisted artists in negotiating prices with dealers. In one case, although a dealer thought the artist was overcharging, the artist would not budge from her position. The dealer passed, only to return to the artist's studio six months later with a client who paid the original asking price.

Another situation involved a better-known artist who had consistently sold a minimum of 75 percent of his work in previous one-person shows. A new show was planned and he wanted to double his prices. However, the dealer was afraid the artist was pricing himself out of the market. A compromise was reached: the artist doubled the prices of the pieces that were near and dear to his heart and increased the prices on the other works by 50 percent. He sold work in *both* price ranges.

I also advise artists to set a value a few hundred dollars over the price they actually want. This way there is bargaining leverage and dealers believe they are participating in pricing decisions.

No More Regional Pricing

Artists sometimes wonder if they should charge certain prices in large cities but lower the prices if the work is shown in the boondocks. The answer is an emphatic no. Regional pricing is insulting. It penalizes your market in large cities and patronizes your market elsewhere. It also supports elitist notions that people in small cities or rural areas are incapable of valuing art.

The chances are, if you are an artist in a rural area or small city and are affiliated with a local gallery, you have been persuaded to price work at what the dealer thinks the local market will bear. If you also connect with a gallery in Chicago, for example, make sure the prices in the local gallery are in accord with what the dealer in Chicago is charging. Prices must be universally consistent, whether your work is sold in Vienna, Virginia, or Vienna, Austria.

Developing Price Lists

When assembling a price list, *always* state the retail price, and make sure the word *retail* appears on the price sheet. The danger in stating a "wholesale price" or "artist's price" is that it gives dealers carte blanche to price your work in any way they see fit. The "wholesale price" is construed as an artist's bottom line, and many dealers feel justified in selling work for as much as several hundred percent above the wholesale price and pocketing the difference. Recently a gallery in New York known for requiring artists to state their wholesale prices sold a sculpture for $25,000. The artist received $2,500! The transaction was completely legitimate because the artist stated in writing a wholesale price of $2,500.

Another problem with wholesale pricing is that it prevents artists from establishing a *real* market value. For example, if you are using wholesale prices and have relationships with more than one gallery or art consultant, it is highly conceivable that your work will sell for vastly different prices in different cities or within the same city.

When establishing a retail price, assume a dealer will take a 50 percent commission. Do not adjust the retail price if a dealer's commission is lower. Do not work with dealers who require a commission higher than 50 percent.

A price list can also state your discount policy. Guidelines for developing a discount policy are described in the following section.

Developing a Discount Policy

Shortly after beginning a consignment relationship with a gallery, an artist named Steven was informed by the dealer that a client was interested in buying one of his paintings. The client had previously purchased work from the gallery, and the dealer offered a 20 percent discount, which she asked Steven to split.

New to the gallery world, Steven was unfamiliar with discounts, an issue that had not been addressed in a consignment agreement issued by the gallery. Steven was confused and talked to a friend with more gallery experience. The friend confirmed that artist/gallery discount splits are usual occurrences.

Steven complied with the dealer's request. The painting was sold and he received a check equaling 40 percent of the retail price—the dealer had deducted a 50 percent commission and another 10 percent that represented Steven's share of the discount.

Many artists split discounts without analyzing what discounts actually symbolize or represent. For a gallery, the main purpose of giving discounts to a collector is to reward loyalty and patronage, and to create an incentive for the collector to remain a client.

As a token of gratitude, awarding a discount is a public-relations gesture. But is it logical or ethical for artists to be required to share or absorb public-relations expenses of a gallery, and if so, under what circumstances?

Steven was a new gallery artist, and the discount he allowed was a public-relations token that directly rewarded the collector's *previous* patronage of the gallery and of *other* gallery artists. How would Steven have responded if he had been required to contribute 10 percent of the painting's sale price toward exhibition announcements for other gallery artists, or toward a generic brochure tooting the horn of the gallery?

If the 50 percent commission charged by most dealers can in any way be justified, this hefty amount provides a very adequate cushion that enables dealers to offer clients discounts without infringing on an artist's profit. It also provides enough flexibility for dealers to split commissions with art consultants and interior designers.

The time to discuss discount splitting is *before* beginning a gallery relationship. This means *before* any work enters the gallery for exhibition and/or consignment and *before* an agreement has been signed. If a dealer insists on splitting all discounts, you have the option of not working with the gallery or suggesting a compromise of splitting discounts only if (1) the client has previously purchased *your* work and/or (2) the client is simultaneously purchasing more than one piece of *your* work. If a dealer is in agreement with this arrangement, it *must* be stated in writing.

Some dealers have been known to deduct a discount from an artist's share of a sale when in actuality a discount has not been given. This situation can be prevented if an artist demands a copy of a *bill of sale* that includes the collector's *signature*, or uses an *artist sales contract*. An artist sales contract is a contract between an artist and collector that not only covers important copyright issues but also states the purchase price of the artwork. Examples of a bill of sale and an artist sales contract can be found in several publications, including the *Legal Guide for the Visual Artist* by Tad Crawford and *The Artists' Survival Manual* by Toby Judith Klayman and Cobbett Steinberg. Pull-out versions of the forms are included in *Business and Legal Forms for Fine Artists* by Tad Crawford. These resources are listed in the Appendix section under "Law."

Of course, an unscrupulous dealer overpowered by greed can always find ways of deceiving both artists and clients even when a sales contract or bill of sale has been used. Once the deed is discovered, however, it is much easier to go to court with a good contract in hand than with a handshake or spoken understanding.

Gallery discount policies vary as much as commission policies. A recent survey[19] of ninety-five commercial galleries in Chicago indicated that 46 percent of the galleries split discounts with artists, 22 percent of the galleries fully absorbed discounts, 2 percent of the galleries required artists to fully absorb discounts, and 30 percent of the galleries either did not address the discount issue or offered miscellaneous comments.

The survey also revealed that galleries that fully absorbed discounts tended to charge artists less of a commission. For example, of the galleries that required splitting discounts, 2 percent charged commissions higher than 50 percent; 73 percent charged commissions of 50 percent; 11 percent charged commissions ranging from 25 to 40 percent; and 14 percent charged varied commissions, but the range was not indicated. Of the galleries that fully absorbed discounts, none charged commissions over 50 percent; 43 percent charged commissions of 50 percent; 33 percent charged commissions ranging from 25 to 45 percent; and 24 percent charged varied commissions, but the range was not indicated. Galleries that required artists to fully absorb discounts charged commissions of 50 percent.

Discounts on Studio Sales

Awarding discounts on studio sales is another issue about which there is much confusion. Over the years a strange protocol has developed according to which artists are *expected* to offer clients a 50 percent discount on work sold from their studios. It is one of those chicken-or-egg situations: which came first, artists volunteering a 50 percent discount or clients demanding a 50 percent discount because the artwork was not being sold in a gallery or through an agent? Regardless of how this precedent started, it should be abolished with haste.

When a studio sale is imminent, it is easy for an artist, seduced by the excitement of the moment, to abandon powers of logic and reason and succumb to some rather unreasonable requests concerning the terms of a sale, such as granting a large discount. To avoid being caught off-guard, vulnerable, or tongue-tied, always keep a price list on hand that states *retail* prices and your *discount policy*. For example, your policy could be the same as that offered to dealers: 10 percent if more than one piece of work is simultaneously purchased, and 10 percent for clients who have previously purchased work.

There are other options, such as offering different discounts to collectors who have previously purchased work and to collectors who are simultaneously purchasing more than one piece. Or you can give discounts based on a sliding scale according to the retail value, say, 10 percent for work priced up to $2,000 and 15 percent thereafter. Or you can have a policy of offering no discounts under any circumstances!

A discount range of 10 to 15 percent provides the flexibility needed to negotiate with clients who insist on a larger discount. Whether or not you acquiesce is a personal decision, but studio discounts should not exceed 25 percent.

Clients who expect a 50 percent discount on studio sales and balk at a lower rate need to be reminded that artists have overhead expenses just like all other businesspeople—and just like art dealers. Consequently, granting discounts of 50 percent is unrealistic and impracticable.

Unfortunately, within the art world, guidelines regarding discounts do not exist. Much of the time, dealers' policies are based on hearsay or greed, and artists' policies are manifestations of confusion and feelings of powerlessness. But although the results of the Chicago survey[20] illustrated that most galleries require artists to split discounts, some dealers are fair and seem to understand a discount's intrinsic meaning. At least this is a beginning, a beginning that could quickly become a norm if more artists refuse to split discounts, or at least specify the circumstances under which they will agree to this practice.

Set the same high standards for pricing work as you do for creating the work. Do not be afraid to negotiate. The extent to which you compromise is a personal decision and greatly depends on the status of your ego and bank account, and how well you are able to exercise powers of logic.

Resources for additional information about pricing can be found in the Appendix section "Pricing."

4

Public Relations: Keep Those Cards and Letters Coming In and Going Out

In the early 1980s, choreographer and artist Laura Foreman and composer John Watts distributed a poster throughout New York City announcing an upcoming collaboration called *Wallwork*. The poster included the dates, place, and times of the performances, as well as a phone number for reservations. However, if you called the number you were informed that there were no seats available and no new names were being added to the mailing list.

The fact was that *Wallwork*, as a dance and music performance, *did not exist*. However, *Wallwork* did exist as a conceptual performance: "a performance which completely emancipated itself from the performance medium. What you see—the poster, the sign, the image, the expectation, the media fantasy—is what you get."[21]

Wallwork could have quietly taken place, its purpose and existence known only to the artists who conceived it. But in order for *Wallwork* to achieve optimum effectiveness, its message had to reach a large audience. So, as posters were being distributed, Foreman and Watts sent out a special news release to members of the press, defining *Wallwork* and its purpose:

WALLWORK aborts the audience's expectations and critiques the medium of performance while using it; . . . creates a found audience of thousands of people—all those who pass by the posters become participants in the (conceptual) creation of the performance.

WALLWORK asks questions such as these: Is art what the artist says it is? Is it publicity or is it "art"? Is art beckoning you into a vacuum? What is the nature of performance? Do the fantasies of artists feed the expectations of an audience? Who is the audience? Why do people most desire that which they can't have? How does an artist "perform"? After a performance, is there anything left? Can an artist create a performance of the mind?[22]

Although it was not the intention of the artists to use *Wallwork* as a self-promotion vehicle, publicity was a key part of the performance and a key to making it a success. Several newspapers in New York covered the story, including the *New York Times*. Critic Jack Anderson wrote:

The final paradox of a paradoxical situation is that *Wallwork*, a non-existent dance, is more interesting than many dances that do exist. It stimulates thought. It conjures up ideas. And one does not have to sit through it in an airless studio or on a hot night. One can think about it at leisure. *Wallwork*, though something of a hoax, has its own strange validity.[23]

Many artists are offended by self-promotion because they believe it taints their work and self-image. Others are offended by some forms of publicity but accept other forms that they consider in good taste. Still others are averse to publicity only because they are not receiving it. And some artists are offended by self-generated publicity but do not question publicity generated by an art gallery, museum, or organization on their behalf. Often, in such cases, an artist does not believe that the gallery, museum, or organization is doing enough.

Writer Daniel Grant gives two perspectives on the publicity issue:

> Publicity has become a staple in the art world, affecting how artists see themselves and how dealers work. On its good side, it has attracted increasing numbers of people to museums and galleries to see what all of the hullabaloo is about and consequently expanded the market for works of art. More artists are able to live off their work and be socially accepted for what they are doing. On the other hand, it has [made] the appreciation of art shallow by seeming to equate financial success with artistic importance. At times, publicity becomes the art itself, with the public knowing that it should appreciate some work because it's "famous," distorting the entire experience of art. [24]

The questions that Grant raises about what constitutes art appreciation and good art and what distorts the art experience have been asked for hundreds of years, many years before the great media explosion came into being. They are questions that will continue to be debated and discussed, within the context of publicity and without. In the meantime, this chapter will discuss basic public-relations tools and vehicles for developing an ongoing public-relations program for your career.

Public appearances, demonstrations, and lectures are vehicles that offer excellent exposure and can also provide income. They are discussed in Chapter 8, "Generating Income: Alternatives to Driving a Cab."

The Press Release

A press release should be written and used to announce and describe anything newsworthy. The problem, however, is that many artists are too humble or too absorbed with aesthetic problems or the bumps of daily living to recognize what about themselves is newsworthy, or they view the media as an inaccessible planet that grants visas only to Barbara Kruger and Roy Lichtenstein.

A press release should be issued when you receive a prize, honor, award, grant, or fellowship. It should be issued if you sell your work to an important local, regional, national, or international collector. Use a press release to announce an exhibition, regardless of whether it is a single show in a church basement or a retrospective at the Whitney Museum or a group exhibition where you are one of two or one of one hundred participants. A press release should be issued to announce a slide and lecture show, demonstration, performance, or event. It should also be issued to announce a commission.

In addition, a press release should be issued after you have lectured, performed, demonstrated, exhibited, completed the commission, et cetera. Some publications are primarily interested in advance information, but others are interested in the fact that something took place—what happened; what was seen, said, and heard; and who reacted.

A press release should also be issued if you have a new idea. New ideas are a dime a dozen, particularly if you keep them to yourself. What might seem humdrum to you could be fascinating to an editor, a journalist, a host of a radio or television interview program, or a filmmaker looking for a subject. Personality profiles also make their way into the news.

Why Bother?

Press releases can lead to articles about you. Articles can help make your name a household word, or at least provide greater recognition. Articles can lead to sales and commissions. Articles can lead to invitations to participate in exhibitions or performances, and to speaking engagements. Articles can help you to obtain fellowships, grants, honors, and awards.

A press release does not have to be published to generate a response. For example, a press release can lead to an invitation from a curator to participate in an upcoming theme show.

Press releases that I wrote and distributed concerning some of my own projects generated articles in the *New York Times, Life, Art Direction, Today's Art, Architectural Forum, House and Garden, Playboy, New York,* the *Washington Post,* and *Progressive Architecture,* and syndicated articles in more than one hundred newspapers throughout the United States (via the Associated Press and United Press International). In Europe, my press releases generated articles in the *International Herald Tribune, Paris Match, Der Spiegel, Casabella,* and *Domus.* These articles then generated invitations to exhibit at museums and cultural centers throughout the United States and in Europe. In addition, some articles led directly to commissions and sales.

An excellent way of keeping track of whether your press release was reprinted, or whether you were mentioned or featured in publications, is to use a clipping service. For a reasonable fee, a clipping service will monitor specific geographic regions and send you copies of articles that mention your name. The names of clipping services can be found in the Yellow Pages under "Clipping Bureaus."

Dos and Don'ts

A press release should tell the facts but not sound like Sergeant Friday's police report. It should whet the appetite of the reader, inspire a critic to visit the show, inspire an editor to assign a writer to the story, inspire a writer to initiate an article, inspire television and radio stations to provide coverage and interviews, and get dealers, curators, collectors, influential people, and the general public to see the exhibition or event.

The fact that an exhibition or event is taking place is not necessarily newsworthy. What the viewer will see and who is exhibiting can be. A press release should contain a *handle,* a two-sentence summary that puts the story in the right perspective. A handle does not necessarily have to have an aesthetic or intellectual theme. It can be political, ethnic, scientific, technological, historical, humorous, and so on. Editors and writers are often lazy or unimaginative about developing handles. Give them some help.

Although a reporter might not want to write an article exclusively about you or your show, your handle might trigger a general article in which you are mentioned.

Press releases have an amazing longevity. Writers tend to keep subject files for future story ideas. Although your release could be filed away when it is received, it could be stored in a subject file for future use. My releases have resulted in articles or mentions in books as much as six years after they were issued!

If writing is not your forte, do not write a press release. Get someone to do it who is good with words, understands the concept of handles, likes your work, and finds the experience of writing in your behalf enjoyable. *You serve as editor.* Too often artists are so excited about a press release that they relinquish control of its content and let a description pass that understates or misinterprets their intentions. On its own, the press has a field day in this area. It does not need any encouragement.

Many artists believe that they do not have anything to say. Use a press release to articulate your thoughts about your work and motivations (see "Artist Statements," page 37). Learning to do so is particularly useful for preparing grant applications and for face-to-face encounters with people who are in a position to advance your career. It is also a good way to prepare for interviews.

Do not use a press release to exercise your closet ego or show off your academic vocabulary. Who wants to read a press release with a dictionary in hand? Avoid using art criticism jargon and long sentences that take readers on a wild-goose chase. Writing over the heads of readers is guaranteed to breed intimidation. This kind of release ends up being filed under "confusion"—in the wastebasket. Here is an example:

> The . . . exhibition presents the work of six differently motivated artists. . . . They each arrive at their own identity through an approach based on the dynamic integration inherent in the act of synthesis, synthesis being the binding factor which deals comprehensively with all the other elements involved in the creative process, leading ideally to

an intuitively orchestrated wholeness which informs both the vision and the process.[25]

What to Include

The headline of the release should capture the handle and announce the show, award, commission, or event.

The average arts-related press release that I receive is destined for the wastebasket because it loses my attention in the first paragraph. For example: "A group exhibition featuring the work of sixteen abstract artists opens at Highgate Gallery on June 1, 1990. The exhibition features paintings, drawings, and sculpture." Although this opening paragraph provides basic information, it does not spur interest in attending the show, except perhaps for the sixteen artists' parents, relatives, and friends.

The first paragraph should contain the handle; use strong sentences that capture reader interest. For example:

Imagine dirigibles hovering over the World Trade Center or a NASA space shuttle parked on your block. These events would never happen in real life unless, of course, they were a project of an ambitious sculptor. Even then, the construction would be very daring if not too costly; however, The Rotunda Gallery's new show, "Sculptor's Drawings," provides sculptors with the opportunity to indulge such fantasies.[26]

In 1979, during performances, New York artist Francine Fels began sketching Alvin Ailey's dance "Revelations." "It had such an ongoing magical effect that I wanted to hold the moment forever, to make the experience constantly alive and give its impact permanency," said the 65-year-old artist. Six years later, Fels completed fifty paintings based on hundreds of her sketches.[27]

So profound is a grain of sand that some people continue to see worlds within these particles of ancient rock. This experience applies to the recent wall reliefs by Lydia Afia, entitled "BEHIND GLASS: Windows of Fallen Light," on exhibition January 4th through 20th, 1988, in the windows of Tiffany & Company.[28]

The lead or second paragraph should also contain information known in journalism as the "five Ws": who, what, when, where, why, and sometimes how.

Subsequent paragraphs should back up the first paragraph. They should contain quotes from the artist and, when possible, from critics, writers, curators, and others. Let them toot your horn; it is more effective.

A short biography should also be included (see "Biographies," page 36). The biography should highlight important credits such as collections, prizes, awards, fellowships, exhibitions, and other significant accomplishments. In addition, it can mention where you were born and/or where you went to school.

Letterhead

When possible, issue a press release under the auspices of the sponsor of your exhibition, event, prize, award, commission, or whatever. Request permission to use the sponsor's letterhead even though the sponsor plans to issue its own release, with the understanding that the sponsor can approve the final copy. The release should include, as a courtesy, a paragraph about the sponsoring organization or gallery—for example, a historical sketch and a description of its activities or purpose.

If the sponsor does not have a qualified person to handle public relations, provide your name and home telephone number and identify yourself as the press contact. To determine whether the sponsor's public-relations representative is qualified, use the following criteria: the person is willing to cooperate and is not threatened by your aggressive pursuit of good press coverage; you have a good rapport with the person; and he or she *really* understands your work.

Additional information about press releases can be found in *Developing the Press Packet*, published by the Media Distribution Co-op, and *Fine Art Publicity: The Complete Guide for Galleries and Artists* by Susan Abbott and Barbara Webb (see the Appendix section "Public Relations/Press Relations").

Publicity for Upcoming Exhibitions
and Performances

If you are invited to exhibit or perform, do not rely or depend on the sponsoring organization to do your public relations. Create an auxiliary campaign (which might end up being the primary campaign). Try to persuade the sponsor to cooperate with your efforts. If the sponsor agrees to collaborate, volunteer and *insist* on overseeing the administration.

Doing your own public relations or taking control of the sponsor's operation is important because of the following: (1) For various illogical reasons, sponsors can be lax, disorganized, and unimaginative in the public-relations area. Many sponsors do not realize that if they develop an effective, ongoing public-relations program they not only promote their artists but also make their institution or gallery better known—both of which can offer prestige and financial rewards in the present and future. (2) If you are in a *group* show or performance, the sponsor will probably issue a "democratic" press release, briefly mentioning each participant, but little more. Your name can get lost in the crowd. Sometimes participants are not even mentioned. (3) Sponsors' mailing lists are usually outdated and full of duplications, and very few lists show any imagination for targeting new audiences. (4) Sponsors can be negligent in timing press releases and announcements so that they coincide with monthly, biweekly, weekly, and daily publication deadlines. Sometimes they do not take advantage of free listings, or if they do they send only one release prior to the opening of the exhibition or performance, even though the show runs for several weeks.

Designing Announcements

A few years ago Braintree Associates of New Jersey, a company that uses Jungian symbolism in fund-raising, placed a small broken-egg symbol on a direct mail solicitation to raise money for a charitable organization. As a result, the dollar amount of contributions its client received increased 414 percent. The broken egg was not mentioned in the fund-raising letter, and, according to a follow-up poll, donors claimed not to have noticed it.

Each month I receive hundreds of exhibition announcements from artists nationwide. But the vast majority of communiqués contain neither a subliminal nor a conscious message that would stimulate my interest in attending the show or inspire me to pick up the phone to request additional information.

This is not to suggest that symbols of broken eggs should be incorporated into exhibition announcements, but the results of the Braintree campaign illustrate the importance of visual information in getting a message across.

The use of exhibition announcements as an extension of an artist's creativity and very special way of looking at the world is all too often a neglected aspect of public relations. For various reasons, artists, curators, dealers, and other exhibition sponsors do not analyze the purpose of an announcement, the results it should achieve, or what it should communicate.

There is a direct correlation between announcement design and exhibition attendance. Well-executed announcements can stimulate interest in an exhibition, and the more people that are in attendance, the greater the chances are of increasing sales and commission opportunities. Creative announcements can also generate press coverage and invitations for more exhibitions.

Generic invitations, those that omit visual information and merely list the name(s) of the artist(s), exhibition title, location, hours, and dates, are frequently used for group exhibitions to resolve the problem of selecting one piece of work to represent all of the exhibiting artists. A generic solution may also be used because some artwork is not photogenic and loses its power when reproduced in photographic form. But the most common reason generic announcements are used is to save money.

Granted, generic announcements are less expensive than four-color cards, but a successful announcement does not need to be in color or contain a photograph of actual work. For example, for an exhibition entitled "Reflections," organized as a memorial to artist Jane Greengold's father, a square of reflective paper was attached to a card accompanied by a text describing *reflections* as a metaphor for her feelings and thoughts after her father's death.

For an exhibition entitled "Paintings at the Detective Office," artist Janet Ziff's announcement contained a drawing of a mask to which two actual sequins were attached.

Taking a more minimal approach, for the exhibition entitled "Lost Watches," artist Pietro Finelli's announcement contained only basic who, when, and where information, but the intriguing exhibition title and text were printed in silver ink on a thick piece of gray cardboard that was pleasurable to read and touch.

In each of the above examples, without using photographs of actual exhibition artwork or costing a lot of money, the invitation did more than announce a show. Each invitation also gave the recipient a sense of the artist, and was in itself an *invitation to respond to the artist's message* with intellect, humor, compassion, pleasure, or whatever emotions and sensations were evoked.

Press releases and exhibition announcements should be given tender loving care. Cutting corners might ease time and money pressures in the short run, but short-term thinking can backfire. Boring publicity tools usually bring boring results.

Advertisements

Dealers pour thousands of dollars into advertising each year. "The art magazines . . . are publicity brochures for the galleries, sort of words around the ads, and [they create] total confusion between editorial and advertising," observes writer and critic Barbara Rose. "The only way you can really get your statement, your vision, out there to the public is to put it up on the wall. And to be willing to be judged."[29] If Rose's observation is correct, and

I am convinced it is, it implies that whoever is buying or exhibiting art on the basis of seeing it published in art magazines cannot differentiate between a paid advertisement and a review or article. Thus, everything that is in print becomes an endorsement.

But according to Nina Pratt, a New York–based art-market advisor, many dealers are misguided when choosing advertisement content and design and when selecting publications where advertisements are placed. She criticizes the use of "tombstone" ads, those without visual information (what I have referred to as generic advertising), and she believes that many galleries lack an overall or specific advertising strategy and rarely employ important target marketing concepts. Dealers repeatedly place ads in the same art periodicals without analyzing whether the readership is actually the primary market or the only market a gallery wants to reach. There is an excellent potential market in non-arts-related publications. For example, a dealer who already has collectors from the business community, or wants to develop such a clientele, would find it advantageous to advertise in publications that businesspeople read, such as the *Wall Street Journal*.[30]

If *you* have to pay for your own advertising space to announce an *exhibition*, think twice about spending your money. (Paid advertising to announce a performance or event for which tickets or reservations are required is entirely different.) Unless you are willing and able to buy multiple ads, week after week, bombarding the public with your name (just as an ad agency launches a campaign to promote Brand X), I am not convinced that paid advertising is a worthwhile investment.

However, if you have no qualms about participating in bribery, sometimes an ad will guarantee that your show will receive editorial coverage. Some of my clients have had firsthand experience in this area. For example, a sculptor telephoned a weekly New York paper about getting press coverage for a group exhibition. She was transferred from department to department until someone in advertising told her that if she bought a display ad there was a good possibility the show would be covered. Another client was approached by the editor of an art publication after he had written an excellent review of her work. He asked her for a payoff. Instinct told her no, and she politely turned down his request, but she had many misgivings about whether she had done the right thing.

On the other hand, if your gallery or sponsor is willing to buy advertising space in your behalf, by all means tell them to go ahead. Many galleries have annual advertising contracts with arts publications (and some publications make sure that their advertisers are regularly reviewed, a corrupt but accepted practice).

Step by Step

The following schedule is based on a six-month time period. Not everyone has six months to plan a public-relations campaign. If you have a year, spread the responsibilities accordingly, but don't start the two-month or three-week plan (for example) until two months or three weeks before the actual opening. If you have only a month to get your plans together, the schedule will have to be condensed, but do not eliminate the following tasks.

Six Months Before Opening

ESTABLISH A PUBLIC-RELATIONS BUDGET. Find out what the sponsor is doing about public relations so that your efforts are not duplicated. Try to coordinate efforts. Make it clear what the sponsor is paying for and what you are paying for. Budgetary considerations should include postage, printing (press releases, photographs, duplication of mailing lists, invitations, posters, catalogs, or any other printed materials), and the cost of the opening. If you are involved in a group show, try to coordinate your efforts with other participants. If the sponsor has little money to appropriate toward public relations, take the money out of your own pocket. Don't skimp. But squeeze as many services out of the sponsor as possible (administrative, secretarial, and clerical assistance; photocopying; use of tax-exempt status for purchasing postage, materials, and supplies; etc.)

PREPARE MAILING LISTS. (See "Mailing Lists—The Usual and Esoteric," page 11.) Study the mailing lists and decide how many press releases, invitations, posters, and catalogs you need. Information listed under "Two Months Before Opening," "Three Weeks Before Opening," et cetera, will help you ascertain who should get what.

WRITE A PRESS RELEASE. (See the section "The Press Release" earlier in this chapter.)

WRITE FREE-LISTINGS RELEASES. Many publications offer a free-listings section. Special releases should be written for these publications and a listings release should be sent to the attention of each publication's listings editor. Free-listings columns use very few words to announce an event. Therefore, your release should contain the basic who, what, where, and when information. Why and how can be included if you can succinctly explain them in one or two short sentences. Otherwise, the description will not be used. Several free-listings releases might be necessary. Write a release for each week the event will take place. For example, if the exhibition or performance is for four weeks, write four listings releases and date each release with the date you wish to have the free listing appear. These dates should correspond to the publication's cover-date schedule.

WRITE COVER NOTES. Write a short note to people with whom you have been in contact. Remind them who you are and where you met or how you know them, and tell them that you hope they can attend the exhibition. Cover notes should accompany invitations, press releases, posters, catalogs, et cetera. But be selective and study your mailing list to ascertain who might need a cover note. Your cover-note list might include critics, curators, gallery dealers, collectors and potential collectors, members of grant agencies, and so forth.

PLAN AND DESIGN INVITATIONS, POSTERS, AND CATALOGS. (See the section "Designing Announcements" earlier in this chapter.)

SELECT PHOTOGRAPHS OF YOUR WORK. Choose photos that you want disseminated to the press (see "Slides and Photographs," page 41). Publications require glossy 8″ × 10″ or 5″ × 7″ photographs. If a publication uses both color and black-and-white photographs, send a selection of both types. Many free-listings columns and gallery guides also publish photographs, so include these publications in your photo mailing.

RESOLVE THE ISSUE OF PAID ADVERTISEMENTS. (See the section "Advertisements" earlier in this chapter.) If you are planning to buy advertising space, decide on the publication(s) and obtain all of the relevant information pertaining to closing dates for text and artwork.

PREPARE A MAILING SCHEDULE. Decide who gets what and when. You may use the following guidelines to help establish the exact mailing dates, but it is important to check with the publications to confirm their closing-date schedules.

Four Months Before Opening

GO TO PRINT. Print photographs and press releases.

MAIL PRESS PACKAGES TO MONTHLY PUBLICATIONS THAT HAVE A THREE-MONTH LEAD. Mail photographs and press releases to monthly publications so that they will be able to cover your exhibition or performance *prior to the opening and/or while the exhibition or performance is in progress.* For this type of press coverage, monthly publications usually have a deadline three months before the cover date, but check with each publication. (Invitations and press releases to critics and staff members of *monthly* publications that *review* work should be sent *three weeks* prior to the opening.)

Three Months Before Opening

GO TO PRINT. Print invitations, posters, catalogs, and any other printed matter that you are using.

MAIL PRESS PACKAGES TO MONTHLY PUBLICATIONS THAT HAVE A TWO-MONTH LEAD. Mail photographs and press releases to monthly publications so that they will be able to cover your exhibition or performance *prior to the opening and/or while the exhibition or performance is in progress.*

One Month Before Opening

SEND PRESS PACKAGES TO WEEKLY PUBLICATIONS. Mail photographs and press releases.

SEND LISTINGS RELEASES TO WEEKLY PUBLICATIONS. Also send photographs to the publications that publish photographs in their listings sections.

Three Weeks Before Opening

SEND INVITATIONS AND PRESS RELEASES TO EVERYONE ELSE ON YOUR LIST. Include critics, curators, art consultants, gallery dealers, collectors, and friends. Send cover notes, catalogs, posters, et cetera, if appropriate.

CONTACT STAFF MEMBERS OF MONTHLY, WEEKLY, AND DAILY PUBLICATIONS THAT *REVIEW* WORK. Send invitations and press releases.

SEND SECOND LISTINGS RELEASES TO WEEKLY PUBLICATIONS.

Two Weeks Before Opening

SEND PRESS PACKAGES TO DAILY PUBLICATIONS.

SEND PRESS RELEASES TO RADIO AND TELEVISION STATIONS.

SEND THIRD LISTINGS RELEASES TO WEEKLY PUBLICATIONS.

One Week Before Opening

SEND FOURTH LISTINGS RELEASES TO WEEKLY PUBLICATIONS.

Press Deadlines

The above schedule is a general rule of thumb, and it is very important to check with the various publications regarding their copy deadlines. For example, some weeklies require listings releases to be submitted ten days before an issue is published, while other weeklies have deadlines as much as twenty-one days before publication.

Openings

Many artists would rather have open-heart surgery than go to their own openings, or to any openings for that matter, and many guests feel the same way. Most openings are lethal: cold, awkward, and self-conscious. But they don't have to be that way. You worked hard to open. Your opening should be your party, your celebration, and your holiday. Otherwise, why bother?

Do not look at the opening as a means to sell your work or receive press coverage. If it happens, great, but many critics boycott openings, and rightfully so, for with all of the people pressing themselves against the walls (hoping they will be absorbed in the plaster), how can anyone really see the art? And many serious buyers like to spend some quiet time with the work, as well as with the artist and dealer, and an opening is not the time or place to do it. Some openings are planned around a lot of booze to liven things up, and while things can get peppy, often in the high of the night people make buying promises they don't keep.

When the exhibition "11 New Orleans Sculptors in New York" opened at the Sculpture Center, the eleven New Orleans artists surprised their guests with a creole dinner. It was an excellent opening, and some of the best openings I have attended (including my own) involved the serving of food (other than cheese and crackers). The menus were not elaborate, but something special, which indicated that the artists actually liked being there and liked having you there; that the artists were in control and were "opening" for reasons other than that it was the expected thing to do. In addition, the breaking of bread among strangers relieved a lot of tension.

Choreograph your opening and be involved in the planning as much as possible. Not all dealers are willing to relinquish control and try something new, but push hard. The opening shouldn't be a three-ring circus structured for hard sell with a little goodie (glass of wine) thrown in as a fringe benefit. This is your show, and the opening should be structured accordingly.

Critics and Reviews: Their Importance and Irrelevance

I have always liked and believed in the adage that "a painting is worth a thousand words." I have never appreciated or enjoyed reading art reviews. I like to know how history affected and influenced art, but I do not care for art history. Such are my own personal biases and interests, and it is tempting to launch into a tirade about the ironies and ambiguities of art criticism and how unintelligent it is that we have allowed subjectivity to have such devastating power to make or break visual artists, writers, and performers. However, as the emphasis on the importance of being reviewed grows so out of proportion to its intrinsic humanistic value, its is necessary to meet the monster head-on and deal with, rather than complain about or worship, its existence.

Critic and curator John Perrault comments:

> I know that artists in general will do almost anything to get a review. I have had artists tell me, "Please write about my show. I don't care if you hate it but write something about it." It's very important for artists to have that show documented in print somehow. Often artists don't think that they exist unless they see their names in print.[31]

Also, some dealers, curators, and collectors don't think an artist exists unless the artist's name is in print!

It is all too easy to say that one should stay clear of *review junkies*, those who depend on the printed word to form their opinions or convictions about whether your work is good, bad, worthy, or unworthy, and whether or not you're a good bet and someone to watch in the future. Many such people have camouflaged their weakness so skillfully that one would never suspect they have less self-confidence than an overweight teenager with pimples. *But a lot of insecure people are currently ruling the art world.* Therefore, it is necessary to pursue media coverage and the attention of critics to please these junkies. But the pursuit should be a routine task using public-relations channels (such as those suggested in this chapter), and at the same emotional level as any other routine. *It is not worthy of obsession.*

My own good breaks came from several different circles: insecure people with power, secure people with heart, and those with both heart and power. Ultimately, I have to take credit for putting this kind of constellation together because dealing with the review system also means putting together a backup system so that *your career can flourish with or without reviews.*

Making New Contacts and Keeping in Contact

Making new contacts and keeping in touch are very important aspects of public relations. Establishing new contacts and reviving old contacts can begin with a few first-class stamps.

It is also important to keep your contacts warm and remind people that you exist. For example, at my urging, a client who was literally destitute, out of work for several months, and being evicted from his apartment contacted a music critic at the *New York Times*. Two years before, the critic had written a highly enthusiastic and flattering review about the musician. He reminded the critic of who he was and laid on the line his current dilemma. Consequently, the critic was instrumental in finding the musician work, which not only helped him over a huge financial crisis, but also helped him restore faith in himself, in his work, and in humanity.

Set aside time each week to make new contacts, by using the telephone or sending presentation packages and letters to solicit and generate interest in you and your work. The more contacts you make, the greater the chances that you will find yourself at the right place at the right time.

Do not underestimate the value of this phenomenon. For example, a sculptor who had recently moved to New York from the West Coast asked me to assist her with contacts. I provided her with a list of exhibition spaces that I thought would be interested in her work. The first alternative space she contacted immediately accepted her work, as it precisely fit into the theme of an upcoming show. Both the sculptor and the show received excellent reviews. The sculptor was then invited to participate in a group exhibition at a museum (as well as another alternative-space gallery); a dealer from a well-known gallery saw the museum show and singled out the sculptor and invited her to exhibit at his gallery. This all took place in less than three months!

Once a rhythm is established for a consistent approach to public relations, the job becomes easier and less time-consuming. The letter that once took you hours to compose will become a snap. And if you keep up on your homework (see "Read, Note, File, and Retrieve," page 9), you will never exhaust the list of people, organizations, and agencies to contact.

Keeping in Touch

There are many ways to keep in touch. Press releases and exhibition/performance announcements are two such ways. But there are other vehicles. One sculptor sends a newsletter a few times a year to collectors, people who have expressed interest in his work, and people in the art world whom he knows personally. The newsletter announces upcoming exhibitions and recaps recent activities.

Another artist recycled a postcard featuring a color photograph of a painting, which had been used as an exhibition invitation, to announce a grant she had received from a private foundation. The postcard was sent to collectors, various art-world associates, and dealers with whom she had been in contact.

The Law of Averages

When sending presentation packages, keep in mind that generally you can expect a 2 percent response.

If you consider the law of averages, the more contacts you make (and reestablish), the more opportunities you create to let people know that you and your work exist, the greater the chances that something will happen that will accelerate your career development. Each time you receive a letter of rejection (or of noninterest), initiate a new contact and send out another package. The "in and out" process feeds the law of averages, increases your chances of being at the right place at the right time, and also puts rejection in a healthier perspective. (Rejection is discussed in Chapter 9.)

Additional resources pertaining to public relations are listed in the Appendix section "Public Relations/Press Relations."

5

Exhibition and Sales Opportunities: Using Those That Exist and Creating Your Own

Now more than ever before there are many opportunities to exhibit and sell work not only outside the commercial gallery system (which is discussed in Chapter 6, "Dealing with Dealers and Psyching Them Out"), but outside your town, city, and country of residence. This chapter describes various exhibition and sales markets, including national and international resources.

Alternative Spaces

The *alternative-space movement* emerged in reaction to the constrictive and rigid structure of commercial galleries and museums. Artists took the initiative to organize and develop their own exhibition spaces, using such places as abandoned and unused factories and indoor and outdoor public spaces that previously had not been considered places to view or experience art. Some alternative spaces acquired a more formal structure, such as artists' cooperatives, and became institutionalized with tax-exempt status.

Alternative spaces mushroomed throughout the United States under such names as the Committee for Visual Arts, the Institute for Art and Urban Resources, and the Kitchen, all in New York City; the Los Angeles Institute of Contemporary Art; the N.A.M.E. Gallery in Chicago; the Washington Project for the Arts in Washington, D.C.; and the Portland Center for the Visual Arts in Oregon.

The alternative-space system continues to spread, providing general exhibition and performance opportunities, as well as exhibition opportunities for specific artists. For example, there are alternative spaces dedicated to black artists, women artists, black women artists, Hispanic artists, and artists born, raised, or living in specific neighborhoods of cities. There are alternative spaces dedicated to mixed media, photography, performance, sculpture, et cetera.

When the original alternative spaces were established, their goals were simple and direct: to "provide focus for communities, place control of culture in more hands, and question elitist notions of authority and certification."[32] While on the surface the goals of the newer alternative spaces might appear to be in harmony with those of their predecessors, many, unfortunately, have other priorities. Although some spaces are still being run by artists, others are being administered by former artists who have discovered that being an arts administrator or curator is a quicker route to art-world recognition and power. Some alternative spaces have been infiltrated by bureaucrats who are self-appointed spokespersons for what's "in" and important in art. They work hardest at attaching themselves to *movements*, believing that every great and successful curator must hitch his or her wagon to a movement. Thus, they seek out and feature only the artists who fit into their bag.

Consequently, the goals of some alternative spaces are not necessarily in the best interests of artists or the communities they were originally intended to serve. An *alternative elite* has arisen, so it should not surprise an artist that the reception he or she receives when contacting an alternative-space gallery could well be reminiscent of the reception encountered at a commercial gallery.

Of course, there are alternative spaces that remain true to the ethic and purpose of what an alternative space is, and generally the alternative-space system has many good attributes.

The biggest and most important difference between an alternative space and a commercial gallery is that the former is nonprofit in intent, and therefore is not in business to *sell* art or dependent on selling for its survival. Basically, its survival depends on grants and contributions, which impose another kind of financial pressure. But without the pressure of having to sell what it shows, the alternative space is able to provide artists with exhibition space and moral support, and feature and encourage *experimentation* (a word that can cause cardiac arrest for many dealers). This is not to imply that work is not sold at alternative spaces, for it is, but an artist is not obligated to pay the ungodly commissions required by commercial galleries. If an alternative space charges an artist a commission, it is usually in the form of a contribution.

Alternative spaces have many other good points. For example, they offer an artist a gallerylike setting in which to show his or her work. This can help a dealer visualize what the work would look like in his or her gallery. Do not underestimate the value of this opportunity: many dealers have remarkably little imagination. Also, alternative spaces are frequented by the media and critics, providing artists with opportunities for press coverage, which, as discussed in Chapter 4, can often be an important factor in career acceleration. And alternative spaces provide artists with a chance to learn the ropes of what exhibiting is all about.

Curators and dealers include alternative spaces in their regular gallery-hopping pilgrimages, for glimpses into *what the future might hold* as well as to scout for new artists. Some of my clients' alternative-space experiences skyrocketed their careers or took them to a new plateau.

Many artists have misconceptions about the value and purpose of an alternative space and regard it as a stepchild of the commercial-gallery system. They think that it should be used only as a last resort. This is not true. While alternative spaces provide valuable introductory experience into the art world and exhibition wherewithal, *it is counterproductive to abandon the alternative-space system once you have been discovered by a gallery.* Balance your career between the two systems. Until a commercial gallery is convinced that your *name alone* has selling power, you will be pressured to turn out more of what you have thus far been able to sell. You might be ready for a new direction, but the dealer won't want to hear about it. Those offering an alternative space do!

Alternative spaces are not closed to artists who are already with commercial galleries. In fact, including more established artists in alternative-space exhibitions adds to the organization's credibility, and for an alternative space whose survival depends on grants and contributions, there is a direct correlation between reputation and financial prosperity.

The names and locations of alternative spaces throughout the United States are listed in the *Art in America Annual Guide to Galleries, Museums and Artists* and in *The National Association of Artists' Organizations Directory* (see the Appendix section "Exhibition/Performance Places and Spaces").

Other Alternative Sites and Spaces

In addition to the traditional types of exhibition spaces in commercial galleries and museums, there are many other kinds of spaces available for artist-initiated exhibitions. Mimi and Red Grooms's "Ruckus Manhattan" exhibition opened in a warehouse in lower Manhattan and ended up at the Marlborough Gallery. Artist Richard Parker turned the windows of his storefront apartment into an exhibition space for his work and received a grant from the New York State Council on the Arts to support the project. Bobsband, a collaborative of artists, convinced New York City's Department of Transportation to let them use the windows of an unused building in midtown Manhattan to exhibit their work and the work of other artists. They started the project with their own money and eventually received financial support from federal and state arts agencies. Banks, barges, restaurants, parks, alleys, rooftops, building facades, and skies are only a sampling of other alternative sites and spaces that artists, dancers, performers, and musicians have used as focal points, props, and backdrops for projects.

Cooperative Galleries

Cooperative galleries are based on artist participation. Artists literally run a cooperative gallery and share in expenses (in the form of a monthly or annual fee) in return for a guaranteed number of one-person shows within a specified period, as well as group exhibitions. Gallery artists make curatorial decisions and select new artists for membership.

Because of its participatory structure, the cooperative system, at its best, offers artists a rare opportunity to take control, organize, and choreograph their own exhibitions and be directly involved in formulating goals, priorities, and future directions of the gallery. At its worst, since a member must accept group decisions, you might find yourself in compromising situations, having to abide with decisions that are in conflict with your own viewpoints. And you might also find yourself spending more time squabbling and bickering over co-op–related matters than on your artwork!

It is always difficult to know what you are getting yourself into, but before rushing into a cooperative, talk to the members to ascertain whether you are on the same wavelength. Obviously, if you receive an invitation to join a co-op, the majority of members approve of you and your work. You should determine whether your feelings are mutual.

Co-op memberships are limited and correspond to the single-show policy and space availability of the gallery. For example, if the co-op agrees that members should have one-person shows for one month every eighteen months, the membership will be limited to eighteen artists. Or if the gallery has the facilities to feature two artists simultaneously, the membership might be limited to thirty-six artists. Some co-ops have membership waiting lists; others put out calls for new members on an annual basis or when a vacancy occurs. In addition, some co-ops have invitationals and feature the work of artists who are not members.

Some cooperatives do not take sales commissions; others do, but the commissions vary and are far lower than those charged by commercial galleries. If commissions are charged, they are recycled back into the gallery to pay for overhead expenses.

In *On Opening an Art Gallery*, Suzanne K. Vinmans describes with refreshing honesty and humor the evolution, trials, and tribulations of a co-op gallery, as well as the events leading up to its demise. Although problems with a landlord were a contributing factor to the closing of the gallery, most of the difficulties were created by the gallery's artists, many of whom shirked responsibility, suffered from an acute case of stinginess, and were overpowered by negative attitudes. "If I had it all to do again, I would . . . make myself the director from the outset. As the person who did most of the work and made most of the decisions, I should have received that recognition," writes Vinmans. "I would search for more committed artists. . . . A gallery such as ours could have worked if each member was committed to the fullest degree."[33]

If you join a co-op gallery, it is important to *know when it is time to leave*. Since artists are guaranteed a set number of single and group exhibitions within a specific time frame, all too often a co-op serves as a security blanket for members afraid to venture out into the world and risk the possibility of being rejected.

The "Cooperative Galleries" section of the Appendix lists resources from which you can learn more about the cooperative-gallery system.

Vanity Galleries

Beware! Not all cooperative galleries are really cooperatives. Opportunists have aligned themselves with the cooperative system and put together galleries that are defined as cooperatives but are really vanity galleries in disguise. Their only selection criterion is the availability of the almighty dollar: "If you've got the bread, have I got a space for you!" And more often than not the space is not remotely like what you envision as a decent exhibition environment.

For a *Village Voice* article, journalist Lisa Gubernick posed as an artist and went undercover to learn more about what artists experience when making the gallery rounds. With a set of borrowed slides, she contacted numerous galleries in New York City, including the vanities. At the Westbroadway Gallery, she was offered a show in the gallery basement, which was called the "Alternative Space Gallery," for $850. In addition, she described her experience at the Keane Mason Woman Art Gallery as follows:

> I had a draft contract in my hands within 20 minutes . . .
> $720 for 16 feet of wall, a mini-solo they called it. The
> date . . . was contingent upon "how I wanted to spread
> out my payments," according to the assistant director. In
> an embarrassingly blatant ploy she put red-dot adhesive
> stickers—the international "sold" symbol—on each of the
> half-dozen slides she deemed suitable for my show, all
> the while emphasizing various corporations' interest in the
> gallery. . . . The shows I saw at Woman Art were hung
> poorly. Wall labeling was crooked, and the gallery gerry-
> mandered with partitions to eke out more space.[34]

Once, when a gallery dealer deflated the ego of one of my clients, he trod over to a (now-defunct) vanity gallery, much against my advice, like the guy who discovers his mate has been unfaithful and marches off to a prostitute. He signed up for a show, signed the dotted line on the contract, and wrote a check for several hundred dollars. In addition to the "exhibition fee," he had to pay for all of the publicity, including invitations, announcements, press releases, and postage, and for the wine served at the opening. Although the show did nothing for his career, he felt victorious. He had shown the dealer!

Vanity galleries located in large cities, particularly those in New York, are very seductive. They appeal to naive, often desperate artists who may believe that having a show in a New York gallery, even if you have to pay for it, provides the path to fame and fortune. Vanity galleries entice artists through advertisements in regional and national art publications that include tempting come-ons such as "New York gallery looking for artists."

Although exhibiting in a nonvanity New York gallery does not guarantee recognition or financial success, the Herculean strength of the mythology surrounding the importance of exhibiting at a New York gallery enables vanity galleries in New York to flourish.

Variations on the Theme

Closely aligned with vanity galleries are an assortment of schemes and methods for getting artists to spend vast amounts of money to exhibit. For example, a gallery in Washington, D.C., charges $95 per month for a one-year contract that entitles an artist to participation in three group shows and inclusion in a slide registry. Artwork is *not* insured, so artists must either carry their own policies in the gallery's plan, for which there is an *additional monthly fee* of 1½ percent of the declared value of each work of art. For example, for a piece of work valued at $2,000, insurance would cost $30 extra per month. In addition, the gallery charges a 50 percent commission if work is sold! So, if a $2,000 piece takes six months to sell, the artist will have paid $750 in insurance and exhibition fees and a $1,000 commission to the gallery, and will be left with a net profit of $250. And on top of paying a monthly gallery fee, insurance charges, and a commission, the artist is responsible for round-trip packing, transportation, and delivery fees, and any installation costs.

Stay clear of vanity galleries and related schemes that place all of the financial risks on artists. If artists made a concerted effort to boycott vanity galleries, these galleries would disappear.

Juried Exhibitions

Hundreds of local, regional, national, and international juried exhibitions are held each year. Juried shows can offer artists opportunities for recognition and exposure, as well as cash prizes and awards. If you were so inclined, you could enter a juried exhibition every day of the year.

But the biggest drawback to entering juried exhibitions is the expense involved. Most shows require entry fees, and these fees have dramatically increased over the years.

The issue of charging fees and other related matters have made juried shows so controversial that the National Artists Equity Association has prepared a position paper, *Recommended Guidelines for Juried Exhibitions*. It states that

> while certain circumstances might necessitate asking the artists who are chosen to share in some of the costs, National Artists Equity suggests that this be done only as a last resort and that the amount to be charged should be published in advance. However, charging fees to *all* prospective artists (entry fees) is considered to be inappropriate and unprofessional.[35]

The National Endowment for the Arts has also had a long-standing position against the charging of fees. A spokesperson for the NEA has stated that "if a show promoter charges fees . . . top calibre artists won't enter the show, and . . . shows requiring entry fees generally don't have good reputations."[36]

Although sponsors have legitimate exhibition-related expenses, such as for administration, transportation, insurance, advertising, jurors' fees, and cash awards, some juried exhibitions use only a small percentage of fees for legitimate expenses, with the bulk of the money going directly into the pockets of the "fat cat" organizers.

For example, one New York gallery sponsors a juried competition in which artists are required to pay a registration fee of

$35 for up to four slides, $5 for each additional slide, a $10 nonrefundable fee for repacking and handling artwork "even if hand-delivered," and a 40 percent commission on all sales!

Some juried shows *appear* to be more prestigious than others, because they are sponsored by highly respected institutions, or because the jury is made up of famous art-world personalities. But keep in mind that *jurors are handsomely paid* to lend their names to exhibitions, and the fact that a famous critic, curator, or gallery dealer is on the jury is *absolutely no indication* that the show has been organized with high standards and in the best interest of artists.

Before submitting work to a juried exhibition, even if it is sponsored by a museum or reputable institution or organization, do your homework. Make sure the sponsor will provide a contract or contractual letter outlining insurance and transportation responsibilities, fee structures, submission deadlines, and commission policies. If you pay an entry fee you should not have to pay a commission on work that is sold, and you should not participate in exhibitions that do not insure work while it is on the sponsor's premises.

The Appendix section "Competitions and Juried Exhibitions" includes a list of resources from which you can obtain additional information on juried exhibitions.

Slide Registries

An active slide registry is used by many people: by curators and dealers to select artists for exhibitions, by collectors for purchases and commissions, and by critics, journalists, and historians for research. It makes a lot of sense to participate in the registry system, but not all registries are equally used. Before going through the expense and energy of submitting slides, find out if the registry is really active.

My first encounter with a registry occurred when I was preparing an exhibition at a museum in New York City and spent a lot of time in the curatorial chambers. The curators meticulously went through their registry, on the lookout for artwork that would fit into a theme show they were preparing (eighteen months in advance). When they found something they liked, regardless of whether the artist lived in Manhattan, New York, or Manhattan Beach, California, they invited the artist to participate.

It is very important to *continually update the slides you submit so the registry reflects your most recent work.* A person reviewing the registry will assume that whatever is there represents your current work, but, unless your slides are up-to-date, this might not be the case. For example, one of my clients was invited to participate in a museum exhibition by a curator who had seen her work in a registry. It would have been her first museum show, but she learned that the curator wanted to show only the work that she had seen in the registry. The artist was mortified: a year earlier she had destroyed the entire body of work, and the curator was not interested in her recent work. It was a big letdown, and the artist was depressed for weeks.

Resource materials on slide registries are listed in the Appendix under "Slide Registries" and "Public Art."

Museums

Generally speaking, museums are leaving their doors more open to new and emerging artists. Some museums are actually leaving their doors ajar. My first exhibitions were sponsored by museums, contrary to the notion held by many artists that one must be affiliated with a commercial gallery before being considered by a museum. In many instances, what initially led to an exhibition at a museum was a set of slides, a résumé, and a show proposal (see the section "Develop and Circulate a Proposal" in this chapter). Other exhibition invitations came as a result of both long- and short-term professional relationships with museum directors and curators.

My own experience in gaining museum shows is not unlike the steps Patterson Sims outlined when he was associate curator of the Whitney Museum:

On the basis of slides and exhibition notices the curators will call for appointments with individual artists for studio visits. . . . Calls from friends, collectors, and gallery owners about the work of an artist are another means of introduction. . . . Conversations with artists, art writers, and museum personnel will bring an artist's name to a curator's attention.[37]

Sims also described how artists are actually invited to exhibit at the Whitney: "Decisions . . . [are] made at curatorial staff meetings. It is up to the individual curators to promote the work of an artist they feel has a fresh style, a sense of quality, and a provocative outline. If a curator can convince others . . . the group will decide to invite an artist to participate."[38]

The unilateral support system that Sims describes is one of the biggest snags in the exhibition process of some museums. It is debatable whether the artist who is presented for consideration on the basis of slides and a studio visit has the same leverage as an artist who was brought to the attention of curators by "friends, collectors, and gallery owners." Many artists believe that the Whitney, for example, is a closed shop to artists not affiliated with well-known commercial galleries. Judging from who *is* invited to participate in the Whitney Biennials, this is a logical conclusion. On the other hand, one of my clients who had no particular gallery affiliation was invited to participate in a Whitney Biennial. She concluded that she was a "small fish that slipped through the net!"

There are curators who have autonomous power and are able to make their own decisions rather than succumb to peer or dealer pressure. Do not let hearsay discourage you from contacting curators, nor should you be fooled by the myth that only artists connected to prestigious commercial galleries can exhibit in museums.

Curators organize exhibitions, assemble collections, and write catalogs and articles. They are under pressure to put contemporary art into a historical context, discover "new movements," and develop thematic exhibitions, and they cannot rely solely on well-known artists to accomplish their goals. And if they are aggressively pursuing a reputation in the art world, they are on a constant quest to discover artists who will reinforce and support a particular point of view.

Curators select artists whose work thematically falls within the parameters of future exhibitions through the use of slide registries (see page 90). In many instances curators have their own personal registries, which are developed, in part, through artist initiative: artists send letters and presentation packages to introduce these curators to their work.

A young artist who was having a one-person exhibition at a suburban library couldn't understand why a museum would possibly be interested in her work. But I convinced her to include curators in the mailing to announce the show. She sent a cover letter, a color postcard featuring a piece of her work, and a press release to curators nationwide, and was utterly amazed that the mailing elicited a response from curators at the Hirshhorn Museum and the Guggenheim Museum. Both curators requested a set of slides to keep for their files.

Resources for obtaining the names of curators are listed in the Appendix sections "Mailing Lists" and "General Arts References."

Colleges and Universities

Colleges and universities are often receptive to sponsoring exhibitions and performances, and their interest is not necessarily limited to alumni, although approaching a college or university of which you are an alumnus or alumna is a good beginning. Colleges and universities have their own network, and from my experience, once you have an exhibition at one of them, word spreads fast and more invitations follow.

The first step is to send college and university gallery directors a presentation package and cover letter, or a proposal. This process is described in the section "Develop and Circulate a Proposal" in this chapter (see page 108).

Exhibiting at colleges and universities can also offer other rewards. Sometimes, as a result of an exhibition, artwork is purchased for the school's collection, and artists are commissioned to do projects for particular campus sites. In some cases, exhibiting artists are invited to present a lecture about their work, for which they receive a fee and travel expenses.

The names and locations of college and university galleries throughout the United States are listed in the *Art in America Annual Guide to Galleries, Museums and Artists* (see "Exhibition/Performance Places and Spaces" in the Appendix).

The Corporate Art Market

The corporate art market offers artists many sales and exhibition opportunities. Over the last fifteen years, there has been a dramatic increase not only in the number of corporate collectors but also in the amount of art being purchased and the money being spent.

Although some corporations buy art primarily for the purpose of investment, the majority buy art to attain a prestigious image, or even for the far nobler reason of improving employee morale. Although some of the motives behind corporate collecting are basically self-serving, the corporate market has become a very viable arena for many artists to sell and exhibit work.

Generally, corporations steer away from work that is political, overtly sexual, religious, or negatively confrontational. Otherwise, the field is open.

The term *corporate market* encompasses a wide range of institutions, ranging from financial corporations and law offices to hospitals and restaurants.

There are several ways to reach the corporate market: through consultants and art advisors, through galleries that work with corporations, through architects and interior designers, and by directly contacting corporations, usually through staff curators.

Art Consultants and Art Advisors

Art consultants are agents who sell work to corporations and individuals. If work is sold or commissioned through the efforts of an art consultant, the artist must pay a commission.

Anyone can become an art consultant. Like gallery dealers, art consultants are unregulated. The occupation of art consultant is often confused with *art advisor*, and often these job titles are used erroneously and interchangeably. Some art advisors are members of the Association of Professional Art Advisors, a national organization that has stringent regulations regarding business practices and professional qualifications. It defines an art advisor as one who is

> qualified to provide professional guidance to collectors on the selection, placement, installation, and maintenance of art. The professional art advisor has an understanding of art history, art administration, the art market, educational concepts, contemporary business practices, public relations, and communications.

Orlando art advisor Brenda B. Harris points out that

> our culture has created a modern-day monster called "consulting" which often is used by those who may have good intentions, but who are not fully qualified or trained to advise or consult. Many of these individuals are unaware of the meaning or responsibilities associated with being an art consultant or advisor. These professional designations are often inappropriately used by gallery or artist sales representatives to indicate expertise and imply that the information is provided in the client's best interest. In reality, it is the product with the greatest profit potential, not artistic quality, that may be promoted.[39]

Art advisors do not receive commissions from artists on work sold or for projects commissioned. They are *paid by their clients* (individuals, organizations, and businesses) to provide information, advice, and related services *without any conflict of interest*. This means that, unlike many art consultants, art advisors do not maintain permanent inventories of art, so they are not "pushing" only the work of artists they have on hand. Also, art advisors accept work on consignment only for the purpose of presentation or approval.

Commissions paid to art consultants can be negotiated, but expect to be asked to pay between 40 and 50 percent on work that has already been created. *Under no circumstances* should you pay more than 25 percent of the *artist's fee* for *commissioned projects* obtained through an art consultant. In other words, do not pay a commission on the overhead expenses of the project (see Chapter 3, "Pricing Your Work: How Much Is It Worth?").

Art consultant Françoise Yohalem gives excellent advice to artists who are being considered for a commissioned project:

> Never make a model, never make a proposal, unless you are paid for it. This is very important. Artists are too often willing to do a lot of work for nothing on the hopes that maybe something good will come out of it—and that is wrong. It gives the wrong impression to the client. It says that the artist is not professional, that the artist is pathetic and wants the job so badly that [he or she] is willing to do anything. I think the client respects the artist more if the artist says I expect to be paid.[40]

If an art consultant or art advisor requests work on consignment, do not let any work leave your studio *before* an artist/agent contract is signed. If a commissioned project has been arranged by an intermediary, you should use an artist/agent contract *in addition to* the commission contract between yourself and the client. The Appendix section "Law" lists publications such as *Legal Guide for the Visual Artist* and *The Artists' Survival Manual* that include artist/agent and commission agreements. For further information on contracts, refer to pages 137–140.

When approaching an art consultant or art advisor, submit a basic presentation package (see Chapter 2), including a cover letter and a self-addressed stamped envelope. The names and addresses of art consultants and art advisors are listed in various publications, including *The International Directory of Corporate Art Collections* and the *Directory of Fine Art Representatives and Corporate Art Collections*. In addition, the index of the *Art in America Annual Guide to Galleries, Museums and Artists* lists corporate consultants and galleries that work with corporations. For additional information about these resources, see the Appendix section "Corporate Art."

Corporate Curators

Generally, corporate curators have the same professional qualifications as museum curators and function in a similar capacity as art advisors, but they are on the staffs of corporations and receive salaries for their services instead of fees. In addition, professional practices of corporate curators are governed by the National Association for Corporate Art Management.

Corporate curators should receive a basic presentation package (see Chapter 2), including a cover letter and a self-addressed stamped envelope. Names and addresses of corporate curators are listed in *The International Directory of Corporate Art Collections* and the *Directory of Fine Art Representatives and Corporate Art Collections* (see the Appendix section "Corporate Art").

Architects and Interior Designers

Many architectural and interior design firms commission artwork or purchase work in behalf of their clients. Some firms delegate a project manager or project designer to select work and/or maintain an artists' slide registry. In some instances a slide registry is organized by a staff librarian.

Architects and interior designers should receive a basic presentation package (see Chapter 2), including a cover letter and a self-addressed stamped envelope.

The names and addresses of architects and interior designers can be obtained in several ways. For example, *The Dodge Report* is a quarterly publication that provides information on every construction project nationwide, including the name of the design firm in charge and whether a budget has been allocated for the purchase or commissioning of artwork. Individual state reports are also available, but the drawback is that even a state report is very expensive.

A less expensive alternative is a publication published by the American Institute of Architects called *Profile*. It profiles architecture and interior design firms nationwide, and indicates whether the designers are involved in public art or percent-for-art programs (see page 100).

In addition, you can obtain the names and addresses of architects and interior designers in your area by contacting local chapters of the American Institute of Architects (AIA) and the American Society of Interior Designers (ASID), or through the national headquarters of the AIA and ASID.

For additional information regarding *The Dodge Report*, *Profile*, the American Institute of Architects, and the American Society of Interior Designers, see the Appendix sections "Corporate Art" and "Interior Design and Architecture."

You can develop a more personalized list of firms by studying architectural, landscape, and interior design publications to look for designers whose work is aesthetically compatible with your own. The names and addresses of these publications in the United States, Canada, and abroad are listed in the Appendix section "Interior Design and Architecture."

Another way of reaching architects and interior designers is to advertise in *The Guild*, an annual publication that contains color photographs of artwork and names, addresses, phone numbers, and biographies of American fine artists and crafts artists. *The Guild* is distributed free of charge to those who attend the national conferences of the American Society of Interior Designers and the American Institute of Architects. Additional information about *The Guild* is contained in the Appendix section "Corporate Art."

Not all artists' sourcebooks are used as frequently or are as reputable as *The Guild*. In the article "Buying Ad Space in Artists' Sourcebooks," published in *ArtCalendar*, Carolyn Blakeslee points out that

> a few questionable publishers have entered the business. There are now encyclopedias, directories, catalogues, surveys—of contemporary art, New York art, living artists, erotic art, West Coast artists, and so on. To pay to have your artwork published in a book: a good investment, or a waste of money?[41]

The article offers good advice to help you determine whether it is worth the effort to advertise in a sourcebook. For example, artists should know what kind of paper the ad will be printed on, at what line-screen ruling the plates will be reproduced, how large the book will be, how many copies of the book will be printed, whether the circulation is audited, and how often the book is published.[42] (Information on obtaining a copy of the article is listed in the Appendix section "Career Management, Business, and Marketing.")

Publicizing and Generating Corporate Sales and Commissions

If your work is purchased or commissioned by a corporation, use public-relations tools such as press releases (see page 62) and photographs (see page 41) to generate publicity and new contacts. *Past accomplishments should always be used as a springboard to solicit new clients and projects.*

Issue a press release to announce a corporate commission or sale. Press releases should be sent to collectors, clients, potential collectors and clients, and people in the art world with whom you are in contact, or people in the art world whom you have always wanted to contact.

Send a press release to *Corporate ARTnews*, a monthly publication that contains the columns "Recent Acquisitions" and "Recent Commissions." Each announcement in these columns includes the artist's name, the title of the artwork, a description, the year the work was completed, the medium, the name of the corporation, and, if applicable, the name of the art consultant responsible for placing the work. If a commission or sale involved the *services of an art consultant or art advisor*, send a press release and photograph to *Art Business News*, a monthly publication that also announces recent corporate acquisitions and commissions. The addresses of *Corporate ARTnews* and *Art Business News* are listed in the Appendix section "Corporate Art."

A press release issued by an artist announcing the acquisition of three photographs by a Canadian bank led to a feature article in a major New York newspaper. A press release issued by an accounting firm, in behalf of a sculptor, announcing the completion of a commissioned piece was sent to various trade publications read by accountants. An article in one such publication announcing the commission led to a commission for the sculptor from another accounting firm.

Public Art Programs

In addition to private and corporate clients, there is a wide range of commission and sales opportunities available to artists through public art programs sponsored by federal, state, and municipal agencies and independent organizations.

There is also a wealth of information available about public art programs. For example: *Competitions Hotline* is a quarterly newsletter that lists public art, architecture, and landscape architecture competitions in the United States and abroad. *Going Public: A Field Guide to Developments in Art in Public Places*, published by the Arts Extension Service of the University of Massachusetts, provides an overview of current issues, policies, and processes in the administration and preservation of public art, with an appendix that includes information on two hundred ongoing public art programs. The *Guidebook for Competitions and Commissions*, published by Visual Arts Ontario, provides guidelines on commissioning public art, and discusses the roles of the sponsor and artist. And the *Percent for Art/Public Places Programs Mailing List* provides mailing labels for city, state, and national programs; postcards to request information; and a master list that includes the names and addresses of each public art program, including the name of the contact person, his or her telephone number, and eligibility requirements. The list is updated several times a year. The addresses of these resources are listed in the Appendix under "Public Art."

Federal Public Art Programs

The federal government commissions artists to produce works of art for various government projects. In the General Services Administration (GSA) Art-in-Architecture Program, artists are commissioned to produce works of art that are incorporated into the architectural design of new federal buildings. In addition, artwork is commissioned for buildings undergoing repair or renovation, as well as for federal buildings in which artworks were originally planned but never acquired.

Commissioned work includes (but is not limited to) sculpture, tapestries, earthworks, architecturally scaled crafts, photographs, and murals.

One half of one percent of a building's estimated construction cost is reserved for commissioned work. Artists are nominated cooperatively by the GSA, the National Endowment for the Arts (NEA), and the project architect.

The architect is asked to submit an art-in-architecture proposal that specifies the nature and location of the artwork, taking into consideration the building's overall design concept.

The NEA appoints a panel of art professionals who meet at the project site along with the architect and representatives of the GSA and NEA. They review the visual materials (which are submitted through the GSA's slide registry) and nominate three to five artists for each proposed artwork. The NEA forwards the nominations to the administrators of the GSA, who make the final decision.

The Veterans Administration's Art-in-Architecture Program is similar to that of the GSA, but it has its own operating budget.

The addresses of these agencies are listed in the Appendix under "Public Art."

Municipal, State, and Independent
Public Arts Programs

The precedent of allocating a certain percentage of the cost of new or renovated public buildings for art, as described in the GSA's Art-in-Architecture Program, has also been legislated by many cities, counties, and states throughout the United States. Canada, too, has similar programs.

The Art in Public Places Program of the National Endowment for the Arts provides grants to nonprofit organizations so that they can commission artists to create art for public spaces. The Public Art Fund, Inc., sponsors installations in public spaces throughout New York City. The Social and Public Art Resource Center in Venice, California, is a multicultural arts center that produces, exhibits, distributes, and preserves public artwork; it also sponsors murals and workshops. Urban Arts in Boston is a public arts agency that houses a nationwide slide registry of artists in all disciplines.

The names and addresses of municipal and state public art agencies and independent organizations are listed in the Appendix section "Public Art."

Public Art Programs
for Transportation Systems

Other public art projects have been initiated in conjunction with mass transit facilities and airports. For example, in New York City there is the Arts for Transit Program, in conjunction with the New York City Transit Authority, the Metro-North Commuter Railroad, the Long Island Rail Road, and the Triborough Bridge and Tunnel Authority. Arts for Transit commissions art for several projects, including Adopt-a-Station, Creative Stations, Percent for Art, Exhibition Centers, Music Under New York, Sounds Grand, and Special Projects. Arts on the Line in Cambridge, Massachusetts, commissions artists and purchases work for the Massachusetts Bay Transit Authority; and Los Angeles has an Art for Rail Transit program sponsored by the Los Angeles County Transportation Commission. In addition, the Tucson International Airport and the Seattle-Tacoma International Airport have public art programs. The addresses of these agencies are listed in the Appendix under "Public Art."

Making National Connections

A recent edition of the *Art in America Annual Guide to Galleries, Museums and Artists* lists 4,814 galleries, alternative spaces, museums, university galleries, private dealers, corporate art consultants, and print dealers throughout the United States, from Anniston, Alabama, to Thermopolis, Wyoming.

The *Annual* lists 594 commercial and not-for-profit galleries in New York City, 133 in Chicago, 70 in Los Angeles, 46 in Boston, 33 in Dallas, and 28 in Atlanta. Although many consider New York to be the art capital of the world (and also make the erroneous assumption that New York artists are more talented than artists elsewhere), the main reason New York is deserving of its title is the large number of exhibition opportunities that are packed into the small island of Manhattan. However, thousands of exhibition and sales opportunities are available throughout the United States and outside of the United States, resources that are consistently overlooked and neglected by the majority of artists.

Artificial barriers and provincial attitudes about the art market restrict artists' career development. Many artists believe that their market is limited to their city of residence, or that some sort of universal censorship is imposed, illogically concluding that there is no market *anywhere* for their work if they are unable to find a receptive audience in their hometown. Additionally, many artists fail to make national contacts because they ponder trivial details and dwell on the logistics of transporting work to other cities and working with out-of-town dealers and art consultants.

It is important to keep in mind that regardless of the varied philosophical or altruistic reasons dealers give to explain their involvement with art, the bottom line is *money*. If someone believes *money can be made from your work*, geographic considerations become inconsequential.

The most effective way to find suitable out-of-town galleries is to travel. The *Art in America Annual* can be a helpful preliminary tool in locating exhibition resources. On a state-by-state, city-by-city basis, it lists the names, addresses, and phone numbers of gallery dealers, alternative spaces, and museums, and for each organization it describes the type of art and/or medium of interest, as well as the names of artists represented or exhibited. Use the *Annual* before traveling to compile a list of galleries that are interested in the kind of work you do (e.g., works on paper, sculpture, photography, painting, decorative arts).

Other publications offer more detailed information about marketing and exhibition resources on a *regional* basis. For example, the *Artists Gallery Guide for Chicago and the Illinois Region* lists exhibition opportunities in Indiana, Missouri, and Wisconsin as well as Chicago and the rest of Illinois; *Washington Art* profiles 158 commercial galleries, 58 art centers and alternative spaces, and 23 corporate art consultants and museums in the Washington, D.C., metropolitan area; the *National Association of Artists' Organizations Directory* lists more than 1,000 organizations in the visual, performing, and literary arts, many of which sponsor exhibitions; and *The Artists' Guide to Philadelphia* describes commercial galleries, cooperatives, alternative spaces, art centers, and arts service organizations in the Philadelphia area. The names and addresses of the publishers of these resource guides are listed in the Appendix section "Exhibition/Performance Places and Spaces."

Visit each gallery on your list to ascertain whether it is *right for you*. (For guidelines on helping you determine whether a gallery is right for you, see page 127.) Eliminate from your list those galleries that fall short of *your standards*, and concentrate on the ones that have made an impression. Try to set up an appointment, mentioning that you are from out of town. New York galleries are notorious for being inaccessible to unreferred artists; galleries in smaller cities are generally more availing. But if you are unable to make an appointment, drop off or mail a presentation package.

If you are unable to visit out-of-town galleries in person, you can get an idea of the type of work some of these galleries exhibit by scanning art periodicals, studying gallery display ads, and reading articles and reviews that are accompanied with photographs.

If you are unfamiliar with a gallery's business reputation, contact artists who are already involved with the gallery before committing yourself to a consignment arrangement and/or exhibition. The names of the artists represented by a particular gallery are listed in the *Art in America Annual*.

Negotiating with out-of-town dealers can be as simple as sending a contract that outlines your requirements and, if necessary, being willing to compromise over certain issues. However, it can also be as complicated as persuading a dealer to use a contract!

You can also make national contacts by writing to out-of-town museums, alternative spaces, public art programs, art consultants, and university galleries and museums.

Developing markets beyond your home city offers many rewards. You should also consider extending your horizons beyond the United States.

Making International Connections

I recently met with an American artist who regularly exhibits at museums and commercial galleries in Germany and Italy. She sells enough work in Europe to afford a studio outside of Rome and another studio in New York City.

She described how well she was treated in Europe, where the occupation of artist is cherished and highly respected, but she concluded that her main problem was that she was without New York gallery representation.

I asked if European galleries or museums were pressuring her to exhibit in New York. The answer was no; it was her idea. Although she detailed the reasons why she needed a New York gallery in a lengthy monologue, the real issue was *validation*. She believed the myth that New York gallery representation equals universal validation.

Since she had been out of the country for several months, I climbed up on my soapbox and gave her an overview of New York galleries. I explained that over the last few years, it has become increasingly difficult to differentiate vanity galleries (see page 86) and what are considered mainstream galleries, because of the incredible exhibition-related costs galleries expect artists to absorb.

The artist realized how fortunate she was to have cultivated professional contacts outside of the United States, contacts who did not look to New York for validation of her talents.

If you are intrigued with the idea of exhibiting and selling work abroad, but don't know how to make the contacts or get started, a variety of resources are available. Unfortunately, no single comprehensive reference book lists and describes international galleries, museums, private dealers, corporate consultants, and alternative spaces in detail, but several useful references are available.

The Art Guide series, published by Art Guide Publications in London, provides good background information about contacting galleries, museums, alternative spaces, the press, arts organizations, et cetera, in selected international cities and countries. The books are distributed in the United States by the Talman Company of New York City. The series includes the *Amsterdam Art Guide, Berlin Arts Guide, Australian Arts Guide, London Art and Artists Guide, Paris Art Guide, Madrid Arts Guide, Glasgow Arts Guide,* and *The Artists Directory: A Handbook to the Contemporary British Art World.*

The *International Directory of Corporate Art Collections*, published by the International Art Alliance and *ARTnews*, contains information on one thousand corporate art collections, including the collections of Japanese and European corporations.

Art Diary and *Photo Diary* list the names, addresses, and phone numbers of artists, critics, galleries, museums, cultural centers, and art periodicals in twenty-seven foreign countries. Although the *Diaries* are published annually, information is not updated on a regular basis and you might need to refer to a second source to obtain correct mailing addresses.

By scanning periodicals that review and/or advertise international galleries you can get an idea of the type of work certain galleries exhibit. International periodicals can be found in bookstores and libraries that have extensive art sections. The names of various foreign art periodicals are listed in *Art Diary* and *Photo Diary*, and in the Art Guide publications.

After compiling a list of museums and galleries, send each contact person a presentation package (see Chapter 2), and include a cover letter stating that you are planning a trip to that person's city and would like to arrange an appointment if the person finds your work of interest. If you receive positive responses, make the trip a reality!

The same guidelines for selecting and working with domestic galleries are applicable to galleries in foreign cities (see page 127). Additional resources for making international connections, including funding organizations, artist-in-residence programs, and studio exchange programs, are listed in the Appendix section "International Connections."

Creating Your Own Exhibition Opportunities

Even though your presentation packages are circulating in registries, museums, commercial galleries, alternative spaces, et cetera, don't sit around waiting to be asked to exhibit and don't depend on someone to suggest a context in which to exhibit your work. Create your own context and exhibition opportunities.

Theme Shows

Curate your own exhibitions or performances, based on themes that put your work into a context. Theme shows can feature your work exclusively or include the work of other artists. A theme show is more than a straightforward exhibition. At their best, theme shows increase and enhance art-viewing consciousness, demand the participation of many of our senses, and help the public as well as the art community understand and learn more about what an artist is communicating and the motivating influences revealed in the work. For example, the group exhibition "A, E, Eye, O, U, and Sometimes Why" contained two-dimensional pieces that used "a variety of media to express the concerns and reactions to different social, informational, and psychological situations, through the combined use of words and images."[43] The theme show "Top Secret: Inquiries into the Biomirror"[44] featured the work of artist Todd Siler and consisted of a "32-foot, 3-dimensional sketch of a Cerebreactor, drawings and detailed studies which introduce Siler's theories on brain and mind, science and art."[45]

Another asset of theme shows is that it is far more likely you will obtain funding for a theme show with *broad educational value* than for a show called "Recent Paintings."

Develop and Circulate a Proposal

A proposal should describe your idea, purpose, intentions, and audience. It should tell why the theme is important, how you plan to develop it, and who will be involved. Supporting materials should include information about the people involved (résumé, slides, etc.) and indicate your space or site requirements. Depending on the intended recipient of the proposal, it could also include a budget and ideas on how the exhibition will be funded.

The proposal should be circulated to museums, colleges, galleries, alternative spaces, cultural organizations, and funding organizations. It could very well be that you will need only one of these groups to complete the project. On the other hand, you might need all of these groups, but for such different reasons as sponsorship, endorsement, administration, facilities, funding, and contributions.

A book published by the Smithsonian Institution Traveling Exhibition Service (SITES) called *Good Show! A Practical Guide for Temporary Exhibitions* is an excellent resource for artists interested in curating exhibitions and is also helpful for proposal writing, as it covers the complete range of factors that need to be taken into consideration (e.g., advance planning, preparation, fabrication, illumination, and installation). The book also includes a good bibliography for each of the subjects it covers. For further information see "Exhibition Planning" in the Appendix.

Artist Fees

Often artists let the excitement of an exhibition opportunity interfere with clear thinking, and overlook various exhibition costs. The most neglected item in budget planning is an artist's *time*—for example, the time spent conceptualizing an exhibition, researching and contacting galleries and museums, and preparing and sending proposals and/or presentation tools. Then there is the time spent preparing, installing, and dismantling the exhibition. The list could go on and on.

Although some alternative and nonprofit galleries pay artists a fee to help offset exhibition expenses, this practice has not been widely adopted, nor is it widely recognized by artists that they have the right to request a fee, particularly a *realistic* fee.

Canada is far ahead of the United States in acknowledging the need for realistic artist exhibition fees. For example, the Canadian arts service organization Canadian Artists' Representation Ontario (CARO) recommends minimum exhibition fees that artists should charge when exhibiting in public or nonprofit museums and galleries. Recommendations take into account a wide variety of exhibiting situations, including single, two-person, three-person, four-person, and group shows; regional, interregional, national, and international touring and nontouring shows; and juried and nonjuried shows. CARO's recommended fees are published in the *CARFAC Recommended Minimum Exhibition Fee Schedule* (see the Appendix section "Exhibition Planning").

Open Studio Events

You can generate exhibition and sales opportunities by opening your studio and/or home to the public. However, a successful open studio event requires careful planning: You must develop an imaginative guest list with many *new* names and have a clear idea of what you want to achieve. Is your main goal exposure, sales, or a combination of both?

Following are guidelines for open studio planning:

DATES. An open studio should be held on a *minimum* of two (not necessarily consecutive) days, preferably including at least one weekend day and one weekday evening.

INVITATIONS AND MAILING LIST. The invitation should include a visual image of your work (see page 69). Invitations should be sent to collectors, potential collectors, contacts within the art world, family, and friends. But most important, *invitations should also be sent to new people.* One way to do this is by telling friends and associates *who admire your work* and are *not* necessarily part of the art world that you want to increase your contacts for the purpose(s) of sales and/or exposure. Ask if they would be willing to write a personal note on the invitation, inviting their friends and associates to attend. If ten people send ten invitations in your behalf, one hundred new contacts will be generated.

USE AN ASSISTANT. All too often, open studios resemble gallery openings, with guests self-consciously glued to the walls. Uncomfortable environments are not conducive to generating sales or exhibiting work; people want to leave as soon as possible. It is important to create a warm and energizing atmosphere. Guests should be introduced to one another. But if you are serving beverages, answering the door, and asking people to sign a guest book, et cetera, you will not have time to meet people in an effective way, introduce guests, talk about your work, or answer questions. Hire a person or ask a friend to help out with all of the various tasks associated with an open studio so that you are free to spend time with people.

PROVIDE PRINTED MATERIALS. Prepare multiple copies of printed materials (as many copies as the number of guests expected), including a résumé (see page 30) or biography (see page 36), an artist statement (see page 37), press clippings (if applicable), and a price list (see page 54). These materials should be placed in a central location.

Selling from Your Studio

Most artists find the experience of selling work directly to the public gratifying on several levels. The intimacy of a studio and direct contact with an artist can create a very positive environment, and for many people direct contact with an artist is a chief factor in buying art.

But other people buy art for many different reasons. Increasing studio sales requires an understanding of basic sales skills particular to selling art, and an understanding of individual buying styles. In her book *How to Sell Art: A Guide for Galleries, Art Dealers, Consultants, and Agents* (see the Appendix section "Career Management, Business, and Marketing"), Nina Pratt, an art market advisor, offers the following advice:

> Learn your own buying style, because it influences your selling style. . . . There are as many different buying styles as there are people. But there are a few main categories that most people fall into . . . [for example,] impulsive versus calculating buyers. . . . There are also people who hate to be told anything . . . as opposed to the ones who want a full biography of the artist; the ones who have to tell you their life stories before they are ready to buy; the apparently timid, docile client with a will of steel; [and] the bargain hunters [who] will ask for a discount at the drop of a hat. Learning how to distinguish each type comes with time and

practice. Until your instincts develop, rely on . . . skillful questions to find out which sort of person you are dealing with.[46]

The questions Nina Pratt recommends include: Does this person buy art? What kind of art? In what price range? Is your work appropriate for this person? Does this person have the authority to buy, or will a spouse have the final say?[47] Pratt points out, however, that "most visitors . . . would be turned off if you boldly grilled them on these subjects. So you must learn to probe delicately but precisely for the information that you need."[48]

6

Dealing with
Dealers and Psyching
Them Out

Although this chapter is primarily about gallery dealers, much of the information and advice and most of the perspectives and views are also applicable to people in other arts-related occupations, including art consultants, curators, critics, administrators, collectors, and artists. Some of my impressions and characterizations might seem severe, but it is not my intention to throw all of the blame for the ills and injustices in the art world on dealers, curators, and the like. *Artists must also accept responsibility for the way things are*, mainly because most artists, overtly, covertly, or inadvertently, participate (or try to participate) in the dog-eat-dog system. Few are trying to change it.

If I had my way, I would replace commercial galleries with a system in which artists exhibited work in their studios and sold it directly to the public. But such a system could work only if artists acquired enough self-confidence not to need gallery validation, and if the public, likewise, had the self-confidence necessary to buy work without gallery validation. Since there is a very remote chance that these events will occur in my lifetime, the next best thing for changing the system is to regulate the business practices of galleries nationwide, including policies affecting commissions, discounts, insurance, and payments to artists. For the time being, since the gallery system is still very much intact and is virtually unregulated, the following opinions, advice, and observations are aimed at helping artists acquire more business savvy, more control over their careers, and more control in their relationships with those who are currently running the show.

Lies, Illusions, and Bad Advice

Artists are constantly bombarded with erroneous, irresponsible, and unethical advice about the art world and art galleries. While some advice is exchanged through word of mouth, much of it is disseminated through articles in trade publications. Some of these articles are written by well-meaning but naive individuals who are connected to the art world in some capacity; others are written by less-than-well-intentioned art-world figures whose motives are self-serving. For example, in an article from *Art in America*, a dealer assures readers that "a minority of dealers are strictly concerned with commercial success."[49] However, he then condones the greedy practice of awarding dealers a commission on *all* studio sales:

> An artist may on occasion sell a work directly from his studio to a friend or to a collector he has known before his gallery affiliation. It is the artist's ethical obligation to report such transactions to his dealer and to remit a reduced commission, commonly 20 percent, to compensate the dealer for a work he cannot offer under the usual terms of their agreement.[50]

Another dealer insinuates that the fastest track into the art world is to work for a famous artist, and tells *ARTnews* readers that "apprentices have instant entrée. They meet collectors and curators."[51] A political scientist *cum* art collector encourag ginners to exhibit only in "small" places when he writes in *A ican Artist*, "Begin building your career at smaller local or regi\ galleries of good repute. It is too bruising to try the larger galleries in major art centers."[52] An arts administrator encourages artists to retreat if they are rejected by galleries, advising, "If your first search is unsuccessful, wait a year or two and try again."[53] And a career consultant to artists states that the reason it is important to dress presentably is "so that you give the impression that you're making money somehow, presumably through your artwork."[54]

Artists also give each other peculiar and bad advice, much of it better suited to the *National Enquirer* than to the "reputable" periodicals that publish it! For example, an artist tells readers of *ARTnews*: "What works best—for success—is if the artist is handsome or very beautiful."[55] In a book profiling contemporary artists, an artist discusses how she uses sex to get ahead: "I've been propositioned a lot: 'I'll give you a show if you sleep with me.' It happens often. Would I do it for a show? Now I would, but when I was younger I wouldn't. I wouldn't because I was a jerk."[56] And another artist tells beginners that "one of the necessary qualities of being an artist . . . is to not expect an awful lot, to be somewhat dense about any thoughts of what you will get out of being an artist."[57]

If you believed everything you read you would conclude that, in order to find a gallery and succeed in the art world, you must be beautiful or handsome, sleep with dealers, and dress as though you have a lot of money. When beginning your career you should work as an apprentice to a famous artist but have low expectations, and exhibit in small, local galleries. You should avoid large cities at all costs. And if you are rejected from galleries, you should retreat and wait a year or two before trying again!

Although in composite form these recommendations sound very silly, many artists, unfortunately, believe the advice to be true.

Dealers and Their Personalities

Arrogant and *temperamental* are adjectives frequently used to describe both artists and dealers. Who started the name-calling first? Was it the arrogance of an artist that forced a dealer to retaliate with the same weapon? Or was it a temperamental dealer who elicited the same response from an artist? Is it a chicken-and-egg situation or a matter of simultaneous combustion?

Arrogance is a self-defense tactic to disguise insecurities, and frustration is often demonstrated through a temperamental personality. Artists and dealers have a lot of insecurities. What about frustration? It is easy to understand and explain why artists are frustrated. Why should dealers be frustrated?

Many dealers are frustrated artists who did not have the tenacity, perseverance, and fortitude to stick it out. Consequently, they are jealous of anyone who did. The wrath of some dealers pours forth when they spot weak work or weak personalities. A weak artist reminds them of themselves, and the memories bring little pleasure. Other dealers behave like bulls that see red: they believe all artists are threatening. They do not differentiate.

Because many dealers are unable to produce provocative work, and *showing* provocative work does not gratify their frustrated egos, they compensate by cultivating provocative personalities. Some dealers are so skilled in verbal delivery that they lead others to believe they know what they are talking about. These dealers begin to believe that their reputations give them the right to make outrageous, irresponsible demands and give outrageous, irresponsible advice. These dealers also believe that reputation alone exempts them from the requirements of morality or integrity, let alone courtesy.

A painter once came to me for advice about his dealer, with whom he had worked for several years. The dealer gave him single shows on a regular basis, and the artist sold well at all of them. However, the dealer, one of the better known in New York, had been badgering the artist for months to stop doing free-lance work for a national magazine. The dealer contended that if the artist continued to work for the magazine he would not be taken seriously as a fine artist. The artist began to question the dealer's judgment only when it infringed on his financial stability. Until then, he let the dealer's opinions influence and control his life.

In response to his problem, I simply stated that it was none of a dealer's business how an artist made money; the artist looked at me as if this were the biggest revelation of the century!

Another client was told by a dealer who had just finished rejecting him to be careful about showing his work to other artists because they might steal his ideas. The artist didn't know what to do with the backhanded compliment. On the one hand, the work wasn't good enough for the dealer. On the other hand, the ideas were good enough to be stolen. Up until that point the artist had not been paranoid about other artists stealing his ideas, but the dealer successfully instilled a fear: beware of the community of artists!

Dealers take great delight in giving artists advice on how their work can be *improved*. The lecture begins with a critique of the artist's work that quickly transforms into an art history class. And artists listen. They listen in agony, but they listen.

It Takes Two to Tango

I am reminded of an artist who called me to make an appointment to discuss her career. She called back a few days later to cancel, saying her slides weren't ready, then quickly changed her mind about the excuse she had offered and lashed into a tirade that ended with: "And who in the hell are you to judge my work? I don't want to be put in a position to be judged."

It took me a while to regain composure, but when I did, I told her that, in my capacity as an artists' consultant, I did not judge work, and even if I did, I hadn't called her, *she had called me* and set up the situation!

Many artists have an "attitude" about dealers and anyone else in the art world who is perceived as an authority figure. In the years that I have worked with artists, I have had to remind clients on several occasions that I am not the enemy!

Once, at a cocktail party where artists were in the majority, a painter used the opportunity to verbally abuse a dealer he had just met for the first time. At the top of his lungs he held the dealer personally responsible for the hard time he was having selling his work, and he tried, unsuccessfully, to goad his colleagues into joining his tirade. The scene served no other purpose than to add some excitement to what, up to that point, had been a very dull party. The dealer left in a huff, followed by the artist, who was angry that he had received no support or encouragement from his peers.

On another occasion, a meeting I had with a client and his dealer centered on the artist's career. As long as this was the case, the artist was enthusiastic and amiable. However, when we finished with the subject at hand and drifted on to other topics, the artist began yawning, squirming in his chair, and nervously rapping on the table. When he saw that neither the dealer nor I intended to respond to his body language, he started ranting that he was bored with our conversation. With one conciliatory sentence the dealer placated the artist so easily and skillfully that I realized how familiar and experienced he was with this kind of behavior.

On the other hand, dealers can be cruel or even sadistic, heaping abuse on artists while the artists masochistically allow it. The following episode illustrates the point loud and clear.

A painter took slides to a dealer. While he was viewing her work, he lit up a cigar. After examining the slides he said that he wasn't interested—her work was "too feminine." He then proceeded to give the artist a lecture on the history of art, all the while dropping cigar ashes on her slides.

The artist watched in excruciating pain, but didn't say a word. When the dealer finished the lecture, the artist collected her slides and left the gallery. But she was so devastated by the symbolism of the ashes on her work that she put herself to bed for three days.

Regardless of whether the dropping of ashes was sadistic or inadvertent carelessness, the question remains, Why didn't the artist say something? For example, "Excuse me, but you are dropping ashes on my slides!"

One wonders: if the dealer had been pressing his foot on her toe, would she have allowed him to continue? When the dealer said that her work was "too feminine," she should have immediately left the gallery (with a curt "Thank you for your time") or stayed to challenge his idiotic statement.

Just as artists tend to forget that, to a great extent, a dealer's livelihood depends on an artist's work, dealers also forget, and they need to be reminded. Reminding them won't necessarily mean that they are going to like your work any more, but it can give you some satisfaction, and it puts things in perspective, something that the art world desperately needs.

Dealers as Businesspeople

Finding gallery representation is a task that requires patience. In New York, for example, many artists are strung along by galleries for as long as ten years. After several rounds of annual studio visits and more rounds of appointment changes or no-shows, a commitment is finally made—an actual exhibition date is scheduled. But the exaltation of gallery status can quickly dissipate when one discovers exactly what being a gallery artist entails.

Nina Pratt, a New York–based art market advisor, observes:

> If those considering opening a gallery or entering a related profession were presented with a checklist of qualities and skills necessary for a successful career, the majority of people would have second thoughts about entering the field![58]

Pratt is knowledgeable about the inner workings of gallery operations, and she sheds light on why so many dealers sink or barely keep their galleries afloat, and live up to neither their own nor artists' expectations. If many of the reasons she addresses sound very familiar, it is because they are the very same reasons that prevent artists from achieving their goals, with or without gallery representation.

Pratt believes the root of the problem is that many dealers believe the myth that art and business do not mix. "Dealers are terrified of being viewed as used-car salesmen. They go to great lengths to disassociate themselves from the 'business' aspects of art."[59] She also points out that many people who open galleries naively assume that an arts-related profession will automatically make them successful. Parallels can be drawn between these dealers and the artists who believe that talent is the only skill necessary to guarantee a constant stream of dealers, curators, and collectors knocking at the door.

Pratt also points out that since a dealer's selling style usually matches his or her personal buying style, he or she frequently hires a staff with a similar selling style. This lack of flexibility can severely cripple sales. "Collectors come with a variety of backgrounds, tastes, and buying power," Pratt says. "They also come with a variety of ways they behave as consumers. A gallery must be able to adapt to the range and differences in consumer habits."[60]

During personal encounters with the public, dealers tend to go to extremes by either not talking at all or talking too much. The cool, nonverbal approach can be perceived as intimidating; overly talkative dealers might not hear what the client is saying. "Important data can be gleaned from listening, including aesthetic leanings, price range, style of buying, and sincerity of interest," Pratt observes.[61]

Citing greed as one of the most self-defeating business practices, and noting dealers' unwillingness to split commissions with other dealers and art consultants, Pratt adds that "dealers should be willing to pass up commissions in order to show clients that they can get them what they want. This can most definitely strengthen a working relationship with collectors, stimulate trust, and encourage future sales. A cooperative spirit between dealers, and between dealers and art consultants, is at an all-time low."[62]

Pratt also faults dealers for their approach to advertising, which is discussed in Chapter 4 (see page 70).

"The Attitude"

New York dealer André Emmerich has said that "good art dealers don't sell art; they allow people to acquire it."[63] Such a statement sets the tone for the way art is often marketed, an attitude conveyed not only in a gallery's selling style, but by its staff.

In a recent article, Grace Glueck, a critic and art editor of the *New York Times*, described some common grievances voiced by the public about galleries.[64] Complaints spanned a range of issues, including the absence of basic civil courtesies and being patronized or treated rudely when purchasing work in the lower end of a gallery's price spectrum.

Dealers, for their part, complained that the public is not knowledgeable about art; they ask too many questions. Dealers further suggested that members of the public do their homework *before* entering a gallery.

The article painted a disheartening picture of the gallery world, primarily in New York City, but the picture is even more disheartening when one realizes how pervasive "the attitude" really is.

Although most dealers are not perceived as used-car salesmen, they often overreact to their fear of being perceived this way by cultivating snobbish airs. However, a haughty attitude coupled with a lack of business acumen often results in a loss of clients and potential clients, and eventually in the loss of their galleries!

Unethical Business Practices

Whether a gallery is ethical depends on its moral and financial integrity. A gallery's immoral practices are not always apparent until an artist is already involved in a formal relationship with it. However, some of the ploys used by morally abusive dealers include playing "mind games," making outrageous demands on artists, and dispensing bad advice. Often, artists are willing to accept a dealer's tyrannical or manipulative behavior as long as they don't feel that the dealer is cheating them financially.

The Martyr Syndrome

Frequently, dealers see themselves as martyrs who are taking a big risk simply by selling art for a living. But many of the dealers who have made their way into the art world in recent years require artists to share the financial risks of running a gallery—without sharing the profits. Because they see themselves as martyrs, dealers also rationalize that it is fair and just to use an *artist's share* of a sale to offset gallery cash-flow problems. Artists are paid when it is convenient—or in some cases they are never paid!

In the last edition of this book, published in 1988, I wrote:

> In the area of finance, there are certain disreputable dealers who are easy to identify, for they blatantly nickel-and-dime artists for every expense that is directly or indirectly related to an exhibition. Up until the time work is placed in a gallery, an artist is financially responsible for the costs of preparing the work for exhibition and transporting the work to a gallery. But once the work is in the gallery, an artist should not have to pay for any costs other than a dealer's commission, and then only if the work is sold!

Tragically, in the 1990s, there would be slim pickings if artists limited themselves only to galleries that pay for all exhibition costs. A recent survey of Chicago galleries[65] showed that 38 percent of the galleries polled require artists *either* to split promotion expenses with the gallery or pay the full amount; 22 percent require artists to split opening costs with the gallery or pay the full amount; and 30 percent require artists to split postage costs with the gallery or pay the full amount.

Although the majority of Chicago galleries still pay for most exhibition-related expenses, the statistics are indicative of *a trend outside of New York City* to make artists more responsible for gallery costs. In New York City, the practice of requiring artists to split or fully absorb exhibition expenses is not a trend, it is a *fait accompli!*

Gallery Hanky-Panky

Sometimes dealers deduct exhibition expenses and/or client discounts from an artist's share of a sale without forewarning the artist of this policy. And sometimes when work is sold artists are paid based on a price they previously set, when in reality the work sold for a higher amount. In many instances artists are oblivious of the deception.

One artist suspected something fishy after his numerous requests to his dealer for copies of sales invoices pertaining to his work went unheeded. He concocted a brilliant scheme to determine whether his suspicions were justified. Knowing that his dealer was out of town, he telephoned the gallery assistant to share a secret: he confided his plans to give the dealer a collage to commemorate his first year as a gallery artist. The collage would incorporate copies of sales receipts pertaining to his work, symbolic of hopes for a continuing prosperous relationship. The artist asked the assistant to cooperate by allowing him to photocopy the receipts. The assistant eagerly complied.

The receipts showed that the artist's suspicions were indeed justified. In one instance, a painting for which he had been compensated based on a selling price of $5,000 had actually been sold for $10,000! The case was settled out of court, and the artist received all of the monies due.

In New York, price manipulation of artwork in galleries was so endemic that in 1988 the city's Department of Consumer Affairs ruled that the prices of artwork in New York galleries must be "conspicuously displayed" for all visitors. Galleries complied, but not without a big fuss. Critic Hilton Kramer wrote a scathing article in the *New York Times* to protest the ruling. His basic point was that galleries are not retail stores and should not be required to display price tags.[66] However, *Times* readers disagreed, and in the following weeks numerous letters to the editor were published contesting Kramer's point of view. One art collector wrote:

> Art galleries are stores. Their proprietors, the art dealers, are merchants. Their primary purpose is to sell art in order

to make a profit. They are not houses of worship. They are not museums. They are not schools. They are not eleemosynary institutions. The dealer is not an altruist dedicated to educate and elevate the public. He is a pragmatic businessman. . . . There is no valid reason why this rule should not apply to galleries so that the collector will get the same information as other consumers.[67]

And an artist wrote:

Mr. Kramer endorses . . . both the "old boy" approach and the "if you must ask the price . . . " snob approach: salesmanship by intimacy and intimidation, respectively, which is exactly what the New York City Department of Consumer Affairs is trying to end. . . . As consumers, we are assured that the amount on whatever price tag is meant for everyone. How strange it is that the art gallery racket is the singular exception to this forthright concept, and how stranger that art dealers should be allowed to hide behind that protective screen of esthetics, of all things.[68]

How Dealers Find New Artists

In the late 1970s *Artworkers News* published the first and only comprehensive survey of New York City galleries that show contemporary art.[69] The study was based on a questionnaire completed by ninety-nine galleries.

Although the main purpose of the study was to investigate the extent to which galleries were excluding artists on sexual or racial grounds,[70] the survey results unearthed some valuable insights into the gallery system in general. For example, the study showed that while seventy-five of the galleries viewed slides of unreferred artists, fifty galleries had not taken on an unreferred artist in the past two years. Twelve galleries reported that they got new artists primarily from viewing slides of unreferred artists. The study also revealed that while the majority of galleries viewed slides, the main intent was not to look for new artists. Reasons cited for viewing slides included not wanting to discourage young artists, keeping in touch with the kind of work currently being done, and looking for artists whose work the dealers would be interested in following over a period of years.[71]

Although you might find the above statistics depressing, do not use the findings to rationalize why it is a waste of time to have your slides reviewed by dealers. Instead, turn the findings around and look at the situation in another light. For example, the study showed that the gallery *slide-viewing system is not a total dead end.* Some galleries *do* invite unreferred artists to exhibit; some galleries *do* want to keep an eye on new artists; and gallery dealers in general *do* want to know what's going on outside their own confines, and logically so, for their livelihood depends on artists, a fact that artists tend to forget.

Referral Systems

The study also revealed that the main ways galleries get new artists are through artist referrals *and* referrals from other "art-world figures." The study indicated, however, that artist referrals are the *primary* source.[72]

The following is a good example of how the artist referral system works: One of my clients, a painter, approached a well-known New York gallery dealer. He set up an appointment, showed his slides, and the dealer responded with the "Come back in two years" routine. Several weeks later, while the painter was working as a waiter, he noticed that a famous artist was sitting at one of the tables. He introduced himself to the celebrity and asked whether the celebrity would come to his studio to see his work. The painter and celebrity exchanged telephone numbers, and within the next few weeks the celebrity paid the artist a visit. The celebrity was impressed with the painter's work, so impressed that he bought a painting and insisted that the painter show his work to a specific gallery dealer, coincidentally the same dealer who had rejected him a few weeks before. The celebrity called the gallery dealer, raved about the artist, and shortly afterward my client returned to the gallery. This time he was greeted with another routine, but one more pleasing to his ear: "Where have you been all my life?"

Relatively few artists are admitted into galleries; assuming that dealers heed mainly the advice of other artists, my contention that artists are not referring each other to the extent to which they should seems accurate.

On the other hand, although artist referrals do exist, I am skeptical as to whether the gallery dealers who responded to the *Artworkers News* questionnaire were honest about artists being the primary referral source. It sounds good for the record, but compared with artist referrals, referrals from other art-world figures offer more mileage. For example: Curator tells dealer that critic wrote an excellent review about artist. Dealer checks out artist and invites artist into gallery. Dealer tells curator that artist is now part of gallery. Curator tells museum colleagues that artist is part of gallery and has backing of critic. Curator invites artist to exhibit at museum. Curator asks critic to write introduction to exhibition catalog in which artist is included. Dealer tells clients that artist has been well reviewed and is exhibiting at museum. Clients buy.

There are other variations on the same theme, including curator/dealer/critic conspiracies, which involve each buying the work of an unknown artist for very little money. Press coverage and exhibition exposure begin, and within a short period of time the dealer, curator, and critic have substantially increased their investment.

Throughout the book *The Art Biz: The Covert World of Collectors, Dealers, Auction Houses, Museums and Critics*, Alice Goldfarb Marquis describes the many entangled, self-serving relationships among art-world figures, pointing out that

the marketplace in stocks and bonds operates under stringent regulations against insider trading and conflicts of interest and insists on considerable openness about buyers, sellers, and prices. Despite occasional lapses, trading is constantly monitored; violators of the rules could end up being frog-marched down the center of Wall Street in handcuffs. By contrast, the art marketplace tolerates—indeed fosters—a sleazy, robber-baron style of capitalism not seen on Wall Street since the Great Depression. . . . If they were dealing in securities rather than one of humankind's noblest endeavors—art—the perpetrators of such egregious conflicts would be in jail.[73]

New York art dealer Richard Lerner acknowledged the importance of the art-world-figure referral system when he discussed his criteria for inviting new artists into his gallery. He described his selection process, which sounds more like a shampoo-judging contest, in this way:

For the benefit of the people that are already in the gallery, it's imperative, if I add names, I add names that already have some luster . . . I mean peer approval . . . who are recognized curatorially, critically as having importance in the mainstream of American art.[74]

Selecting Galleries

The most common advice given to artists about selecting galleries is to start small and avoid big cities. The advice is not based on any great truism or profound knowledge; it is simply the way things have been done. However, there is no guarantee that if you start with a small, obscure gallery you will end up in a large, high-profile gallery, just as there is no certainty that if you start big you will automatically be turned away. Since neither of the formulas is guaranteed to work, *approach all galleries that meet your criteria.* Keep all of your options open and do not let supposedly pragmatic advice narrow the possibilities.

Criteria for Selecting Galleries

Deciding whether the gallery is right means paying attention to big and little details. Obviously, respecting the work of gallery artists is an important consideration, but do not limit your selection to those galleries featuring work that is similar to your own. Although it seems like a logical criterion by which to select a gallery, logic does not often prevail in the art world, and a dealer might respond by saying, "We have someone doing that already!" Select galleries with whose artists you *share an affinity*.

The physical properties of a space, including size, ceiling height, and light quality, are another important consideration. Envision your work in the gallery space. Would it be exhibited to its best advantage? Does the gallery have a cluttered or spacious feeling?

Another important factor to consider is a gallery's price range. A gallery should offer you pricing *breadth*. Even though your work might currently be priced in a lower range, you want to be able to gradually increase your prices. Therefore, you need a gallery that sells work in a flexible price range. Many galleries have a price ceiling based on what they think their constituency will spend on art.

Let Your Fingers Do the Walking, and Wear a Disguise

The *Art in America Annual Guide to Galleries, Museums and Artists* is a helpful tool for locating galleries throughout the United States. Other publications offer more detailed information on a *regional* basis, including the *Artists Gallery Guide for Chicago and the Illinois Region*; *Washington Art*, which profiles galleries in Washington, D.C., and the surrounding area; *The Artists Guide to Philadelphia*; and *Access: A Guide to the Visual Arts in Washington State*. The names and addresses of the publishers of these resource guides are listed in the Appendix section "Exhibition/Performance Places and Spaces."

Use the *Annual* and/or regional publications to compile a list of galleries corresponding to the various descriptions that apply to your work (e.g., works on paper, sculpture, photography, painting, decorative arts).

Follow up by visiting each gallery to ascertain whether it is right for you. Consider this to be an "exploratory" visit—not the time to approach a dealer about your work. On the contrary, *disguise yourself as a collector*. You can glean much more valuable information about the gallery if the dealer thinks you are there to buy! By asking the right questions, you can learn quite a lot about a gallery's profile, including its price range, the career level of artists represented, and whether the dealer and/or his or her sales force is effective.

On the basis of your experiences during personal gallery visits, eliminate from your list the galleries that are no longer of interest and concentrate on approaching those that have made an impression. Guidelines for contacting out-of-town galleries are described in "Making National Connections" (see page 103) and "Making International Connections" (see page 105).

What a Gallery Can Do

A gallery has the *potential* to provide artists with many important amenities that are valuable in the present as well as the future. The optimum services to artists can include selling work through single and group exhibitions and on consignment; generating publicity; establishing new contacts and providing entrée into various network systems; developing and expanding markets in all parts of the world; arranging to have work placed in collections; arranging exhibitions in museums and other galleries; and providing financial security in the form of cash advances and/or retainers.

The minimum gallery services can include selling work on consignment (without an exhibition), providing general gallery experience, and adding résumé credits.

Naively, artists either (1) believe that once they are accepted into a gallery, the optimum services will automatically be provided, or (2) enter a gallery relationship without any expectations, thus missing the amenities that a gallery could provide. Keep in mind that dealers in big galleries do not provide any more or fewer amenities than dealers in small galleries. *It really depends on the dealer.*

There are various reasons why some dealers are more supportive than others. In some instances, it is because a dealer is so busy promoting one particular artist that other gallery artists are treated like second-class citizens. Often it is a case of downright laziness. For example, an artist was told by his dealer that he had been nominated for *Who's Who in American Art*, but the dealer had let the deadline pass for providing the required biographical data. In addition, for more than two months she had been "sitting on" sixty-five written inquiries that had resulted from the artist's work being published in a magazine.

Since there are no guidebooks available that evaluate dealers by strengths or weaknesses, the best way to track down this information is to talk to artists who are with a gallery or artists who have left one.

Finally, don't be afraid to leave a gallery if you find that it is no longer serving your best interests. Give a dealer a chance to respond to your needs or requirements, but if he or she is unresponsive, leave.

Presenting Yourself and Your Work

Dealers are so whimsical: I mean, who knows who is going to like what? I just tell people that I know it's a humiliating, horrible process. I don't approve of it at all, the way artists have to trundle around with their wares. I hate being in a gallery when an artist is in there showing slides. It makes me sick to my stomach—I mean, whoever the artist is. But the fact remains, that's how it works and I'm not going to be able to change it singlehandedly. If artists get upset about it, maybe they will do something about it.[75]

Most artists can probably identify with the circumstances

and feelings described here by author and critic Lucy Lippard. But showing your work to a dealer doesn't have to be a painful, gut-wrenching experience. Doing everything possible to put yourself on the offensive will make the process easier.

The first step is to understand that many dealers play games. *Just realizing that games are being played will give you an edge,* making it less likely that the games will be played at your expense. Having an edge can give you the self-confidence and perception necessary to respond with precision, candor, wit, or whatever the circumstances call for. Compare this power with the many times you have walked out of a gallery thinking of all the brilliant retorts you wished you had said while you were there. Keep in mind that one reason why dealers appear to be in control, even when they are hostile, is that they have a lot of experience talking to artists. Dealers have much more contact with artists than artists have with dealers. The more face-to-face encounters you have with dealers, the more quickly you will be able to psych them out, and the more rapidly your tongue will untwist. Practice makes perfect!

How you contact a gallery can also put you on the offensive. You can walk in cold, lukewarm, warm, or hot. Walking in cold means that you are literally coming off the streets without setting up an appointment or bothering to inquire whether the dealer has regular viewing hours. Chances are you will be interrupting one of the numerous tasks and appointments that consume a dealer's day. Walking in cold leaves you vulnerable to many uncertainties, except the fact that you will receive a cold reception.

Walking in lukewarm means that you have sent a presentation package (see Chapter 2) or you have set up an appointment in advance. If you mail a package, follow up with a telephone call two weeks later. Keep calling until you get a reaction. Dealers complain that they are pestered with phone calls, but phone calls are the only way to circumvent procrastination and vagueness. As long as the package remains unopened, you are losing valuable time; the package could be in the process of review elsewhere. One of the advantages of using a brochure in lieu of slides (see page 44) is that you do not have to wait for it to be returned to contact other people.

Walking in warm means that you have been personally referred by an artist or art-world figure. In other words, someone is allowing you to use his or her name. You still might have a hard time getting an appointment, but be persistent. Persistence is not making one telephone call and giving up.

Walking in hot means that a person who is well respected by a dealer has taken the initiative to personally contact the dealer in your behalf.

Don't Show Your Work to Subordinates

Under no circumstances should you show your work to any gallery subordinate (e.g., receptionist, secretary, gallery assistant, manager, assistant manager) unless you have previously met with the dealer. Although there are exceptions, subordinates rarely have any power to influence a dealer's decision, and you should not put them in a position to interpret their boss's tastes. Too many artists make the mistake of allowing their work to be judged by gallery underlings. Subordinates are capable of giving compliments, but your ego is in sad shape if you need to hang on to the opinion of each and every staff member who happens to be hanging out at the gallery. Everyone on the staff, except the dealer, is basically an apprentice. Always get the final word straight from the horse's mouth!

Additionally, do not let subordinates discourage you from seeing a dealer. There are always a million excuses why an appointment is impossible. For example: "Mr. Smith is much too busy; he's going to Europe." "He's just returned from Europe." "He's preparing an opening." Don't assume that this overprotectiveness of the boss is necessarily maternalistic or paternalistic. On the contrary, it can be one of the many gimmicks used by people who feel powerless to usurp what they don't have. In some cases, subordinates want to see your work so *they* can reject it. In other cases, subordinates derive pleasure simply from informing an artist that a dealer is unavailable. Of course, not all subordinates are involved in these power games, and there are those who are sincerely interested in seeing your work. But keep in mind that subordinates are not in a position to make the decision as to whether your work will be accepted by the gallery. Their enthusiasm or discouragement is opinion, not gospel.

There are cunning ways to penetrate the protective shields that surround a dealer. Lying is one method, for instance, "What a coincidence. I'm on my way to Europe, too. I *must* talk to Mr. Smith before he leaves so that we can get together over there!" Name-dropping can also work. And then there is basic honesty, letting the person know that *you know* that he or she is playing a power game and why. Honesty is a very effective tool in disarming someone.

Don't Send a Substitute

Even if a friend, mate, spouse, or relative is trying to be supportive and offers to take your work around to galleries, turn the offer down. Do not send a substitute; it is unprofessional and it weakens your position. A dealer wants to know, and has every right to know, with whom he or she is dealing. Likewise, an artist has the same rights and should have the same concerns. If a dealer delegates the responsibility to see an artist's work to a subordinate, an artist will not feel that he or she is being taken seriously. And if an artist is unwilling to confront a dealer, the dealer could conclude that the artist is not serious about exhibiting at the gallery.

Agents

The use of agents is an accepted practice and has sometimes proved to be effective for marketing and selling art that is *commercially used*. For example, photographers, illustrators, and fashion and graphic designers use agents ("reps") to establish contacts, obtain commissions, and sell their products.

In such cases, the artist pays a commission to a rep, but not to anyone else. For an agent to make a decent living, he or she must represent several artists simultaneously. The nature of the commercial art business makes this feasible. A rep may work with many publishers, whose business requires and needs many artists, with different styles and different areas of expertise. Thus, a rep can handle many artists without anyone being neglected (although I am sure some commercial artists would argue with me on this point).

However, in the field of fine arts the use of agents is complicated. Dealers do not like to split commissions, and usually if an agent is involved it means the dealer will receive less money on a sale. And if a commission is paid to an agent from an artist's share of a sale, ultimately the artist pays more money in commissions than he or she receives for the sale of the work. For example, if a dealer's commission is 50 percent, and an agent's commission is 20 percent of the artist's share, for a painting priced at $5,000 the dealer receives $2,500, the agent receives $500, and the artist receives $2,000!

Over the last several years, a new type of agent has emerged, one who bypasses galleries and sells work directly to museums, corporations, and individuals. Many of the new agents are former gallery owners who found that it was more cost-effective to represent artists without high gallery overhead costs, and to use their contacts and networks in a new way. Essentially, an agent who works this way goes directly to the client, and two commissions are not involved. Unlike an art consultant, this type of agent represents a limited number of artists, and is likely to be interested only in artists with proven track records.

Some artists are using managers. Although a manager functions as an agent, he or she works with only one artist, and is paid a salary or fee in lieu of a commission.

In Chapter 9 (see page 168), I describe an artist's fantasy of finding the perfect agent. It is important to learn to *manage your own career* because the odds are too low that you will find the fantasy agent, or even one who works well with dealers and splits commissions with them; who takes on emerging artists; who is an effective businessperson; and who works with a small number of artists, giving each of them tender loving care and individual attention.

Studio Visits

Believe it or not, dealers dread studio visits as much as artists dread having them visit. Both parties are nervous and uncomfortable. Dealers are uneasy because they do not like to be put on the spot on an artist's turf. They feel more comfortable rejecting an artist or being vague in their own territory. Dealers also feel anxious about the reception they will receive. They fear that an artist will use the studio visit to give the dealer a taste of the same medicine the artist received in the gallery!

Artists are nervous about the judgment that a studio visit implies. They are anxious about being rejected, or they feel hostile, thus validating a dealer's worst fears that the studio visit will be used as an opportunity to "get even."

One dealer told me that she had to prepare herself mentally weeks in advance of a studio visit. "They are always a nightmare. Artists are so arrogant and hostile." I asked her how she coped with such situations. "I am indecisive and unresponsive. This drives them crazy!"

Don't go out of your way to be cold and bitter. If you find it comes easily, be restrained. You have the power to set things up so that the studio visit accomplishes something positive. In some instances, you also must take some of the responsibility if the visit turns out to be unsatisfactory. A successful studio visit should not depend on whether the dealer offers you an exhibition. Many of my clients have been able to score excellent referrals through studio visits. Although the dealers didn't believe that the work was right for their galleries, they were impressed enough to contact other dealers or curators in the artists' behalf, or offered to let artists use their names to set up appointments (enabling them to "walk in warm").

When you host a studio visit, be yourself and don't turn your life upside down. A curator who had spent a concentrated month visiting artists' studios observed that artists who lived and worked in the same space often made a conscious effort to create an atmosphere that suggested their lives were devoid of other living entities. Although the curator saw relics and signs that indicated that the premises were inhabited by dogs, cats, babies, children, and other adults, the studios were conspicuously cleared of all of these other forms of life. She felt very uneasy, as if the artists had a special life-style reserved for curators. She sensed that the artists viewed her as subhuman. The strange atmosphere actually diverted her attention away from the art. She couldn't give the artists or their work her undivided concentration.

Avoid extremes. Don't brownnose dealers or pretend that you are preoccupied with more important matters. Even though you might not yet have had a gracious or civilized gallery experience, treat a dealer the way you would want to be treated when you enter his or her domain.

As soon as the studio visit begins, *take control* by diffusing tension. Tell the dealer that you understand this is only a preliminary visit and you do not expect a commitment.

Sometimes circumstances are beyond your control. The worst studio visit I ever had involved a well-known art critic who came to look at my work for the purpose of writing an article in a national news magazine. The meeting was going well, but just as he began to select photographs to accompany the article, our meeting was interrupted by an emotionally unstable artist acquaintance who had decided to pay me a visit. Before I had a chance to make introductions, the artist lashed into a series of incoherent insults, *impersonally* directed at anyone who happened to be in the room.

While the art critic quickly packed up his gear, I tried to make apologies. The critic was unresponsive. He had assumed that the artist's insults were directed at him because he was a critic. He departed and I never heard from him again, although I wrote a letter of apology. I was guilty by association.

At first my anger was directed at the artist, but the more I thought about it, the more I realized that the critic and artist had much in common: they were both devoid of clarity and powers of reason.

I lost the article, but I also lost my awe of the critic. This was an important gain.

Artist-Gallery Agreements

Beware of dealers who won't use contracts. Requesting someone to enter into a formal agreement does not imply that you are distrustful. It merely attests to the fact that being human lends itself to being misunderstood and misinterpreted. Contracts can help compensate for human frailties.

Also beware of contracts prepared by dealers. Just because a contract is *ready*, don't assume that its contents are "professional" or necessarily in your best interests. In fact, over the years, most of the dealer-originated contracts that I have screened have not been at all in the best interests of artists. For the most part they have been narrow in scope and have not taken into account the very realistic scenarios that can develop in an artist/gallery relationship. A contract is a *symbol* that a transaction is being handled in a "professional" manner. What the contract contains is the heart of the matter.

All negotiated points (as well as unnegotiated points) *must* be put into writing. The section on "Law" in the Appendix lists resources for obtaining legal advice and *sample* contracts for various situations that involve artists and dealers. I emphasize *sample* because the contracts should be used as *guidelines*. No two artists or their situations are 100 percent similar, and contracts should reflect these distinctions accordingly.

Consignment and Consignment/Exhibition Agreements

A consignment agreement and a consignment/exhibition agreement are the most common types of contracts between an artist and a dealer. Many artists mistake a consignment *sheet* for a contract. A consignment sheet should be *attached* to a consignment agreement or consignment/exhibition agreement; it provides an inventory of the work in a dealer's possession and states the retail value of each piece. A consignment *agreement* should cover basic issues, including the length of time the contract is in effect, whether a dealer is limited to selling your work within a specific geographic region, where in the gallery your work will be displayed, the range of sales commissions to be awarded a dealer under *various circumstances*, transportation and packaging responsibilities of the artist and dealer, financial arrangements for rentals and installment sales, artist payment due schedules, and gallery discount policies.

In addition, a consignment agreement should protect an artist against the assignment or transfer of the contract, and address the very important issues of moral rights, arbitration, copyright, and insurance.

A consignment/exhibition agreement should cover all of the issues just raised, but it should also outline the exhibition-related responsibilities of an artist and dealer. Does the gallery pay for advertising, catalogs, posters, announcements, postage for announcements, press releases, postage for press releases, special installations, photography sessions, opening parties, and private screenings? Or are all or some of these costs split between the artist and gallery—or fully absorbed by the artist?

Artist Sales Contract

An artist sales contract is an agreement between an artist and a collector. Although dealers do not sign this contract, the fact that an artist requires a sales contract as a condition of sale can be a provision in a consignment agreement, consignment/exhibition agreement, or artist/agent contract (see page 96).

Some dealers are vehemently opposed to the use of an artist sales contract because they are naive and are unilaterally opposed to all artist-related contracts. Other dealers are opposed to the contract because it states the price actually paid for the work. If a dealer is involved in hanky-panky, the last thing he or she wants an artist to know is the work's real selling price. Probably the most common reason some dealers are opposed to the use of the contract is they fear that if an artist knows the name and address of a collector, the artist will try to sell more work to the collector without the dealer's involvement. You can placate some dealers by assuring them that you would much rather be in your studio creating work than going behind their backs trying to sell work. Making an effort to address a dealer's fear often resolves the situation.

From an artist's point of view, a sales contract or artist transfer sales agreement (see below) is very practical. Not only does it provide you with a record of who owns your work at any given time, but it reminds collectors that they cannot alter or reproduce your work without your permission. The contract also states that the artist must be consulted if restoration becomes necessary. And if the work is transferred to a new owner, the sales contract is also transferred.

Artist Transfer Sales Agreement

An artist transfer sales agreement includes all of the provisions of an artist sales contract, but it goes one step further: it requires the collector to pay the artist a percentage of the increase in the value of a work *each* time it is transferred. The amount of the percentage can vary.

In California, which is the only state that has enacted a resale royalties act, artists are entitled to a *5 percent* royalty on the gross sale price when work is resold in California or by a California resident. This ruling applies to any work created after January 1, 1977, that is sold for more than $1,000 and more than the seller's original price. The California act applies only to paintings, sculpture, and drawings, and the artist must be either a United States citizen or a two-year resident of California at the time of resale.

Some artists are using *7 percent*, which was the amount required in the Resale Royalties Act that was proposed but defeated in New York State. Others are using *15 percent*, an amount suggested in what is known as the Projansky Agreement, drafted several years ago by New York attorney Robert Projansky.

Recently, the United States Congress commissioned the Registrar of Copyrights at the Library of Congress to conduct a study on the feasibility of enacting national resale royalties legislation and establishing a collection agency or agencies to monitor its enforcement. In an article about the Library of Congress study, La Jolla, California, arts attorney Peter H. Karlen discussed the pros and cons of resale royalties:

> There are practical and theoretical reasons for resale royalties. The typical visual artist is one of the most underpaid individuals in our society. The commissions that artists pay to dealers and other agents are terribly high, and sales of artworks are often at extreme discounts. Why shouldn't a consumer of an artwork have to pay a royalty based upon each new "consumption" of the work, in the same way that purchasers of books pay the author (via the publisher) upon each new purchase.
>
> Nonetheless, unless the attitudes of dealers and collectors change so that they fully understand artists' residual rights in their works and the theory behind resale royalties, enacting a national resale royalty law is only likely to create a new expensive bureaucracy. It will be much to do about nothing simply because the costs of collecting resale royalties from recalcitrant dealers and collectors may exceed the royalties.[76]

In the meantime, since there is no bureaucracy monitoring or collecting royalties for visual artists, an artist transfer sales agreement is a document based on trust, not law. Each artist makes his or her own personal decision on whether or not to use this contract.

Checking Up on Dealers

Before committing to a consignment and/or exhibition relationship with a dealer, request a contract. If a dealer is unwilling to use a contract, do not get involved. If a dealer provides you with a contract that he or she has prepared, compare it with one of the sample contracts referred to in the Appendix section "Law." If necessary, amend the dealer's contract to include any important provisions that are missing.

If you have successfully negotiated a contract but are unfamiliar with a gallery's business reputation, talk to other artists represented by the gallery. If you do not know the names and whereabouts of other gallery artists, ask the dealer. *It is about time that artists begin requesting references!* If you are still unable to get a clear picture of a gallery's business reputation, contact a local chapter of the Better Business Bureau. Ask whether complaints have been registered against the gallery. You should inquire about the gallery's reputation from both an artist's and a client's point of view.

Dealing with Dealers: In Summary

Over the years, I have met with thousands of artists, often serving as a coach to help them iron out gallery-related problems. And over the years I have had at least one client in approximately 90 percent of the galleries in New York City that exhibit contemporary work. These experiences have provided me with an unusually broad perspective on what has gone on behind the scenes at many galleries since the late 1970s and what is going on today. I have been privy to intimate information about how artists are treated and mistreated, who is suing whom and why, the names of the dealers who do not pay artists or do not pay on time, et cetera.

I still cringe when I hear or learn about some of the unintelligent remarks and value judgments made by dealers, or the outrageous rudeness they display. Those rare occasions when an artist praises a dealer for being fair and wise give me hope that perhaps things are changing for the better.

More often, though, I have trouble responding when I am asked to name dealers I respect *both* as businesspeople and as human beings. In New York, which has more than five hundred commercial galleries, the dealers on my list could be counted on one hand!

Although for many reasons I consider the gallery system in New York to be the most decadent, New York is certainly not the only place that attracts art dealers with questionable moral and business ethics. Many artists around the country have trying and cumbersome relationships with dealers. Given the continuing decline of morale between artists and dealers in the United States, galleries located in foreign cities might be the only palatable option left to artists interested in exhibiting in commercial galleries.

If artists do not learn to *cultivate their own market* and become less dependent on galleries for sales and exposure, they will find themselves paying commissions in the neighborhood of 75 percent and up, just to support dealers in the style to which they are accustomed! But it is also highly likely that if you total the amount of money a dealer currently receives for the sale of work and the amount of money some artists are now required to spend for exhibition-related expenses, the day of the 75 percent commission might have already arrived!

It is important that artists develop an autonomous posture and make their own career decisions rather than wasting time waiting for something to happen. The chances are remote that you will find the perfect agent or be introduced to galleries through an art-world-figure referral system, and the so-called artist referral system is virtually nonexistent, because most artists are too paranoid and competitive to refer each other.

You *can* find a gallery without being referred and without an agent. But do not rely on representation by *one* gallery to provide the exposure or livelihood you are seeking. Build a network of many galleries located throughout the United States and the world. Because you can expect an acceptance rate of *2 percent* (see page 43), building such a network requires time and patience. But it can be done.

7

The Mysterious World of Grants: Fact and Fiction

He who hesitates watches someone else get the grant he might have gotten.
—Jane C. Hartwig,
Former Deputy Director,
Alicia Patterson Foundation

W ho gets grants and why? The *real* answers to these questions can be provided by jurors who select grant recipients. All other answers are speculative and have more to do with hearsay than reality. When I asked members of various grants panels about their selection criteria, their answers were simple and direct: they liked the artist's work or they liked the project under consideration and thought that the artist was capable of undertaking the work. When I probed further, the answers were predictably numerous, varied, and subjective, and boiled down to "taste buds."

Artists who are apprehensive and skeptical about applying for grants have many misconceptions about who receives them. Skeptical artists deem themselves ineligible for various reasons, such as being too old or young, lacking sufficient or impressive exhibition or performance credits, or lacking the right academic background. They believe that the kind of work they are doing isn't considered "in" or that they lack the right connections, which implies that juries are rigged!

It is perfectly conceivable and probable that some artists have been denied grants by some foundations because of some or all of the above-mentioned factors. However, on the basis of my own experiences as a grant recipient and juror, as well as the experiences of my clients (the majority of whom would not measure up to the tough stereotype that many artists have of "the perfect grant-winning specimen"), I am convinced that, for the most part, grant selection is a democratic process—meaning that everyone has a *real* chance. Many artists believe that because they have applied for the same grant year after year without success, it is a waste to continue to apply. Images are conjured up of a jury sitting around a table moaning, "Oh, no, not him again!" Or conversely, there are artists who believe that one must apply for the same grant at least three or four times before it will be awarded: "It's her fourth application, let's give her a break!" But contrary to the notion that jurists remember who applied for a grant each year, most panels have new members each time they convene. Each time you apply you have a fresh chance.

Since grant selection in the arts is based on taste, and like taste buds, the grants world is mysterious, whimsical, and fickle, you should not depend on or view grants as the only means of providing the opportunity to do what you really want. Grants should be looked upon as "cream" to help alleviate financial pressures, provide time and new opportunities to develop your career, and add another entry to your list of endorsements.

Projects and ideas should not be tossed aside if funding agencies or foundations reject your application(s). Remember, the selection criteria are subjective and *ultimately you must be the judge* of whether your work and ideas have merit. A grant is not the deciding factor.

Also remember that juries are composed of human beings, and humans can't always predict a "winner." In fact, we have quite a track record of not recognizing talent (until someone dies), while scandalously putting some rather untalented people on a pedestal.

The grants world might seem mysterious, but hundreds of artists each year who take the time and energy to investigate grant possibilities and complete well-thought-out applications are reaping the benefits.

Big Grants and Little Grants

If Your Mother Is an Eskimo, Have I Got a Grant for You! Grants come in many different shapes, sizes, and forms. Although grants and fellowships sponsored by the National Endowment for the Arts, the National Endowment for the Humanities, and state arts councils are the best known in the performing and visual arts fields, there are many other grants available. Because they are less well known, often fewer people apply for them.

There are grants for visual and performing artists with broad-based purposes and specific project grants for well-defined purposes. For example, there are grants for artists who are women, artists who are mothers, artists with a particular ethnic or religious background; grants for artists born in certain regions, states, and cities; grants for artists involved with conceptual art or traditional art; grants for travel; grants for formal study; grants for independent study; grants for apprenticeship; and grants for teaching.

From year to year grant agencies and foundations open and fold, cut budgets, increase budgets, change their funding interests and priorities, emphasize one arts discipline over another or one socioeconomic group over another. It is important to keep abreast of these changes. A grant that is not applicable to your current situation and interests could be suitable in the future.

Even when budgets are being cut, don't hesitate to submit grant applications. A case in point: In the 1980s, while federal arts budgets were being slashed, I received a large matching grant from the National Endowment for the Arts. I was not optimistic that I would receive a grant when I submitted the application. Not only was I surprised that I received the grant, I was also surprised that I was awarded every penny that I requested. However, it was pointed out to me by a person familiar with the inner workings of the NEA that when government arts funding is cut, people are reluctant to submit grant applications. Thus, the competition is reduced. In many instances, people have a better chance of receiving a grant when the financial climate is restrained.

The section "Grants and Funding Resources" in the Appendix lists some resources from which you can learn more about grants in the visual and performing arts.

Art Colonies and
Artist-in-Residence Programs

Acceptance in an art colony, also known as a retreat or an artist-in-residence program, is a form of a grant, since the sponsoring organization subsidizes the artists it selects.

Such retreats are scattered throughout the United States and the world. They offer an artist the opportunity to work on a project for a specific amount of time, free from life's daily burdens, responsibilities, and distractions.

Subsidization can be as comprehensive as payment of transportation expenses, room and board, and a monthly stipend. Or it can be limited to partial payment of room and board, with the artist required to pay a small fee.

Some colonies, such as the American Academy in Rome and the Bellagio Study Center in Italy, sponsored by the Rockefeller Foundation, offer luxurious creature comforts. Other colonies offer a summer-camp ambience and are based on a communal structure.

There are colonies that specialize in one particular arts discipline as well as those that include visual and performing artists and writers.

Artist-in-residence programs can include teaching opportunities (described in the next chapter) as well as international exchanges. For example, Partners of the Americas sponsors an exchange program for visual and performing artists in the United States, Latin America, and Caribbean countries. Resource lists and additional information about art colonies, artist-in-residence programs, and exchange programs are in the Appendix sections "Art Colonies and Artist-in-Residence Programs" and "International Connections."

Nonprofit and Umbrella Organizations

There are more grants available to nonprofit arts organizations than to individual artists, and the dollar value of the grants available is substantially higher. For this reason, when I was working as an artist I turned myself into a nonprofit, tax-exempt organization. The tax-exempt status also allowed individuals to receive tax breaks on any contributions and donations they made to my projects.

Although there were many advantages to being a nonprofit, tax-exempt organization, there were also disadvantages. For example, while my organization was in operation, I found myself spending a disproportionate amount of time completing the various forms and reports that were required by federal and state agencies. Another drawback was having to contend with a board of directors, which diminished, to a certain extent, the autonomy that I had enjoyed while working on my own. I also spent a lot of time meeting with board members and sustaining their enthusiasm for fund-raising.

Carefully evaluate your situation before taking steps to form a nonprofit organization. For further information about forming a nonprofit organization and working with a board of directors see the Appendix section "Nonprofit Organizations."

If you personally do not wish to go nonprofit, there is an option available that allows you to bypass the tax-exemption route: use the services of an *umbrella organization*. Umbrella organizations are nonprofit, tax-exempt groups that let you apply for a grant under their auspices. If a grant is awarded, the umbrella organization receives the award and in turn pays you.

Umbrella services can vary from a minimum of signing a grant application to bookkeeping, managerial advice, preparation of annual, federal, and state reports, assistance with publicity and promotion, and fund-raising. In return for these services, a percentage of any grant that is awarded to an artist or a group of artists goes to the umbrella organization.

Umbrella organizations do not take all artists under their

wings. They consider the nature of an artist's project and the impact it will have on the community. Umbrella groups rely on grants to pay their overhead and salaries, and their ability to receive grants depends largely on the success of the projects they sponsor.

The best way to learn about umbrella organizations in your area is to contact your local state arts council.

Increasing Your Chances of Being Funded

Preapplication Research

Before completing a grant application, learn as much as possible about the funding organization. Your homework should include learning about eligibility requirements, funding priorities, the long-term goals of the organization, and the maximum and minimum amount of the grant. Jane C. Hartwig, former deputy director of the Alicia Patterson Foundation, emphasizes the importance of homework: "The fact that you have done your homework, even at the earliest stage, is impressive, and appreciated by the foundation. It will also save you time, money, and possibly grief."[77]

When you receive your application instructions and the background information about the agency or foundation, the kind of language used will give you a strong indication of the types of art and arts projects that are funded. For example, if you are told that the purpose of a grant is "to foster a high standard in the study of form, color, drawing, painting, design, and technique as expressed in modes showing a patent affinity with the classical tradition of Western culture,"[78] it is very clear what the foundation giving the grant is looking for. If your work or project involves anything other than "the classical tradition of Western culture," it is a waste of time to apply to this foundation.

Submitting Visual Materials

Grant applications in visual arts usually require that slides or photographs of the artist's work accompany a written application. Although some funding agencies request to see the actual work once an artist passes a semifinal stage, most organizations make their final selections on the basis of slides or photographs.

Too often artists place great importance on a written application and give too little attention to the photographic material. Both are important for completely different reasons. Here are some guidelines to follow in submitting visual materials. In addition, review the section "Slides and Photographs" in Chapter 2.

(1) All photographic material should be of *top quality:* clear and crisp, with good lighting and tone.

(2) Submit photographs of your most *recent* work. Funding agencies do not want to see a retrospective of your last ten years. They want a strong, clear indication of your current interests and directions.

(3) Select photographs or slides that represent the *best* of your recent work. *You decide what is best.* If you are indecisive about what to submit, consult with someone whose taste you respect.

(4) Even if the funding agency does not require photographic materials to be labeled, *label* each and every slide or photograph with your name and the title, medium, date, and dimensions of the work. Also include a directional indication showing the top of the work. This information could decide whether your work is rejected or enters the next stage of judging. Photographs or slides should seduce the judges, but if they are confused and can't "read" what is going on, they will not take time to look up your written application in hopes of clarification.

Completing Applications

When you first encounter a grant application, it can seem like Egyptian hieroglyphics. Mastering grant applications *is* like learning a new language, and the more experience you have the easier it becomes.

In addition to carefully following instructions, the best posture to take when filling out an application is to *put yourself in the shoes of a jurist*. In other words, you want to read applications that are legible and clear and that come quickly to the point. You do not want to have to reread an application for clarity. Applications should hold the judges' attention.

I am often called upon to review *unsuccessful* grant applications. These applications tend to have in common one or all of the following mistakes:

(1) They reflect a negative tone, implying that the artist has a chip on his or her shoulder (e.g., "The world owes me a grant").

(2) The description of the grant purpose and/or project talks over the heads of the readers, rambles on with artsy language, and goes off on irrelevant tangents.

(3) Funds are requested for inappropriate or "off-the-wall" purposes, basically insulting the intelligence of the judges.

Recently I was one of eight jury members who met to select a public art project. The proposal I liked best was very imaginative and had a wonderful sense of scale. It would have been relatively easy to install, maintenance free, and able to withstand inclement weather. It was also the least costly of all of the proposals submitted.

However, the project did not win because the artist antagonized the jury! Leaving most of the application questions unanswered, except for a project description, the artist wrote (in barely legible longhand) one arrogant sentence implying that the drawings that accompanied the application would make the sculpture's design and meaning clear to all but the dumbest of viewers.

Although most jurors agreed that this project was the most appealing, they also concurred, based on the attitude expressed in the application, that the artist would probably be difficult to work with during the planning and installation stages. Whether or not that would have been true is open to speculation, but the fact of the matter is that the way in which the artist completed the application prevented her from receiving the commission.

Judging Procedures

Most funding agencies use the first round of judging to sort through applications to make sure that artists have complied with all of the instructions, rules, and regulations. Consider this the "negative" stage of judging, as the agency is on the lookout for applicants who do not follow instructions. This hunt has no deeper purpose than to make the judges' work easier by reducing the number of applications to be considered.

The next round of judging is based on viewing slides and photographs. For example, the Artist Fellowship selection in the Visual Arts Division of the National Endowment for the Arts works as follows: Four or five panelists view ten slides of one artist's work. The slides are projected on a screen, five at a time. Each artist is rated on the basis of a point system, and artists who receive the highest ratings go on to the next judging round. The same ten slides are shown again, and the artist is rated again. The same process continues until the panel has narrowed down the selection of artists for the final stages of judging. At this point the written application is reviewed.

"Say the Secret Word and Win One Hundred Dollars"

Probably as a result of the many tests one is subjected to in school, artists approach a grant application as an aptitude or IQ test. It is felt that ultimately the application is trying to trick you with double meanings. The fact is that there are definitely "wrong" answers, such as those I have described from the unsuccessful grant applications, but there is no one "right" answer.

For example, the National Endowment for the Arts fellowship applications request information on *educational background* and *salary*. Those artists who believe their formal education is inadequate, in terms of establishment credentials, often believe that they will have virtually no chance of being funded. I have also heard artists ponder the question of what to state for salary, thinking that if they put their real salary it will be considered too high ("She's making a bundle and doesn't deserve a grant") or too low ("If he's making so little, he couldn't possibly be talented"). The truth of the matter is that during the judging process the NEA does not even look at educational background or salary information. The information is used *only* for *statistical* purposes to provide taxpayers with a profile of federal grant recipients.

Although there are grants available that are specifically designed to assist impoverished or low-income artists, this requirement is specified in a foundation's statement of purpose. If it is not stated, one can safely assume that the grant is awarded on the basis of merit and not financial need.

Another part of the "secret word" syndrome is how much money to ask for. Arriving at a funding-request figure is not like competing in a jelly-bean-counting contest—you don't have to guess down to the exact penny how much you think the foundation will give you.

Some foundations give a set amount of money (e.g., twenty grants of $5,000 each). Other foundations state a maximum amount, but say that smaller grants will also be given, the amount of which will be left to the discretion of the jury. For example, the National Endowment for the Arts offers fellowships of $25,000 each, with a limited number of $5,000 fellowships for emerging artists. Many artists believe that they have a better chance of receiving an NEA fellowship if they request a smaller amount of money. However, the NEA clearly states in its grant guidelines: "All applicants should apply for the major fellowship amount of $25,000." (You might think you are in the process of emerging, but a jury might believe that you have already arrived!)

There are also foundations that offer project grants. They specify the maximum amount given and ask you to provide a budget and/or statement of your needs.

If you are required to provide a budget, it should be logical and realistic. Spend time investigating real project costs, item by item. If you are awarded a grant and your budget isn't accurate, you could end up in the frustrating position of having to dig into your own pocket to complete the project. Also, a realistic budget makes a jury feel more secure that you know what you are doing and that the project has a real chance of being implemented and completed.

Do not be shy about allocating money in the budget for *your time* ("artist's fee"), and don't undervalue your time. Many applications I have reviewed requested funds only for materials and did not include compensation for the artist's time or studio expenses (rent, electricity, etc.), or, if an artist fee was requested, it was equivalent to a minimum-wage scale. Undervalued artists' fees can imply to a jury that you do not believe in your own worth, so why should they give you money?

Letters of Recommendation

When foundations request that an applicant include a letter or letters of recommendation, it means that they are asking for testimony from other people that your work is good and/or that your project has merits and is relevant and important. I often encounter blank expressions when I ask applicants whom they are going to use as a reference. They believe there is not one person available to help. Of course, it is impressive if you are recommended by an art-world superstar. However, if such a person is not part of your network, do not let this become a stumbling block. Jane C. Hartwig puts it this way:

> You certainly shouldn't shy away from using someone well known in your field if that person happens to know you and your work and has indicated a willingness to write a letter in your behalf. Just don't think that you haven't a

chance if you don't know any luminaries. Happily, it doesn't matter.[79]

In summary, if you were on a grant panel, what would impress you more? An insipid but well-meaning letter of recommendation from a celebrity, or a perceptive and analytical letter from someone you have never heard of?

There is a range of possibilities for obtaining letters of recommendation: a critic who has given you a good review, the director or curator of a museum where your work has been shown, the director of a gallery where your work has been shown, a former teacher, another artist, an art historian, a collector of your work, or the director of an arts organization.

Remember, the worst thing that can happen is that the person you ask to write the recommendation will say no. Although this happens, it doesn't happen that often, because most everyone has been in the position of asking for help.

An Untraditional Grantsmanship Route

The traditional way to apply for grants is to rely on a foundation to announce the availability of a grant and submit an application. However, there is an untraditional route, which I have personally used with very successful results.

Corporate Detective Work

I obtained corporate sponsors for many exhibitions and projects by taking the initiative and contacting companies, regardless of whether they were in "the grants business." I first located corporations that either provided services or manufactured goods and materials that had some relationship to my project or exhibition. I began my detective work at the library by using *Standard & Poor's Rating Guide*, a massive directory that lists major American corporations, cross-referenced according to product and/or service.

In one instance, I was planning an exhibition of sculpture in which aluminum would be used extensively. Through *Standard & Poor's* I came up with a list of major aluminum companies, their addresses, and the names of key officers and public- or corporate-relations directors.

I sent a letter to each public- or corporate-relations director, with a copy to each key officer; I indicated on each original letter that company officers were also receiving the letter.

The letter detailed the purpose of the exhibition, told where it was being held, and included a description and a budget. I also included a sentence or two about what the company would receive in turn for its sponsorship, namely public-relations benefits. *Within six weeks* I landed a sponsor.

Value of Sending Copies

Sending copies of the sponsorship request to key corporate officers is very important. It increases the chances that the letter will really be given careful consideration and it decreases the chances that a sponsorship decision will be blocked by one person. For example, if only the public-relations director receives a letter and that person, for one reason or another, is unmoved, the request dies a quick death. By submitting the request to many officers, you increase the chances that you will find an ally with clout!

Yes, You Can Fight City Hall

For four consecutive years I applied for a grant from a state arts council for three different projects. Each year I was rejected. After the fourth rejection, I launched my own investigation and learned that one staff member was blocking my application, but for reasons that were so petty I could attribute them only to a "personality conflict." Venting my frustration, I wrote to the director of the arts council, detailing the four-year history of grant applications, documenting all the hours spent on applications, answering questions, meetings, appointments, interviews, letters of recommendation, and more letters of recommendation. But most important, I reiterated the merits of the project that I wanted funded. I also named the staff member who had been giving me such a hard time and sent a copy of my diatribe to that person. About three weeks later I received a letter from the arts council stating that it had reversed its decision—the project would be funded.

Generating Income:
Alternatives
to Driving
a Cab

Being able to support yourself as an artist, and maintain a high-quality life through finances generated from your work, can and does happen all the time. But rarely does it happen overnight, and realistically, until your career gets rolling, it is necessary to earn a living through other means. This chapter covers the assets and drawbacks of conventional jobs, and it discusses some job opportunities and ways of generating income within the fine arts field. It also provides ideas for minimizing business expenses and saving money.

Assets and Drawbacks of Conventional Jobs

To solve the problem of supporting yourself as an artist you must take into account your financial and emotional needs and your physical capabilities. Whether the options suggested in this chapter are appealing or you prefer traditional forms of employment that offer more financial security depends on your personality, temperament, and energy level. What works for one artist doesn't necessarily work for another. But the *common goal* is to generate income that simultaneously allows you to maintain a good standard of creature comforts, a good state of mind and health, energy for your own projects, and energy to develop your career. Each of these criteria is equally important. One should not be sacrificed or compromised for another.

However, in the name of art and the "myth of the artist," compromises and sacrifices are constantly made. Contrary to the teachings of the myth, you are entitled to what you want, and there are ways to get it.

Before jumping into employment, assess carefully and *honestly* what you are looking for and why. Does the job provide a *real means to an end,* or is the job likely to annihilate your end? For example, two of my clients took jobs with arts service organizations. Both jobs provided the artists with sufficient income as well as opportunities to meet people related to their profession and expand contacts and networks. One job involved low-pressure, routine duties. Although the artist was not mentally stimulated, she had energy to sculpt and develop her career because her responsibilities were minimal. The other job was full of responsibilities. It was demanding and stimulating. Although the artist found the work fulfilling, at the end of the day she was drained and did not have the energy for her artwork.

Some of the best publications around to help you assess what you are looking for and what you would be good at are the books *Work with Passion: How to Do What You Love for a Living* by Nancy Anderson, and *What Color Is Your Parachute? A Practical Manual for Job Hunters and Career Changers* by Richard Nelson Bolles. Although these books are not specifically addressed to artists, artists will derive a great deal of valuable information and ideas from them. They explain how you can discover your latent skills and talents and expand your concept of what you can do to earn a living. These publications are listed in the Appendix section "Employment Opportunities."

If you want to work within the arts, there are some good resources available. The *National Arts Jobbank* is a biweekly newsletter that lists employment opportunities in the visual and performing arts, literature, education, and arts administration. *The*

College Art Association's Listing of Positions contains a listing of arts-related jobs, mainly in museums, colleges, and universities. *Artsearch*, published by the Theatre Communications Group, is a national employment bulletin for the performing arts. It includes art and arts-related positions in education, production, and management. *National Arts Placement* is published eight times a year by the National Art Education Association and lists positions in arts councils, colleges, museums, schools, and universities. *Jobs in Arts and Media Management: What They Are and How to Get One* by Stephen Langley and James Abruzzo is a guide to the job market in the entertainment industry. In addition, Opportunity Resources for the Arts, Inc., is a national organization that serves as a placement service for administrative positions in museums; art centers; art councils; theater, opera, and ballet companies; symphonies; et cetera. For further information about these resources, see "Employment Opportunities" in the Appendix.

Using Your Career to Generate Income

Teaching: A Boon or a Trojan Horse?

Teaching is attractive to artists for several reasons: it offers financial security as well as the fringe benefits of health insurance, life insurance, sick leave, vacation pay, and long vacations. In addition, it is a highly respected occupation.

Because of these attractions, the competition to teach is horrendous—so horrendous that, unless one is a superstar, getting a job usually necessitates returning to school for more degrees. On the other hand, even if your qualifications are superlative, there is no job guarantee. There are more qualified artists than teaching positions available in colleges and universities and within school systems.

The scarcity of jobs is not the only drawback. When you are an artist and a teacher, you wear two hats. If teaching consisted only of lecturing, critiquing, and advising students, it would be relatively simple. However, teaching means a lot more. It means extracurricular involvement with faculty politics and yielding to the special demands and priorities of academia. Theoretically, these roles should be compatible and supportive, but often they are not.

Artists who teach *and* want to develop their careers must contend simultaneously with the occupational hazards of both professions. The situation is particularly complex because many of the demands and priorities of the art world and academic world are in conflict. Often, artists involved in the academic world face peer pressure based on how much they know about the past rather than what they are doing in the present. Sometimes artists are forced to change their methods of teaching and/or style of work to conform to current academic trends and ideology. Getting tenure often becomes the most important goal in life. Academia also puts demands on teachers to publish articles, essays, and books about art history and art criticism. An artist may have little time for his or her personal work.

On the other hand, some teaching opportunities are available that allow artists autonomy and flexibility. These opportunities exist both within and outside academic compounds. Some of these opportunities are described on the following pages.

Artist-in-Residence Programs

There are various forms of artist-in-residence programs. Some have the fundamental purpose of providing artists with opportunities to live in an environment in which they may work unimpeded by life's daily worries (see page 146). Other artist-in-residence programs pay artists to teach on a temporary, part-time, or full-time basis in school systems and communities throughout the United States.

Among the national programs is the Arts in Education Program of the National Endowment for the Arts, which, through state agencies, places visual and performing artists and writers in educational settings to work and demonstrate artistic disciplines. Affiliate Artists, Inc., places performing artists in eight-week residencies. The program is available to actors, dancers, instrumentalists, and singers. Artists receive a fee that covers salary, travel costs, and administrative expenses. Independent Curators, Inc., arranges long-term residencies for visual artists, choreographers, dancers, and musicians. Hospital Audiences, Inc., brings visual and performing artists to individuals confined in institutions such as mental health facilities, senior citizens' homes, drug rehabilitation facilities, and correctional centers.

For information regarding artist-in-residence programs on the local level, contact local and state arts councils. In addition, the Mid Atlantic Arts Foundation publishes the directory *Visual Arts Residencies: Sponsor Organizations*, which describes programs in the mid-Atlantic region. The addresses of the above organizations can be found under "Employment Opportunities" in the Appendix.

Lectures and Workshops

Lectures, slide presentations, demonstrations, and workshops are excellent means of generating income. They also offer exposure and serve as good public-relations vehicles.

Colleges, universities, social-service agencies, and civic, cultural, and educational organizations often hire artists for "guest appearances."

You can base presentations on your own work alone or also discuss the work of other contemporary artists, art history, and art criticism. Subjects and themes of arts-related presentations are unlimited.

The financial rewards of public appearances can be considerable if you repeat your performance several times. For example, although I conduct some workshops in my home city, others involve a great deal of traveling. Once I receive an out-of-town invitation I use the opportunity to create more opportunities by contacting other educational or cultural institutions in the same area. What starts out as a one-shot engagement ends up as a lecture tour. This generates more revenue and exposure, and since the institutions involved split my travel expenses (apart from the fees I am paid), they all save money.

Setting Up Artist-in-Residence Positions, Lectures, and Workshops

The best way to approach an organization or institution about sponsoring an artist-in-residence position, public appearance, or workshop is to provide a concrete proposal that describes the purpose of your idea or program, why it is relevant, and what the audience will gain. If you are applying for an artist-in-residence position, include a proposal, even if the application does not require one. A proposal for a lecture workshop should not be limited to a title. It should elaborate on the contents of your presentation, including the purpose, relevance, and benefit to the audience.

The value of preparing a proposal in advance is that you avoid having to rely on the institution or organization to figure out a way to use your talents. This could take months.

The other value of preparing a proposal is that it can be used to generate residencies, public appearances, and workshops independent of organizations and institutions that sponsor such programs. In other words, it is not necessary, for example, to go through the Arts in Education, Independent Curators, or Hospital Audiences program to get work. You can initiate contacts yourself.

Send proposals to schools, colleges, universities, social-service agencies, and educational and cultural organizations. Corporations are also receptive to sponsoring lectures and workshops, and many organize educational and cultural programs specifically for their employees.

Generating Income Through the Printed Image

Mail art, book art, rubber-stamp art, Xerox art, and postcard art are art forms created by artists exploring the tools and resources of mass communication and the electronic age. Not only do these art forms respond to the aesthetic sensibilities of mass communication, they *are* mass communication and are mass-produced.

Thus, they are art forms with nonexclusive price tags and have the potential to broaden the art-buying market.

A market and marketing vehicles for these art forms have developed over the last fifteen years. This can be attributed to the efforts of Printed Matter, which was founded in New York City in 1976. This shop/gallery and mail-order service exhibits and sells a vast range of artists' books and other types of artist-created printed materials. The address of Printed Matter and other artists' book resources are listed in the Appendix section "Artists' Books."

More traditional forms of printed materials also offer artists many ways to generate income and exposure. These include signed, unsigned, limited, and unlimited editions of prints, posters, and lithographs.

There is already a large demand for works on paper, and sales do not depend on commercial galleries. You can be your own publisher and do your own marketing, or go through a print publisher. The *Printworld Directory of Contemporary Prints and Prices* is an excellent source for the names and addresses of print publishers and distributors. Usually a distributor will take work on a consignment basis, but if your work sells well, it is possible that the distributor will commission you for specific projects and pay the printing costs. For further information about the *Directory* and other print-related resources, see the Appendix section "Prints and Printmaking."

On the other hand, I have sold numerous prints and posters through my studio, just on the basis of distributing a press release. In one instance I was involved with a silk-screen series consisting of five prints based on one theme. Press releases announcing the series and availability details were sent to arts-related publications and museum shops. Except for the prints that I retained for myself, the entire series sold. Marketing involved neither paid advertising nor a middleperson.

There are many potential markets for artists' work. If you limit yourself to one-of-a-kind objects, your market is one-of-a-kind buyers, those who consider exclusivity and scarcity important and are willing and able to pay for it. However, there are many others who appreciate and want to buy art and are not concerned with these issues.

Minimizing Expenses

I was able to afford an investment in the silk-screen series described above, as well as in other print projects that I initiated, by minimizing my overhead expenses. There are many ways to keep expenses low in order to afford the necessary initial financial investment to launch projects. Some of these ways are described below.

Bartering

Bartering has been in existence for thousands of years. Artists can trade their artwork and special skills for employment- and career-related supplies, materials, and equipment. You can save money on various daily living expenses so that you can allocate more funds for your career.

Some of my clients have bartered with doctors, dentists, restaurants, food stores, plumbers, carpenters, and electricians. I have arranged barters with printers to pay for the overhead expenses involved with various poster and print series.

The bartering phenomenon has expanded into big business, and barter organizations and clubs exist throughout the United States. The names of barter organizations can be found in the Yellow Pages directory under "Barter and Trade Exchanges." For additional information about bartering, consult *Personal and Business Bartering* by James Stout (see "Career Management, Business, and Marketing" in the Appendix).

Apprentices

You can save money and time by using the services of an apprentice. Apprenticeship programs provide artists with students who want studio or work experience. Some apprenticeship programs are structured as a barter: free assistance in return for learning and developing new skills. Other programs require an artist to pay the apprentice a reasonable hourly wage.

Local and state arts councils can provide information on apprenticeship programs. College and university art departments are also good sources. In addition, the Great Lakes College Association sponsors a student-intern apprenticeship program, which makes available apprentices in the visual arts, theater, writing, music, dance, and media. In the visual arts, apprentices are available in painting, sculpture, photography, crafts, all areas of design and commercial art, and architecture. In the theater field, apprentices work with producers and directors and with set-, costume-, and lighting-design personnel. In music, dance, and media, apprentices are available in composition, choreography, production, management, recording, criticism, animation, art, lighting, and editing. For additional information about apprenticeship programs, see the Appendix section "Apprentices and Interns."

Surplus-Material Programs

You can save money on equipment, supplies, and materials by using surplus-material programs. These programs are located throughout the United States and are administered by various arts agencies. Their main source of supply is the General Services Administration, which donates to public agencies and nonprofit organizations a variety of materials, machine tools, office machines, supplies, furniture, hardware, construction equipment, et cetera. In turn, many of the agencies make the supplies and equipment available to artists. A surplus-property agency exists in every state. Contact your local arts agency for further information, and see "Surplus-Material Programs" in the Appendix.

9

Rationalization, Paranoia, Competition, and Rejection

Rationalization

If you want to avoid fulfilling your potential as an artist, it is easy to find an excuse. When excuses linger unresolved too long they become rationalizations. Webster defines the word *rationalize* as "to attribute [one's actions] to rational and creditable motives without analysis of true and especially unconscious motives," and "to provide plausible but untrue reasons for conduct."

Rationalization in one form or another is common to the human species, and sometimes it can be used constructively. However, when rationalization is used to evade fulfilling one's potential, it is being used to disguise a lack of self-confidence and/or fear of rejection.

The most common kinds of rationalizations practiced by artists are rationalizations to *avoid the work process* and rationalizations to *avoid getting work out of the studio and into the public domain,* the marketplace.

Avoiding Work

"I'll get going once I find a work space" and "I'll get going when I have the right working environment" are rationalizations I hear most often from artists who want to postpone or avoid knuckling down. Artists who engage in this form of rationalization do little or nothing, financially or motivationally, in order to attain their goal of finding a suitable work space.

There are many variations on the theme: One artist tells me he can't begin work until he can afford stationery embossed with his studio address. He believes that no one will take him seriously until he has a business letterhead. Another artist, who has spent the last four years traveling, tells me she needs more life experience in order to paint. Another artist tells me that he is waiting for technology to invent the right material that he needs for sculpture. Chances are that when the letterhead, life experience, and new technology are attained, the artists will quickly find another excuse to avoid confronting their work. As psychotherapist and artist Bruce M. Holly puts it:

> For some of us, the risk of choosing and failing in life and in art is a loss of self-esteem which outweighs the potential satisfaction of success so completely that we are locked into immobility by fear. It is this that causes creative death far more frequently than heart disease. There is a quiet courage demanded of all of us with each breath we take. In art, this courage is manifested each time we choose to move toward a new creation.[80]

For the artist who chronically finds an excuse to avoid work, the consequences of rationalization are not limited to getting nothing accomplished. Guilt sets in because you are not doing what you think you want to be doing and because you are practicing self-deceit. Animosities and tensions develop internally and toward others, whom you blame for your circumstances. Jealousy and contempt rear their miserable heads, directed toward any artists (and nonartists as well) who have managed to put their lives together in such a way that they are accomplishing, or are really trying to accomplish, their goals.

With so much negativity festering, no wonder work is impossible. The distance between what you want to achieve and what you are actually achieving grows wider. And if you try to work you find each product of self-expression tainted and influenced by your anger and hostility. Creativity is used to vent frustration and addresses nothing else.

Avoiding Public Exposure

Some artists have no problem working but begin the rationalization process when it comes time for their work to leave the studio and enter the marketplace. To insure yourself against experiencing any form of rejection, you begin to rationalize: your work isn't ready, you don't have enough work to show, you don't fit into the latest trend, you're working for your own pleasure and do not want to derive money from art, and no one will understand your work anyway—it's too deep!

One of the more popular rationalizations is the *perpetual search for the perfect agent*. Once this person is found, he or she will take your work to the marketplace. This person, you tell yourself, will shield you from criticism and rejection; schlepp your slides from gallery to museum; bargain, negotiate, and establish your market value; arrange exhibitions; write letters; attend cocktail parties; and make important connections. In addition, the agent will have excellent press contacts and your work will be regularly featured in leading publications, with critics fighting among themselves for the opportunity to review your shows. And of course, this agent will fill out grant applications on your behalf and will be very successful in convincing foundations to subsidize your career. And when cash flow is a problem, the agent will tide you over with generous advances. When your ego needs stroking, the agent will always be on call. All you have to do is stay in your ivory tower and work.

I estimate that 75 percent of my clients have the notion in the backs of their minds that I will fulfill this fantasy and provide the buffer zone they are seeking. Apart from my belief that within the visual-arts field this fairy godperson is practically nonexistent (or inaccessible to artists who have not yet been "discovered" and have not obtained a high market value), I strongly believe that artists are their own best representatives.

Meanwhile, the search for the perfect agent, the supposed saint of all saints, continues while the artist's work accumulates in the studio, to be seen only by four walls.

Rationalization can become a style of life—an art unto itself. Artists who use rationalization as a style of living tend to associate with other artists who are skilled at the same game, supporting and reinforcing each other, pontificating in unison that "life is hell," and that it's everyone or everything else's fault. It's less lonely going nowhere fast in a group than by yourself.

Paranoia

Rationalization has a twin: paranoia. Webster defines *paranoia* as a "tendency on the part of an individual or group toward excessive or irrational suspiciousness and distrustfulness of others."

Sometimes the twins are inseparable and it is difficult to know where rationalization ends and paranoia begins. Sometimes rationalization is the aggressor and paranoia takes over, and other times paranoia prevails on its own. But the twins always meet again at the same junction, called *insecurity*.

For example, a painter tells me she dislikes showing her work to dealers because when she invites them to her studio she believes that her invitation is interpreted as a sexual proposition. I asked whether she had encountered this kind of experience. "No," she replied, "but I know what they are all thinking." Consequently, dealers are not invited for studio visits. Thus, she eliminates any possibility of being rejected or hearing that her work isn't good enough. Another artist, who was part of a group that I was assisting with public relations for an upcoming exhibition, told me that he did not want press coverage in certain newspapers and on television out of fear that the "wrong kind of people" would come to the show. I could never figure out who the "wrong kind of people" might be—street gangs, muggers? Nor could the artist shed light on the subject when I asked for an explanation. But in his mind there was a special group of people who were not meant to view or buy art.

The belief that there *is* a special group of people who are not meant to view or buy art is common among artists. It translates into the "creating art for friends" syndrome, a principle that, on the surface, sounds very virtuous, but all too often means that anyone who likes your work is worth knowing, and anyone who doesn't isn't. It is a tidy black-and-white package: a handpicked audience that you create for the purpose of lessening the possibility that you will be rejected and increasing your sense of security and self-esteem.

I don't mean to understate or underrate the importance of support and compliments, but there are many dangers in being paranoid about new audiences. In addition to propagating elitist notions about art, it also creates incestuous attitudes and incestuous results. To continually create only what you know will please your peanut gallery impedes your creative growth and limits your creativity. The fear of new audiences also applies to artists who are afraid to leave their galleries or expand into new local, regional, national, and international territories.

One area where paranoia runs rampant is within the so-called community of artists. Artists are often fearful of ideas being stolen, competition, and losing the status quo. By this reasoning every artist is a potential enemy.

An artist who served as an apprentice for two years to a well-known sculptor was preparing a grant application and needed three letters of recommendation. He felt comfortable asking his former employer for a letter because on numerous occasions the sculptor had praised his talents. Yet the sculptor turned him down, saying that on principle he does not give artists letters of recommendation.

Reading between the lines, it is likely that the younger artist posed a threat to the sculptor's status. The sculptor felt that there was no more room at the top, and just to ensure that no one else would inch his or her way up, he thwarted every opportunity that might give someone else upward mobility.

A painter who had recently moved to New York and was eager to begin making gallery contacts told me that she had a good friend who was with an established New York gallery where she would like to exhibit. I suggested that she ask her friend for a personal introduction. "I already did," she glumly replied. "But she said that *she* would be heartbroken if the dealer didn't like my work."

In this example, the artist tried to disguise her own insecurities with a protective gesture. She would not allow herself to be put in a position where her "taste" would be questioned, and/or she saw her friend as a potential threat to her status in the gallery— a realistic enough threat to warrant cutting her friend out of a network.

I once asked a sculptor who was sharing a studio with other artists whether her colleagues were supportive and helped each other with contacts. "Oh, no," she replied, "just the opposite. Whenever one of the artists has a dealer or curator over for a studio visit, the day before the appointment she asks us to cover up our work with sheets." Then she added, "I don't blame her. If I were in her position I would do the same."

In this example there is little room to read between the lines. It is a blatant example of paranoid behavior. Oddly enough, her studio mates complied with the outrageous request because they deeply identified with and understood the artist's fear.

Paranoia also manifests itself in the hoarding and concealment of information. I have seen artists smother in their bosoms any tidbit of information or leads that they believed would be a *weapon in the hands of other artists*. A dancer told me that she holds back information from colleagues about scheduled auditions. A sculptor complained that his best friend entered a competition whose theme was very relevant to his own work; when he learned of the opportunity only after the deadline closed, his friend nonchalantly said, "Oh, I thought I mentioned it to you." A photographer suspiciously asked me how many other photographers I had advised to approach a certain gallery.

Overreacting to Competition

Some of the examples cited above might sound familiar—so familiar and ordinary that you most likely never thought to consider them examples of rationalization and paranoid behavior. This is part of the problem. In the art world, illogical and unsubstantiated fears and scapegoating have become the norm.

One of the basic reasons why rationalization and paranoia are condoned in the art world is overreaction to competition. Everyone tells us how competitive the art world is, how competitive being an artist is. We hear it from critics, curators, dealers, educators, our parents, and other artists. We enter contests and juried shows; vie for the interest of dealers, collectors, patrons, and critics; fight for grants, teaching jobs, and commissions. We write manifestos to be more profound than others.

Competition is an occupational hazard in every profession; it is not exclusive to the art world. But all too often in the art world we have let rivalry assume the predominant role in how we relate to one another. Although for some artists the mere thought of being judged is so overwhelming that they won't even allow themselves to compete, others plunge into the match but let a dog-eat-dog mentality pilot their trip. These are artists who backstab, hoard information, and exercise selective memories.

Some artists try to deal with competition by establishing elitist values, adamantly contending that only a select few were meant to understand their work. Trying to win the interest of a select audience makes competition seem less threatening. Other artists have concocted a myth that dealers, curators, and collectors are incapable of simultaneous appreciation of or interest in more than a few artists. Such artists cultivate a brutal "It's me or you" attitude.

The main reason competition has become so fierce is that many artists really believe only a limited number of artists *can* achieve success. Although it might be true that only a limited number of artists do achieve success, the *potential number* of artists who can succeed *is not limited*. Achieving success has nothing to do with "beating out the competition" through deception, lies, manipulation, and viciousness. Artists who succeed have beaten out the competition through exercising powers of perseverance and discipline, and by cultivating good marketing skills.

Until competition in the art world is recognized for what it really is, rationalization and paranoia will continue to be used by many artists as tools of the trade. They are odious, unproductive, and self-defeating props that are dangerous to your health, career, and the present and future of the art world.

There is no need to expound on why it is unhealthy to live a life predicated on fear, lies, and excuses and what it can do to us physically and mentally. Some artists are at least consistent, allowing self-destruction and self-deceit to govern all facets of their existence. But other artists have a double standard: honesty, intellect, courage, discipline, and integrity are their ruling principles, except when it comes to their art and careers!

Those who let rationalization and paranoia rule their careers in order to avoid rejection, assuage insecurity, and fend off competition must face the fact that their careers can come to a screeching halt, limp along in agonizing frustration, or be limited in every possible sense. Their work suffers (reflecting lies, excuses, and fears) and their network of friends and contacts degenerates to the lowest common denominator, as they stop at nothing to eliminate what is perceived as a possible threat.

Dealing with Rejection

An artist described her experience with rejection in this way: "I, like most young artists, romanticized the idea of 'being an artist' and in so doing anticipated a degree of rejection, but had I known the degree of rejection that would be in store . . . I might have chosen to become a doctor instead. Frankly, I don't get it."[81]

There are many reasons why an artist's work is rejected. Artists are constantly turned down from galleries, museums, alternative spaces, juried shows, and teaching jobs. A bad review is a form of rejection; so is not being reviewed.

Some artists are rejected for reasons for which they are *ultimately responsible*, and for these artists rejection can be an asset. It might be the only indication an artist has that his or her career is being mismanaged.

Artists who are responsible for rejection include those who make no effort to improve their chances by taking the initiative or creating career opportunities. Examples of such artists have been described throughout this book: those who haphazardly enter the marketplace, those who prepare poor presentations, and those who can't abandon "the myth of the artist."

Some artists rely on moods to enter the marketplace. A burst of energy tells them it is time to make contacts and take action, and for a week or two, or perhaps a month, they are sincerely dedicated to showing their work around. But the goal is instant gratification, and if expectations are not rewarded, they retreat. Depending on the artist, it can take months—sometimes years—for anything constructive to happen.

Artists who are controlled by moods further encourage self-defeat by drawing the conclusion that rejection is an absolute: once they are rejected, a museum's or gallery's doors are always closed. Consequently, these artists will not return with a new body of work.

But there are many instances in which artists are not responsible for rejection. These instances are caused by subjective forces, including "taste buds," trends, norms, and other people's priorities. These forces can be illogical and arbitrary, and are, by nature, unfair.

I once had a grant application rejected. The grant's panel had confused me with another artist whose name was similar. That artist had previously received a grant from the same foundation, but had misused the funds. It was only by accident, and many months later, that I learned what had happened.

This was luxurious rejection: I could not take it personally or hold myself responsible, and I was able to learn the *real* reason. It is rare, though, that artists know the real reasons why they are rejected. Consequently, they think they are untalented and that their ideas are without merit.

The side effects of rejection are more horrendous than the actual rejection. For this reason, once you have ascertained that you are no longer responsible for the situation, it is important to build up an immunity against being affected by rejection.

Artist Billy Curmano described his immunity system in *Art-workers News*: "One day, while reflecting on . . . accumulated rejections, I composed an equally impersonal rejection rejection and have begun systematically sending it to everyone in my file. . . . Striking back immediately becomes a ritual to look forward to."[82] Here is the letter Mr. Curmano composed:

Hello:

IT HAS COME TO OUR ATTENTION that you sent a letter of rejection concerning BILLY CURMANO (hereinafter the "Artist") or his work dated ____ to the Artist.

BE IT KNOWN TO ALL, that the said MR. CURMANO no longer accepts rejection in any form.

KNOW YE THAT, this document, as of the day and year first written, shall serve as an official rejection rejection.

IN WITNESS WHEREOF, Artist and Counsel have set their hands and seals as of the date above first written.[83]

Mr. Curmano provided space for his signature as well as his counsel's and ended his rejection rejection notice with: "We are sorry for the use of a form letter, but the volume of rejections received makes a personal response impossible."[84]

One starting point for developing an immunity to rejection is to look at rejection in terms of its counterpart—acceptance, or what is commonly referred to as *success*. Rejection and success are analogous for various reasons. What artists define as rejection and success are usually borrowed from other people's opinions, values, and priorities. Artists who measure success and rejection in terms of what society thinks have the most difficult time coping with both phenomena.

Both success and rejection are capable of producing an identity crisis. Some artists who attain success find themselves stripped of goals, direction, and a sense of purpose. The same holds true for artists who are rejected.

Stagnation is a by-product of success and rejection. Artists who are rejected can be diverted and blocked in their creativity. Artists who attain success can lose momentum and vision.

It *is* possible for artists to be unscathed by rejection or success, and continue with new goals, directions, and explorations, irrespective of other people's aesthetic judgments.

The sooner you lose an obsession with rejection, the sooner your real potential develops, and the better equipped you will be to handle success.

If you accept the premise that the reasons for rejection are not truths or axioms, analyze rejection under a microscope. Reduce it to its lowest common denominator. Who is rejecting you? What does the person or entity mean relative to your existence? Is this entity blocking your energy, self-confidence, and achievements? Are you so vulnerably perched that other people's opinions can topple you?

When you can have a good laugh over the significance you had once placed on the answers to these questions, you will be able to respond to rejection the same way you respond to any other form of junk mail.

Building Immunities to Rejection

Keep in mind that generally it takes fifty presentation packages of the same body of work to generate one positive response (see page 43). A number less than fifty does not even begin to approach an effective market penetration level that justifies any sense of defeat or rejection.

Each time you receive a letter of rejection, initiate a new contact, send out another presentation package, or pick up the phone. Replace feelings of rejection with a sense of anticipation. This process increases the odds of acceptance and keeps your psyche in good shape.

Stop putting all of your eggs in one basket. Submitting one grant application a year or seeing one gallery every six months is only a gesture; strong, affirmative results do not come from gestures. Create opportunities for things to happen. Think big and broad. Make inroads in many directions. *What you want are lots of baskets filled with lots of eggs.*

Appendix of Resources

The following list of contacts and resources includes the addresses of organizations and agencies and the details of publications cited in this book. It also includes other resources pertaining to specific topics. This list is a beginning and by no means covers the infinite number of resources and amount of information available to artists. But it is a good starting point from which to develop a library of materials and contacts to launch (or relaunch) and sustain your career.

Accounting/Bookkeeping

PUBLICATIONS

The Art of Deduction: Income Taxation for Performing, Visual and Literary Artists. California Lawyers for the Arts, Fort Mason Center, Building C, Room 255, San Francisco, California 94123, revised 1985.

The Artist in Business: Basic Business Practices by Craig Dreezen. Arts Extension Service, Division of Continuing Education, University of Massachusetts, Amherst, Massachusetts 01003, 1988. See "Practicing Business Basics."

ArtistHelp: The Artist's Guide to Work-Related Human and Social Services, compiled by the Research Center for Arts and Culture, Columbia University. Neal-Schuman Publishers, 23 Leonard Street, New York, New York 10013, 1990. Identifies agencies offering financial and other human services to artists; lists addresses, phone numbers, and names of contacts, and provides cost information.

The Artist's Tax Workbook by Carla Messman. Lyons and Burford, 31 West 21st Street, New York, New York 10010, revised annually. A step-by-step guide for preparing tax returns, focusing on the special tax situations artists are likely to encounter. It also includes information on record keeping, IRS reporting requirements, sale of business equipment, and home studio deductions.

Bookkeeping for Artists. Chicago Artists' Coalition, 5 West Grand, Chicago, Illinois 60610, revised 1985.

The Business of Art, edited by Lee Caplin. New York: Prentice Hall, revised 1991. See "Understanding Everyday Finances" by Robert T. Higashi and "Preparing for Taxes and Other Atrocities" by Ira M. Lowe and Paul A. Mahon.

Interpretation Bulletin. Published by Revenue Canada. Available from CARO, 183 Bathurst Street, Toronto, Ontario, Canada M5T 2R7, updated regularly. Includes most recent interpretations of the Income Tax Act for visual artists and writers in Canada.

Legal Guide for the Visual Artist by Tad Crawford. Allworth Press, 10 East 23rd Street, Suite 400, New York, New York 10010, revised 1989. See "Income Taxation," "Income Taxation II," "The Hobby Loss Challenge," "The Artist's Estate," and "The Artist as Collector."

A Practical Business and Tax Guide for the Craftsperson by Fred Bair and James Norris. Publishing Horizons, 2950 North High Street, P.O. Box 02190, Columbus, Ohio 43202-9990, revised 1986.

The Professional Artist's Manual by Richard Hyman. New York: Van Nostrand Reinhold, 1980. See "Bookkeeping."

The Tax Workbook for Artists and Others by Susan Harvey Dawson. ArtBusiness, Inc., 223 North Saint Asaph Street, Alexandria, Virginia 22314, revised annually.

Taxation and the Arts: A Practical Guide by Arthur B. C. Drache. Published by the Canadian Conference of the Arts, 1987. Available from CARO, 183 Bathurst Street, Toronto, Ontario, Canada M5T 2R7. Provides guidelines for making a living and paying taxes in the arts.

"Taxes and The Artist" by Carolyn Blakeslee, *ArtCalendar*, P.O. Box 1040, Great Falls, Virginia 22066, April 1989.

ORGANIZATIONS

Artists for Tax Equity, c/o Graphic Artists Guild, 11 West 20th Street, 8th Floor, New York, New York 10011.

Austin Lawyers and Accountants for the Arts, P.O. Box 2577, Austin, Texas 78768.

Business Volunteers for the Arts, 1200 One Union Square, Seattle, Washington 98101.

Business Volunteers for the Arts/Miami, Suite 2500, Museum Tower, 150 West Flagler Street, Miami, Florida 33130.

Community Accountants, University City Science Center, 3508 Market Street, Philadelphia, Pennsylvania 19104. Offers free services to qualified artists.

Lawyers and Accountants for the Arts, The Artists Foundation, Inc., 8 Park Plaza, Boston, Massachusetts 02116. Offers accounting advice to artists.

St. Louis Volunteer Lawyers and Accountants for the Arts, c/o St. Louis Regional Arts Commission, 3540 Washington, St. Louis, Missouri 63108.

Texas Accountants and Lawyers for the Arts, 1540 Sul Ross, Houston, Texas 77006.

Volunteer Lawyers and Accountants for the Arts Program, c/o Cleveland Bar Association, 113 St. Clair Avenue, Cleveland, Ohio 44114-1253.

Apprentices and Interns

PUBLICATIONS

Internships and Job Opportunities in New York City and Washington, D.C. The Graduate Group, 86 Norwood Road, West Hartford, Connecticut 06117, revised annually.

Internships in Federal Government. The Graduate Group, 86 Norwood Road, West Hartford, Connecticut 06117, revised annually.

Internships in State Government. The Graduate Group, 86 Norwood Road, West Hartford, Connecticut 06117, revised annually.

Internships Leading to Careers. The Graduate Group, 86 Norwood Road, West Hartford, Connecticut 06117, revised annually.

National Directory of Arts Internships, edited by Warren Christensen. National Network for Artist Placement, 935 West Avenue 37, Los Angeles, California 90065, revised regularly. Lists more than twenty-one hundred internship opportunities in the arts.

New Internships. The Graduate Group, 86 Norwood Road, West Hartford, Connecticut 06117, revised annually.

ORGANIZATIONS

Apprentice Alliance, 151 Potrero Avenue, San Francisco, California 94103. Brings together apprentices and masters in all disciplines.

Arts Apprenticeship Program, New York City Department of Cultural Affairs, 2 Columbus Circle, New York, New York 10019.

Great Lakes College Association, Ohio Wesleyan University, Delaware, Ohio 43105.

Great Lakes College Association Program in New York, 305 West 29th Street, New York, New York 10001.

Art Colonies and Artist-in-Residence Programs

PUBLICATIONS

Artist Colonies. Arts Resource Consortium Library, 1 East 53rd Street, New York, New York 10022, updated regularly. List of thirty-four artists' colonies located in nineteen states.

Artist-in-Residence Programs, compiled by Caroll Michels, 491 Broadway, New York, New York 10012, updated annually. Includes the names, addresses, phone numbers, names of contacts, and descriptions of more than one hundred national and international artist-in-residence programs and colonies for visual and performing artists and writers.

Artists' Workspace Guide. New York City Department of Cultural Affairs, 2 Columbus Circle, New York, New York 10019, 1988. Includes information on studio space available in conjunction with artist-in-residence programs in the New York City area.

The Handbook for Clay Artists, edited by Alexandra B. Trub and Jimmy Clark. The Clay Studio, 139 North 2nd Street, Philadelphia, Pennsylvania 19106, 1989. Includes information on artists' residencies.

Money for Film and Video Artists, compiled by the American Council for the Arts. Allworth Press, 10 East 23rd Street, Suite 400, New York, New York 10010, 1991. Includes information on artists' colonies.

Money for Visual Artists, compiled by the American Council for the Arts. Allworth Press, 10 East 23rd Street, Suite 400, New York, New York 10010, 1991. Includes information on artists' colonies.

"The Solitude to Create: The MacDowell Colony" by Drew Steis, *ArtCalendar,* P.O. Box 1040, Great Falls, Virginia 22066, July/August 1990.

The Visual Arts Handbook. Visual Arts Ontario, 439 Wellington Street

West, Toronto, Ontario, Canada M5V 1E7, revised 1991. A comprehensive guide to resources for artists, including artists' colonies.

Visual Arts Residencies: Sponsor Organizations. Mid Atlantic Arts Foundation, 11 East Chase Street, Suite 2A, Baltimore, Maryland 21202-2524, 1990. Describes organizations that sponsor visual artists' residencies in the mid-Atlantic region. Lists the name, address, phone number, and contact person for each sponsoring organization.

ORGANIZATIONS

Affiliate Artists, Inc., 37 West 65th Street, New York, New York 10023.

Arts in Education Program, Office for Public Partnership, National Endowment for the Arts, 1100 Pennsylvania Avenue, NW, Washington, D.C. 20506.

Hospital Audiences, Inc., 220 West 42nd Street, New York, New York 10036.

Independent Curators, Inc., 799 Broadway, New York, New York 10003.

Also see "International Connections."

Artists' Books

PUBLICATIONS

Off the Shelf: A Marketing and Distribution Guide for Independent Literary and Artist Book Publishers by Joan Murray. Published by Writers and Books, 1989. Available from the American Council for the Arts, 1 East 53rd Street, New York, New York 10022. Offers tips and advice on business plans, marketing and promotion, media and advertising campaigns, direct mail tactics, distribution agreements, retail sales, library acquisitions, audience development, and funders' perspectives.

ORGANIZATIONS AND DISTRIBUTORS

Artists Book Works, 1422 West Irving Park Road, Chicago, Illinois 60613. A nonprofit organization that promotes the art of handmade books through exhibitions, workshops, and a slide registry.

Book Artists International, 8375 Leesburg Pike, #217, Vienna, Virginia 22180. Membership organization that sponsors a slide registry and newsletter.

Bookworks, Washington Project for the Arts, 400 7th Street, NW, Washington, D.C. 20004. Houses a bookstore that carries artists' books and sponsors an annual bookwork show.

Burning Books, 690 Market Street, San Francisco, California 94104. Distributes and exhibits artists' books.

Califia, 2266 Union Street, San Francisco, California 94123. Distributes and exhibits artists' books.

Center for Book Arts, Inc., 626 Broadway, New York, New York 10012. Nonprofit educational and exhibition facility. Offers classes and production facilities for artists' books. Publishes quarterly newsletter, *Book Arts Review*.

Franklin Furnace, 112 Franklin Street, New York, New York 10013. Nonprofit membership organization. Archive and repository for artists' books. Sponsors exhibitions.

Nexus Press and Bookshop, P.O. Box 54661, Atlanta, Georgia 30308-0661. Production facility for artists' books.

Printed Matter, 77 Wooster Street, New York, New York 10012. Exhibits and sells artists' books.

Printworks Gallery, 311 West Superior, Suite 105, Chicago, Illinois 60610. Exhibition space for artists' books and other works on paper.

Woodland Pattern and Art Works, 720 East Locust, Milwaukee, Wisconsin 53212. Distributes and exhibits artists' books.

Artists' Housing

PUBLICATIONS

"ArtHouse: Finding 'Live/Work' Spaces for Artists" by Drew Steis, *ArtCalendar*, P.O. Box 1040, Great Falls, Virginia 22066, September 1990.

Artists' Housing: Creative Live/Work Space That Lasts by Mike Pipske. Publishing Center for Cultural Resources, 625 Broadway, New York, New York 10012, 1989.

The Artists' Studio and Housing Handbook by Dino Tsantis. CARO, 183 Bathurst Street, Toronto, Ontario, Canada M5T 2R7, 1985. A guide to the rights and obligations of artists leasing studio space under a commercial lease in Canada.

Artists' Workspace Guide. New York City Department of Cultural Affairs, 2 Columbus Circle, New York, New York 10019, 1988. Lists artist-in-residence programs and work space, including space available to nonprofit organizations and commercial work space available to artists.

Creating Space: A Real Estate Development Guide for Artists by Cheryl

Kartes. Allworth Press, 10 East 23rd Street, Suite 400, New York, New York 10010, 1991. A comprehensive guide that shows artists how they can develop their own spaces for living and working. Includes techniques for assessing a studio/housing project, identifying resources, and organizing tenants. Also provides information on financing strategies, legal structures and requirements, design issues, and management.

Live/Work: Form and Function by Jennifer Spangler, ArtHouse, 25 Van Ness Avenue, Suite 430, San Francisco, California 94102, revised 1990.

ORGANIZATIONS

ArtHouse, 315 West 9th Street, Suite 1101, Los Angeles, California 90015. Nonprofit organization with three branches created to address the problem of live-work space for artists. A telephone hot line provides information on available space. See below for other locations.

ArtHouse, P.O. Box 31474, Oakland, California 94604.

ArtHouse, 25 Van Ness Avenue, Suite 430, San Francisco, California 94102.

Artists Housing Program, Philadelphia Historic Preservation Corporation, 1616 Walnut Street, Suite 2210, Philadelphia, Pennsylvania 19103.

The Artists' Housing Service, New York City Department of Cultural Affairs, 2 Columbus Circle, New York, New York 10019.

Arts Legislation and Artists' Advocacy

ORGANIZATIONS

American Council for the Arts, 1 East 53rd Street, New York, New York 10022. National organization that provides information on legislative issues and government policies affecting the arts.

Artists for a Better Image (ArtFBI), 1440 East Baltimore Street, #2E, Baltimore, Maryland 21231-1404. A national information-gathering and advocacy organization that collects and monitors examples of stereotypical portrayals of artists in literature and the media, in order to promote a more realistic image of the artist in society. Offers workshops, lectures, and educational programs.

Arts for America, National Assembly of Local Arts Agencies, 1010 Vermont Avenue, NW, Suite 920, Washington, D.C. 20005. Promotes the development of the arts by strengthening the role of local arts agencies.

National Artists Equity Association, P.O. Box 28068, Central Station, Washington, D.C. 20038. National organization with local chapters. Involved at federal, state, and local levels; concerned with legislative issues that affect artists economically and socially.

National Association of Artists' Organizations, 918 F Street, NW, Washington, D.C. 20004. A membership organization made up of organizations and individual artists. Provides information on legislative issues and governmental policies affecting artists and arts organizations.

National Campaign for Freedom of Expression, P.O. Box 50245, Washington, D.C. 20004. Coalition of artists' organizations, artists, and other individuals working together to protect the First Amendment and freedom of expression. Chapters are located throughout the United States.

Arts Service Organizations

PUBLICATIONS

Access: A Guide to the Visual Arts in Washington State, edited by Claudia Bach. Allied Arts of Seattle, 107 South Main Street, Seattle, Washington 98104, 1989.

Artlines 1991–1992: An Annotated Guide to Organizations and Publications Essential to Artists. National Network for Artist Placement, 935 West Avenue 37, Los Angeles, California 90065, revised 1990. Lists arts organizations that lend support to artists.

Asian American Arts Organizations in New York. Asian American Arts Alliance, Inc., P.O. Box 879, Canal Street Station, New York, New York 10013-0864, 1990.

Directory of Hispanic Artists and Organizations. Association of Hispanic Arts, Inc., 173 East 116th Street, New York, New York 10029. Lists artists and organizations involved with dance, literature, media, music, theater, and visual arts. Published bimonthly.

Directory of Minority Arts Organizations, edited by Carol Ann Huston. Division of Civil Rights, National Endowment for the Arts, 1100 Pennsylvania Avenue, NW, Washington, D.C. 20506, revised 1987. Lists art centers, galleries, performing groups, presenting groups, and local and national arts service organizations with leadership and constituencies that are predominantly Asian American, Black, Hispanic, Native American, or multiracial.

Directory of the Arts. Canadian Conference of the Arts, 189 Laurier Avenue East, Ottawa, Ontario, Canada K1N 6P1, 1991. A complete listing of Canadian cultural departments and agencies, national arts associations, arts councils, and cultural agencies.

Directory of Visual Arts Organizations in New Jersey. P.O. Box 2195, Westfield, New Jersey 07090, updated regularly. Lists regional and county arts councils, cultural and heritage commissions, and museums.

Media Arts Resources Directory. Mid Atlantic Arts Foundation, 11 East Chase Street, Suite 2A, Baltimore, Maryland 21202-2524. Provides information on media arts resource organizations, including types of services offered.

National Association of Artists' Organizations Directory. National Association of Artists' Organizations, 918 F Street, NW, Washington, D.C. 20004, revised regularly. Describes alternative spaces and arts service organizations. Each entry includes a description of programs, disciplines, exhibition and/or performance spaces, and proposal procedures, and the name of a contact.

National Directory of Multicultural Arts Organizations, edited by Johanna L. Misey. National Assembly of State Arts Agencies, 1010 Vermont Avenue, NW, Suite 920, Washington, D.C. 20005, 1990. Contains more than twelve hundred entries; includes listings for service organizations.

Organizing Artists, edited by Lane Relyea. National Association of Artists' Organizations, 918 F Street, NW, Washington, D.C. 20004, 1990. A critical examination of the evolution of artists' organizations and the artist-space movement, tracing the history of artist activism in the United States from 1905 to 1990.

Performing Arts Presenter Directory. Mid Atlantic Arts Foundation, 11 East Chase Street, Suite 2A, Baltimore, Maryland 21202-2524, revised annually. Profiles not-for-profit presenters in the mid-Atlantic region. Each profile includes a description of objectives, budgets, and disciplines; facility information; and information on fees paid for performances and workshops.

The Visual Arts Handbook. Visual Arts Ontario, 439 Wellington Street West, Toronto, Ontario, Canada M5V 1E7, revised 1991. A comprehensive guide to resources for artists and artists' associations.

Whole Arts Directory, edited by Cynthia Navaretta. Midmarch Art Books, 300 Riverside Drive, New York, New York 10025, 1987. Includes information on visual arts; performance art; film, electronic, and print media; craft organizations; and support services and resources.

NATIONAL ORGANIZATIONS

American Council for the Arts, 1 East 53rd Street, New York, New York 10022. National organization whose programs address underlying problems and key policy issues regarding the arts. Sponsors the Arts Resource Consortium Library and Visual Artist Information Hotline. Publishes *Vantage Point* and reference materials for artists and arts organizations.

American Craft Council, 72 Spring Street, New York, New York 10012. National organization that sponsors exhibitions, seminars, workshops, and international exchange and communications programs. Publishes *American Craft*.

Artists for a Better Image (ArtFBI), 1440 East Baltimore Street, #2E, Baltimore, Maryland 21231-1404. A national information-gathering and advocacy organization that collects and monitors examples of stereotypical portrayals of artists in literature and the media, in order to promote a more realistic image of the artist in society. Offers workshops, lectures, and educational programs.

Arts Extension Service, Division of Continuing Education, University of Massachusetts, Amherst, Massachusetts 01003. Serves as a catalyst for better management of the arts in communities through continuing education for artists and arts organizations. Sponsors programs in arts management, business development, fund-raising, advocacy, leadership, and marketing. Publishes and distributes books, guides, and pamphlets.

Arts Resource Consortium Library, 1 East 53rd Street, New York, New York 10022. A national information and referral service for artists and arts managers. Sponsors the Visual Artist Information Hotline (800-232-2789), a toll-free information service covering a variety of subjects including funding sources, health insurance, legal issues, arts service organizations, and technical assistance.

Asian American Arts Alliance, Inc., P.O. Box 879, Canal Street Station, New York, New York 10013-0864. Sponsors exhibitions, publications, and programs for Asian-American artists.

Association of Hispanic Arts, Inc., 173 East 116th Street, New York, New York 10029. Offers a variety of services geared toward professional Hispanic artists and arts organizations.

Association of Independent Video and Filmmakers, Inc., 625 Broadway, 9th Floor, New York, New York 10012. Provides creative and professional opportunities for independent video and filmmakers.

Association of National Non-Profit Artists' Centres, 183 Bathurst Street, Toronto, Ontario, Canada M5T 2R7. Represents artist-run centers throughout Canada. Assists Canadian artists and promotes their work. Encourages cooperation and collaboration among artists and artists' centers in Canada.

ATLATL, 402 West Roosevelt, Phoenix, Arizona 85003. A national nonprofit organization dedicated to the preservation, promotion, growth, and development of contemporary and traditional Native American arts. Provides a Native American Resource and Distribution Clearinghouse. Offers employment referrals, reference and referral information, and publishes *Native Arts Update*.

Canadian Crafts Council, 189 Laurier Avenue East, Ottawa, Ontario, Canada K1N 6P1. Provides information and services to artists.

Interfaith Forum on Religion, Art and Architecture, 1777 Church Street, NW, Washington, D.C. 20036. A national organization dedicated to pursuing high standards in art and architecture for sacred, worship, and liturgical teaching spaces.

International Sculpture Center, 1050 Potomac Street, NW, Washington, D.C. 20007. Nonprofit service organization for professional sculptors. Offers health and studio insurance, provides a computerized data bank, and organizes international and national exhibitions. Publishes *Sculpture*.

Museum Reference Center, Smithsonian Institution Libraries, Office of Museum Programs, Arts and Industries Building, Room 2235, 900 Jefferson Drive, SW, Washington, D.C. 20560. Provides technical assistance, workshops, conferences, and information on museums and visual arts. Sponsors an internship program and publishes book lists and guides.

National Artists Equity Association, P.O. Box 28068, Central Station, Washington, D.C. 20038. National organization with local chapters throughout the United States. Benefits include group medical insurance, studio and work insurance, promotion of arts-related legislation, model contracts, and publications.

National Association of Artists' Organizations (NAAO), 918 F Street, NW, Washington, D.C. 20004. Composed of organizations and individuals that sponsor the production and presentation of contemporary artists' work and/or artists' services.

National Center on Arts and the Aging, National Council on the Aging, 409 Third Street, SW, 2nd Floor, Washington, D.C. 20024. Serves as a clearinghouse on public and private arts and aging agencies. Provides reference materials and technical assistance. Sponsors conferences, workshops, and exhibitions. Maintains an artists' registry. Publishes *Collage* and books on arts and the aging.

National Conference of Artists, Gallery Row, 409 7th Street, NW, Washington, D.C. 20004. The oldest national organization for African-American artists in the United States. Devoted to the preservation, promotion, and development of the work of African-American artists through its various services, publications, and programs.

Photographic Resource Center, 602 Commonwealth Avenue, Boston, Massachusetts 02215. A membership organization providing a range of programs and services for photographers, journalists, critics, curators, students, and other individuals and organizations interested in photography.

Women's Caucus for Art, Moore College of Art, 20th and Parkway, Philadelphia, Pennsylvania 19103. National organization with regional chapters throughout the United States. Represents the professional and economic concerns of women artists, art historians, educators, writers, and museum professionals. Sponsors conferences and exhibitions and publishes a newsletter.

REGIONAL ORGANIZATIONS

Arts Midwest, 528 Hennepin Avenue, Suite 310, Minneapolis, Minnesota 55403. Regional arts organization serving Illinois, Indiana, Iowa, Michigan, Minnesota, North Dakota, Ohio, South Dakota, and Wisconsin. Provides services, publications, workshops, exhibitions, and grants.

Canadian Artists' Representation Ontario (CARO), 183 Bathurst Street, Toronto, Ontario, Canada M5T 2R7. Association of professional visual artists in Ontario working to improve the financial and professional status of artists.

Consortium for Pacific Arts and Cultures, 2141C Atherton Road, Honolulu, Hawaii 96822. Helps state arts agencies in the Pacific Basin develop multistate and international programs. Sponsors workshops, residencies, and educational programs.

Mid-America Arts Alliance, 912 Baltimore Avenue, #700, Kansas City, Missouri 64105. Provides recognition and opportunities for artists, performers, and arts institutions in Arkansas, Kansas, Missouri, Nebraska, Oklahoma, and Texas. Sponsors exhibitions, performances, workshops, residencies, grants, and other services.

Mid Atlantic Arts Foundation, 11 East Chase Street, Suite 2A, Baltimore, Maryland 21202-2524. Serves artists and arts organizations in Delaware, the District of Columbia, Maryland, New Jersey, New York, Pennsylvania, Virginia, and West Virginia. Sponsors performances, fellowships, and residencies, and provides other services.

New England Foundation for the Arts, 678 Massachusetts Avenue, Suite

800, Cambridge, Massachusetts 02139. Serves artists and arts organizations in Connecticut, Maine, Massachusetts, New Hampshire, Rhode Island, and Vermont. Sponsors exhibitions, performances, workshops, residencies, and publications, and provides other services.

Ontario Crafts Council, 35 McCaul Street, Toronto, Ontario, Canada M5T 1V7. Provides information and assistance to artists through seminars, conferences, publications, and exhibitions.

Resources and Counseling for the Arts, 429 Landmark Center, 75 West 5th Street, Saint Paul, Minnesota 55102. Provides business-related information, advice, and technical assistance to artists in Minnesota and surrounding states through workshops, consultations, and other support services.

Southern Arts Federation, 1293 Peachtree Street, NE, Suite 500, Atlanta, Georgia 30309. Serves artists and arts organizations in Alabama, Florida, Georgia, Kentucky, Louisiana, Mississippi, North Carolina, South Carolina, and Tennessee.

Visual Arts Ontario, 439 Wellington Street West, Toronto, Ontario, Canada M5V 1E7. A resource center with books, reports, periodicals, and catalogs. Sponsors artists' business seminars. Services also include group insurance plans, slide registry, color xerography center, international art programs, and art placement programs.

Western States Arts Foundation, 236 Montezuma Avenue, Santa Fe, New Mexico 87501. Serves artists and arts organizations in Alaska, Arizona, California, Colorado, Hawaii, Idaho, Montana, Nevada, New Mexico, Oregon, Utah, Washington, and Wyoming. Sponsors exhibitions and performances, and provides other services.

OTHER ORGANIZATIONS

Artists Foundation, 8 Park Plaza, Boston, Massachusetts 02116. A statewide nonprofit organization devoted to enhancing the careers of individual artists and the position of artists in society. Sponsors exhibitions and performances and provides other services.

Arts for Greater Rochester, 335 East Main Street, Rochester, New York 14604. A coalition of arts organizations, artists, businesses, and county government. Provides support services to individual artists, including promotion, consultations, management workshops, volunteer legal assistance, group health insurance, and a slide registry.

Arts Resource and Information Center, Minneapolis Institute of Arts, 2400 Third Avenue South, Minneapolis, Minnesota 55400. A clearinghouse for information on visual, literary, and performing artists in Minnesota. Houses a cross-disciplinary library on arts organizations, speakers, museum objects, et cetera. Sponsors conferences and workshops. Provides an employment referral service and slide registry.

Artswatch, 2337 Frankfort Avenue, Louisville, Kentucky 40206. Sponsors exhibitions, performances, workshops, educational programs, and residencies.

Boston Visual Artists Union, 33 Harrison Avenue, 7th Floor, Boston, Massachusetts 02111. Service organization that supports artists' work through exhibitions, a slide registry, a resource center, a newsletter, and special programs.

Boulder Center for the Visual Arts, 1750 13th Street, Boulder, Colorado 80302. Sponsors exhibitions, performances, publications, workshops, and educational programs.

Center for Contemporary Arts, 291 East Barcelona Road, Santa Fe, New Mexico 87501. Mailing address: P.O. Box 148, Santa Fe, New Mexico 87504. Sponsors exhibitions, performances, workshops, residencies, publications, educational programs, and studios, and provides other services.

Center for Photography at Woodstock, 59 Tinker Street, Woodstock, New York 12498. Sponsors exhibitions, fellowships, lecture/workshops, and publications for photographers, video artists, and filmmakers.

Center on Contemporary Art, 1309 First Avenue, Seattle, Washington 98101. Sponsors exhibitions, performances, publications, educational programs, and residencies.

Chicago Artists' Coalition, 5 West Grand, Chicago, Illinois 60610. An artist-run service organization for visual artists that offers members a slide registry, lectures, job referral services, and workshops. Publishes *Chicago Artists' News*.

Chicano Humanities and Arts Council, Inc., P.O. Box 2512, Denver, Colorado 80201. Provides technical assistance on proposals and promotion, and offers workshops on the business of art and marketing techniques.

City Without Walls, One Gateway Center, Plaza Level, Newark, New Jersey 07102-5311. Sponsors exhibitions, publications, workshops, and educational programs.

Contemporary Arts Center, 900 Camp Street, New Orleans, Louisiana 70130. Mailing address: P.O. Box 30498, New Orleans, Louisiana 70190. Sponsors exhibitions, performances, publications, workshops, educational programs, and grants, and provides other services.

Contemporary Arts Institute of Detroit, 414 West Oakridge, Ferndale, Michigan 48220. Sponsors exhibitions, performances, publications, workshops, and educational programs, and provides other services.

Cultural Alliance of Greater Washington, 410 8th Street, NW, Suite 600, Washington, D.C. 20004. Membership organization that sponsors workshops and seminars. Provides health insurance for members. Publishes *Art Washington Newsletter.*

The Delaware Center for the Contemporary Arts, 103 East 16th Street, Wilmington, Delaware 19801. Sponsors exhibitions, publications, workshops, educational programs, residencies, and studio space.

Detroit Artists Market, 1452 Randolph, Detroit, Michigan 48226. Promotes and assists Detroit-metropolitan-area artists. Sponsors exhibitions, publications, and an educational program.

Diverse Works, Inc., 1117 East Freeway, Houston, Texas 77002. Sponsors exhibitions, performances, publications, and workshops.

Florida Center for Contemporary Art, P.O. Box 75184, Tampa, Florida 33605. Primarily represents emerging artists in Florida. Services include a slide registry, legal referrals, studio space, and networking information.

Individual Artists of Oklahoma, 5224 Classen Boulevard, Oklahoma City, Oklahoma 73118. Sponsors exhibitions, performances, publications, and workshops.

Maryland Art Place, 218 West Saratoga Street, Baltimore, Maryland 21201. Sponsors exhibitions, performances, publications, workshops, educational programs, and residencies.

Memphis Center for Contemporary Art, 416 South Main Street, Memphis, Tennessee 38103. Sponsors exhibitions and performances, and provides other services.

New Hampshire Art Association, P.O. Box 3096, Boscawen, New Hampshire 03303. Sponsors exhibitions, publications, workshops, and educational programs.

New Organization for the Visual Arts (NOVA), 4614 Prospect Avenue, #410, Cleveland, Ohio 44103. Artists' membership organization. Provides art marketing program to corporations and sponsors exhibitions, lectures, and workshops.

Nexus Contemporary Art Center, P.O. Box 54661, Atlanta, Georgia 30308. Sponsors exhibitions, performances, publications, workshops, residencies, educational programs, grants, and studios, and provides other services.

Oklahoma Visual Arts Coalition, 5224 Classen Boulevard, Oklahoma City, Oklahoma 73118. Sponsors publications, workshops, and educational programs, and awards grants to Oklahoma artists.

Organization of Independent Artists, 19 Hudson Street, #402, New York, New York 10013. An artists' service organization that sponsors exhibitions in public places, a slide registry, and information services;

provides curating opportunities for artists; and publishes a newsletter.

Painted Bride Art Center, 230 Vine Street, Philadelphia, Pennsylvania 19106. Sponsors exhibitions, performances, publications, and workshops.

Pro Arts, 461 9th Street, Oakland, California 94607. Nonprofit membership organization serving artists of all disciplines in the Bay Area. Offers technical assistance, consultations, service library, seminars, workshops, artist-in-residence programs, and exhibitions.

Real Art Ways (RAW), 56 Arbor Street, Hartford, Connecticut 06106. Sponsors exhibitions, performances, publications, educational programs, residencies, and grants, and provides other services.

1708 East Main, 1708 East Main Street, Richmond, Virginia 23223. Sponsors exhibitions, performances, publications, and workshops.

South Florida Art Center, 924 Lincoln Road, Miami, Florida 33139. Sponsors exhibitions, publications, workshops, educational programs, and residencies.

Texas Fine Arts Association, 3809-B West 35th Street, Austin, Texas 78703. Membership organization for Texas artists. Provides statewide and national art exhibits, information, and referrals. Publishes *News*.

Visual Arts Center of Alaska, 713 West 5th Street, Anchorage, Alaska 99501. Provides Alaskan artists access to tools, equipment, space, and technical expertise. Sponsors exhibitions, performances, publications, workshops, and residencies, and provides other services.

Visual Studies Workshop, 31 Prince Street, Rochester, New York 14607. Provides services for artists working in photography, artists' books, video, and independent film, including educational and publishing programs, exhibitions, residencies, and grants.

Washington Project for the Arts (WPA), 400 7th Street, NW, Washington, D.C. 20004. Sponsors exhibitions, performances, publications, and residencies.

Wisconsin Painters and Sculptors, Inc., 341 North Milwaukee Street, Milwaukee, Wisconsin 53202. Sponsors exhibitions, performances, publications, workshops, and educational programs.

The Woman's Building, 1643 18th Street, Santa Monica, California 90404. Provides women artists with opportunities to gain skills, encouragement, and professional exposure. Sponsors exhibitions, performances, publications, workshops, and residencies, and provides other services.

Women and Their Work, 1137 West Sixth Street, Austin, Texas 78703. Sponsors exhibitions, performances, workshops, educational programs, and publications.

Women's Art Registry of Minnesota, 2402 University Avenue West,

Minneapolis, Minnesota 55114-1701. Membership organization serving women visual artists in Minnesota. Maintains a slide registry and administers a mentor program that matches emerging women artists with more established women artists for a period of one year.
Also see "Disabled Artists."

Artwork Care and Maintenance

PUBLICATIONS

The Care of Photographs by Siegfried Rempel. Lyons and Burford, 31 West 21st Street, New York, New York 10010, 1988. Includes information on proper storage techniques and criteria for preparing museum-quality matting and framing.

Caring for Your Art by Jill Snyder. Allworth Press, 10 East 23rd Street, Suite 400, New York, New York 10010, 1991. Covers the best methods to store, handle, mount, frame, display, document, inventory, photograph, pack, transport, insure, and secure art. Also discusses proper environmental controls to enhance longevity of work.

Curatorial Care of Works of Art on Paper by Anne F. Clapp. Lyons and Burford, 31 West 21st Street, New York, New York 10010, revised 1991. Includes advice on conservation techniques and describes the effects of light, acid, and temperature on works on paper.

Matting and Hinging of Works of Art on Paper by Merrily A. Smith. The Consultant Press/The Photographic Arts Center, Limited, 163 Amsterdam Avenue, New York, New York 10023, 1989. Describes mounting and matting techniques used at the Library of Congress.
Also see "Exhibition Planning."

Career Management, Business, and Marketing

PUBLICATIONS

Annotated Bibliography for the Professional Visual Artist. CARO, 183 Bathurst Street, Toronto, Ontario, Canada M5T 2R7, 1988. Lists and describes books available on various career-related topics for visual artists.

The Art Biz: The Covert World of Collectors, Dealers, Auction Houses, Museums, and Critics by Alice Goldfarb Marquis. Chicago: Contemporary Books, Inc., 1991.

ArtCalendar, P.O. Box 1040, Great Falls, Virginia 22066. Comprehensive listing of opportunities for artists, including exhibitions, grants, art colonies, juried shows, alternative spaces, conferences, slide registries, and book reviews. Also features marketing, career management, and legal advice. Published eleven times a year.

The Artist in Business: Basic Business Practices by Craig Dreesen. Arts Extension Service, Division of Continuing Education, University of Massachusetts, Amherst, Massachusetts 01003, 1988. Includes information on record keeping, legal issues, and obtaining funds from grants, commissions, competitions, and teaching.

The Artist's Forum, 1211 Metze Road, #B-5, "The Quarters," Columbia, South Carolina 29210. Marketing newsletter for professional artists. Published quarterly.

Artist's Market, edited by Susan Connor. Cincinnati: Writer's Digest Books, revised annually.

Artists' Resource Book. Chicago Artists' Coalition, 5 West Grand, Chicago, Illinois 60610, revised 1991. Provides information on exhibiting, marketing, materials, and space.

The Artists' Survival Manual: A Complete Guide to Marketing Your Work by Toby Judith Klayman and Cobbett Steinberg. New York: Charles Scribner's Sons, revised 1987.

The Business of Art, edited by Lee Caplin. New York: Prentice Hall, revised 1991. See "An Artist's Way of Life" by James Rosenquist, "Practical Planning" by Bruce Besley, "Setting Up Business" by Harvey Horowitz, and "Preparing Your Portfolio" by Kate Keller and Mali Olatunji.

The Business of Being an Artist by Daniel Grant. New York: Allworth Press and the American Council for the Arts, 1991. Available from Allworth Press, 10 East 23rd Street, Suite 400, New York, New York 10010.

"Buying Ad Space in Artists' Sourcebooks" by Carolyn Blakeslee, *ArtCalendar*, P.O. Box 1040, Great Falls, Virginia 22066, July/August 1991.

The Crafts Report: The News Monthly of Marketing, Management and Money for Craft Professionals, 87 Wall Street, 2nd Floor, Seattle, Washington 98121. Published eleven times a year.

The Entrepreneurial Artist by Zella Jackson and Judy Cunningham. The Consultant Press/The Photographic Arts Center, Limited, 163 Amsterdam Avenue, New York, New York 10023, 1991.

For the Working Artist: A Survival Guide for Artists by Judith Luther. National Network for Artist Placement, 935 West Avenue 37, Los Angeles, California 90065, revised 1991.

How to Sell Art: A Guide for Galleries, Art Dealers, Consultants, and Agents by Nina Pratt. Succotash Press, 116 Pinehurst Avenue, #F65, New York, New York 10033, 1992.

Information for Artists, edited by Sarah Yates. CARO, 183 Bathurst Street, Toronto, Ontario, Canada M5T 2R7, 1988. Includes practical information on basic business practices.

Marketing the Fine Arts by Marcia Layton. The Consultant Press/The Photographic Arts Center, Limited, 163 Amsterdam Avenue, New York, New York 10023, 1992.

Media Arts Presenter Directory. Mid Atlantic Arts Foundation, 11 East Chase Street, Suite 2A, Baltimore, Maryland 21202-2524, revised regularly. A tool for distributors and filmmakers interested in reaching new audiences. Provides information on programs, audiences, and budgets of regional media arts presenters.

Personal and Business Bartering by James Stout. TAB Books, Inc., Blue Ridge Summit, Pennsylvania 17294-0850, 1985.

Photographer's Market, edited by Sam Marshall. Cincinnati: Writer's Digest Books, revised annually.

Photographing Your Artwork: A Step-By-Step Guide to Taking High-Quality Slides at an Affordable Price by Russell Hart. Cincinnati: North Light Books, 1987. Provides examples of the results of various types of lighting and camera angles; discusses photographing challenging artwork, including three-dimensional pieces, miniatures, and installations; also discusses masking and cleaning slides.

Photographing Your Craftwork: A Hands-On Guide for Craftspeople. Madrona Publishers, P.O. Box 22667, Seattle, Washington 98122, 1986.

Profitable Crafts Marketing: A Complete Guide to Successful Selling by Brian T. Jefferson. Madrona Publishers, P.O. Box 22667, Seattle, Washington 98122, 1986.

The Road Show: A Handbook for Successful Booking and Touring in the Performing Arts by Rena Shagan. American Council for the Arts, 1 East 53rd Street, New York, New York 10022, 1985. A complete manual to help soloists and companies in all the performing arts plan and execute out-of-town engagements.

The Selling Art with a Higher Mind: No More Art Sharks by Barbara Scott. Ichor, 2021 California Avenue, #5, Santa Monica, California 90433, 1990. The title promises more than the book delivers. Discusses the application of spiritual principles and values to selling art.

The Selling of Art by Zella Jackson. The Consultant Press/The Photographic Arts Center, Limited, 163 Amsterdam Avenue, New York, New York 10023, 1992.

Sources and Resources for the Visual Artist. San Francisco Arts Commission, 25 Van Ness Avenue, Suite 240, San Francisco, California 94102, 1991. A guide that assists visual artists in developing portfolios and receiving technical assistance.

Supporting Yourself as an Artist: A Practical Guide by Deborah A. Hoover. New York: Oxford University Press, revised 1989.

Taking Charge: Management and Marketing for the Media Arts. Media Alliance, c/o WNET, 356 West 58th Street, New York, New York 10019, 1988. Provides information and step-by-step guidance in the areas of management, marketing, and fund-raising for media projects.

ORGANIZATIONS

Arts Resource Consortium Library, 1 East 53rd Street, New York, New York 10022. A national information and referral service for artists and arts managers. Sponsors the Visual Artist Information Hotline (800-232-2789), a toll-free information service covering a variety of subjects including funding sources, health insurance, legal issues, arts service organizations, and technical assistance.

Caroll Michels, Artists' Career Development Consultant, 491 Broadway, New York, New York 10012.

National Network for Artist Placement, 935 West Avenue 37, Los Angeles, California 90065. Nonprofit organization dedicated to bringing career counseling, employment services, and survival skills to visual and performing artists.

Resources and Counseling for the Arts, 429 Landmark Center, 75 West 5th Street, St. Paul, Minnesota 55102. Runs ongoing workshops related to artist career management and provides other services.

Also see "Organizing Paperwork," "Periodicals," and "Public Relations/ Press Relations."

Competitions and Juried Exhibitions

PUBLICATIONS

Art Competition Handbook by John M. Anglelini. Cincinnati: North Light Books, 1986.

ArtCalendar, P.O. Box 1040, Great Falls, Virginia 22066. Includes a comprehensive listing of juried exhibitions and competitions. Published eleven times a year.

"Entry Fees" by Carolyn Blakeslee, *ArtCalendar*, P.O. Box 1040, Great Falls, Virginia 22066, June 1991.

Exhibition Directory. The Exhibit Planners, Box 55, Delmar, New York 10254. Lists national and regional juried art and photography exhibitions. Contains information on entry dates, media, awards, fees, and method of art delivery.

Guidebook for Competitions and Commissions. Visual Arts Ontario, 439 Wellington Street West, Toronto, Ontario, Canada M5V 1E7, 1991.

Guidelines for Professional Standards in the Organization of Juried Exhibitions. Toronto: CARO/CARFAC, revised 1988. Available from CARO, 183 Bathurst Street, Toronto, Ontario, Canada M5T 2R7.

"Juried Shows: Boosting Your Show Acceptance Rate" by Carolyn Blakeslee, *ArtCalendar*, P.O. Box 1040, Great Falls, Virginia 22066, June 1991.

National Calendar of Open Competitive Art Exhibitions. Henry Niles, 5423 New Haven Avenue, Fort Wayne, Indiana 46803. Published quarterly.

Recommended Guidelines for Juried Exhibitions. National Artists Equity Association, P.O. Box 28068, Central Station, Washington, D.C. 20038, 1991.

"Staging an Exhibition—Texas Style" by Drew Steis, *ArtCalendar*, P.O. Box 1040, Great Falls, Virginia 22066, April 1990.

Cooperative Galleries

PUBLICATIONS

The Artists' Survival Manual: A Complete Guide to Marketing Your Work by Toby Judith Klayman and Cobbett Steinberg. New York: Charles Scribner's Sons, revised 1987. See "Cooperative Galleries."

"How to Organize an Artists' Cooperative Enterprise" by Patricia Thompson, *ArtCalendar*, P.O. Box 1040, Great Falls, Virginia 22066, September 1990.

On Opening an Art Gallery by Suzanne K. Vinmans, 2701 Commercial Avenue, Madison, Wisconsin 53704, 1990.

ORGANIZATIONS

Association of Artist-Run Galleries, 63 Crosby Street, New York, New York 10012. Provides information regarding artist-run galleries including requirements for membership, dues, and exhibition opportunities.

Corporate Art

PUBLICATIONS

"Acquiring Minds" by Elizabeth Venant, *Los Angeles Times Magazine*, 19 June 1988.

Art Business News, 60 Ridgeway Plaza, Stamford, Connecticut 06905, published monthly.

Art in America Annual Guide to Galleries, Museums and Artists. Art in America, 575 Broadway, New York, New York 10012, published annually each August. See "Corporate Consultants" in index.

"Art, Inc.: The Photograph in the Gray Flannel Suit" by Mary Anne Staniszewski, *Manhattan, Inc.*, May 1986.

"The Art World: Medicis, Inc." by Calvin Tompkins, *The New Yorker*, 14 April 1986.

"The Benefits of Working with Art Advisors" by Brenda Bradick Harris. *ArtCalendar*, P.O. Box 1040, Great Falls, Virginia 22066, April 1990.

"The Big Payoff in Corporate Art" by Faye Rice, *Fortune*, 25 May 1987.

The Business of Art, edited by Lee Caplin. New York: Prentice Hall, revised 1991. See "Art Advisory Services—The Age of the Art Advisor" by Jeffrey Deitch and "Art Collections in Corporations" by Mary Lanier.

Corporate ARTnews, 48 West 38th Street, 9th Floor, New York, New York 10018. Published monthly.

"Corporate Interest in Collecting Art Growing," *Arts Management*, 408 West 57th Street, New York, New York 10019, Summer 1985.

Directory of Fine Art Representatives and Corporate Art Collections. Directors Guild Publishers and The Consultant Press, P.O. Box 369, Renaissance, California 95962, 1989. Lists more than 1,350 art consultants and 650 corporations. Organized by state; also includes Canada and Europe.

The Dodge Report. McGraw-Hill, 1221 Avenue of the Americas, New York, New York 10019, revised regularly.

The Guild. Kraus Sikes, Inc., 228 State Street, Madison, Wisconsin 53703, published annually. A resource directory for architects and interior designers. Contains names, addresses, phone numbers, and photographs of American fine arts and craft artists as well as biographical information. Distributed free of charge to attendees of the American Society of Interior Designers and the American Institute of Architects national conferences.

International Directory of Corporate Art Collections. Published by *ART-news* and International Art Alliance, revised 1989. *ARTnews*, 48 West 38th Street, New York, New York 10018. Lists more than one thousand corporate art collections throughout the United States and abroad, with addresses, key personnel, and descriptions of interests.

"Interview with F. David Fowler" by Drew Steis, *ArtCalendar*, P.O. Box 1040, Great Falls, Virginia 22066, March 1990.

"Interview with Françoise Yohalem—Art Consultant" by Drew Steis, *ArtCalendar*, P.O. Box 1040, Great Falls, Virginia 22066, May 1990.

"Making a Business Out of Art for the Office" by Paula Span, *The Wall Street Journal*, 11 July 1985.

"More Corporations Becoming Working Museums" by Thomas J. Lueck, *The New York Times*, 15 September 1985.

Post- to Neo- by Calvin Tompkins. New York: Henry Holt and Company, 1988. See "Medicis, Inc."

Profile. American Institute of Architects, 1735 New York Avenue, NW, Washington, D.C. 20006, revised biannually.

Washington Art: A Guide to Galleries, Art Consultants and Museums by Lorraine Arden, Carolyn Blakeslee, and Drew Steis. Art Calendar, P.O. Box 1040, Great Falls, Virginia 22066, 1988. Profiles twenty-three art consultants in the Washington, D.C., area.

"What Big Business Sees in Fine Art" by Grace Glueck, *The New York Times*, 16 May 1985.

ORGANIZATIONS

American Institute of Architects, 1735 New York Avenue, NW, Washington, D.C. 20006.

American Society of Interior Designers, 1430 Broadway, New York, New York 10018.

Association of Corporate Art Curators, P.O. Box 11369, Chicago, Illinois 60611.

Association of Professional Art Advisors, 2150 West 29th Street, Denver, Colorado 80211.

National Association for Corporate Art Management, P.O. Box 78, Church Street Station, New York, New York 10008.

Also see "Interior Design and Architecture."

Disabled Artists

PUBLICATIONS

Crafts Report. Jewish Guild for the Blind, Cassette Library, 15 West 65th Street, New York, New York 10023. Newsletter in cassette form. Published monthly.

For Your Information. New York Foundation for the Arts, 5 Beekman Street, Room 600, New York, New York 10038, Spring 1991. Special issue devoted to artists with disabilities.

ORGANIZATIONS

Deaf Artists of America, 87 North Clinton Avenue, #408, Rochester, New York 14604. Nonprofit arts service organization for deaf artists.

Disabled Artists' Network, P.O. Box 20781, New York, New York 10025. Support group for disabled professional visual artists. Publishes a newsletter.

National Endowment for the Arts, Office for Special Constituencies, 1100 Pennsylvania Avenue, NW, Washington, D.C. 20506.

National Theatre Workshop of the Handicapped, 105 West 56th Street, New York, New York 10019. Provides professional training for adults with disabilities.

Resources for Artists with Disabilities, 77 Seventh Avenue South, Suite PHG, New York, New York 10011-6645. Sponsors a slide registry and juried exhibitions.

Employment Opportunities

PUBLICATIONS

Artlines 1991–1992: An Annotated Guide to Organizations and Publications Essential to Artists. National Network for Artist Placement, 935 West Avenue 37, Los Angeles, California 90065, revised 1990. Lists arts organizations lending support to artists, including those offering employment opportunities.

Artsearch. Theatre Communications Group, 355 Lexington Avenue, New York, New York 10017. Published biweekly, this is a national employment-service bulletin for performing artists that lists jobs in arts and arts-related education, production, and management.

Aviso. American Association of Museums, 1225 I Street, NW, Suite 200, Washington, D.C. 20005. Lists museum-related positions. Published monthly.

The College Art Association's Listing of Positions. College Art Association, 275 Seventh Avenue, New York, New York 10001. Published five times a year, this is a listing of arts-related jobs, mainly in colleges and museums in the United States and Canada.

Jobs in Arts and Media Management: What They Are and How to Get One by Stephen Langley and James Abruzzo. American Council for the Arts, 1 East 53rd Street, New York, New York 10022, revised 1990.

Money Talks: The Complete Guide to Creating a Profitable Workshop or Seminar in Any Field by Dr. Jeffrey Lant. Jeffrey Lant Associates, Inc., 50 Follen Street, Suite 507, Cambridge, Massachusetts 02138, revised 1990.

National Arts Jobbank, 236 Montezuma Avenue, Santa Fe, New Mexico 87501. Biweekly newsletter listing available employment in the visual and performing arts, literature, education, and arts administration.

National Arts Placement. National Art Education Association, 1916 Association Drive, Reston, Virginia 22091. Features positions in arts councils, colleges, museums, schools, and universities. Published eight times a year.

Performing Artists Discipline Directory. Mid Atlantic Arts Foundation, 11 East Chase Street, Suite 2A, Baltimore, Maryland 21202-2524, revised annually. Profiles professional performing artists and companies who tour the mid-Atlantic region. Includes information on each artist's discipline and fee range, and a description of each artist's work.

Performing Arts Presenter Directory. Mid Atlantic Arts Foundation, 11 East Chase Street, Suite 2A, Baltimore, Maryland 21202-2524, revised annually. Profiles not-for-profit organizations that sponsor performing artists in the mid-Atlantic region; includes information on budgets, disciplines presented, facilities, and fees paid for performances and workshops.

Survey of Arts Administration Training: 1989–90, edited by E. Arthur Prieve. American Council for the Arts, 1 East 53rd Street, New York, New York 10022, 1989. Identifies and describes graduate degree programs in arts management throughout the United States.

Visual Arts Residencies: Sponsor Organizations. Mid Atlantic Arts Foundation, 11 East Chase Street, Suite 2A, Baltimore, Maryland 21202-2524, 1990. Describes organizations that sponsor visual arts residencies in the mid-Atlantic region. Includes the name, address, phone number, and contact person of each sponsoring organization.

What Color Is Your Parachute? A Practical Manual for Job Hunters and Career Changers by Richard Nelson Bolles. Berkeley: Ten Speed Press, revised regularly.

Work with Passion: How to Do What You Love for a Living by Nancy Anderson. Published by Carroll & Graf Publishers, Inc., and Whatever Publishing, Inc., revised 1987. Distributed by Publishers Group West, 5855 Beaudry Street, Emeryville, California 94608.

ORGANIZATIONS

Affiliate Artists, Inc., 37 West 65th Street, New York, New York 10023.

Artists Work, Chicago Artists' Coalition, 5 West Grand, Chicago, Illinois 60610. An employment service offered free of charge to Chicago Artists' Coalition members.

Arts in Education Program, Office for Public Partnership, National Endowment for the Arts, 1100 Pennsylvania Avenue, NW, Washington, D.C. 20506

Hospital Audiences, Inc., 220 West 42nd Street, New York, New York 10036.

Independent Curators, Inc., 799 Broadway, New York, New York 10003.

National Network for Artist Placement, 935 West Avenue 37, Los Angeles, California 90065. Nonprofit organization dedicated to bringing career counseling, employment services, and survival skills to visual and performing artists.

Opportunity Resources for the Arts, 500 Fifth Avenue, New York, New York 10017. National organization that provides placement services for administrative positions in museums; art centers; art councils; theater, opera, and ballet companies; symphony orchestras; et cetera.

Also see "Apprentices and Interns" and "Art Colonies and Artist-in-Residence Programs."

Exhibition/Performance Places and Spaces

PUBLICATIONS

Access: A Guide to the Visual Arts in Washington State, edited by Claudia Bach. Allied Arts of Seattle, 107 South Main, Seattle, Washington 98104, 1989. Lists commercial galleries, college and university galleries, nonprofit and alternative spaces, and museums. Also includes percent-for-art agencies.

American Craft Guide to Craft Galleries and Shops USA. ACC Publications, 72 Spring Street, New York, New York, 10012, revised regularly.

Art in America Annual Guide to Galleries, Museums and Artists. Art in America, 575 Broadway, New York, New York 10012, published annually each August. Alphabetical listing of American museums, galleries, and alternative spaces, arranged by state and city. Each entry includes the address, phone number, business hours, names of key staff members, and a short description of type of art shown.

Art Now Gallery Guide. Art Now Inc., 320 Bonnie Burn Road, P.O. Box 219, Scotch Plains, New Jersey 07076. A national publication with up-to-date information on exhibitions in galleries and museums. Special geographic editions are also available for New York City, Boston/New England, Philadelphia, Chicago/Midwest, the Southwest, the Southeast, California, and Europe. Published eleven times a year.

Artists Gallery Guide for Chicago and the Illinois Region. Chicago Artists' Coalition, 5 West Grand, Chicago, Illinois 60610, 1990. A comprehensive and well-organized guide to commercial and alternative galleries, museums, university galleries, and arts organizations in Chicago, north central and south central Illinois, southeast Wisconsin, St. Louis, and northwest Indiana.

The Artists' Guide to Philadelphia by Amy Orr. The Artists' Guide, P.O. Box 8755, Philadelphia, Pennsylvania 19101, revised 1991. Profiles commercial galleries, alternative spaces, art centers, organizations, and resources in the Philadelphia area; each entry includes a description of facilities, price range, type of work exhibited, appointment procedures, and the name of a contact person.

Artist's Market, edited by Susan Connor. Cincinnati: Writer's Digest Books, revised annually.

Artlines 1991–1992: An Annotated Guide to Organizations and Publications Essential to Artists. National Network for Artist Placement, 935 West Avenue 37, Los Angeles, California 90065, revised 1990. Lists arts organizations lending support to artists, including those offering exhibition and performance space.

Craft Studios in the Sunshine State. Florida Craftsmen Inc., 235 Third Street South, St. Petersburg, Florida 33701, 1991. A guide to craft studios and galleries in Florida.

Directory of Artist Associations and Exhibition Spaces, Art Commissions, Museum Curators, and Art Critics. Directors Guild Publishers and The Consultant Press, P.O. Box 369, Renaissance, California 95962, 1990.

Directory of Galleries for the Fine Artist. Directors Guild Publishers and The Consultant Press, P.O. Box 369, Renaissance, California 95962, 1990. Lists more than thirteen hundred galleries, with detailed information on media and review requirements.

The Handbook for Clay Artists, edited by Alexandra B. Trub and Jimmy Clark. The Clay Studio, 139 North 2nd Street, Philadelphia, Pennsylvania 19106, 1989. Includes information on exhibition opportunities.

Information for Artists, edited by Sarah Yates. CARO, 183 Bathurst Street, Toronto, Ontario, Canada M5T 2R7, 1988. Lists a variety of alternative venues for exhibition and sale of work.

International Directory of the Arts. Wittenborn Art Books, Inc., 1018 Madison Avenue, New York, New York 10021-0163, revised biennially. Two-volume guide to museums, universities, associations, dealers, galleries, publishers, and others involved in the arts in Europe, the United States, Canada, South America, Asia, and Australia.

National Association of Artists' Organizations Directory. National Association of Artists' Organizations, 918 F Street, NW, Washington, D.C. 20004, revised regularly. Describes alternative spaces and arts service organizations. Each entry includes a description of programs, disciplines, exhibition and/or performance spaces, and proposal procedures, and provides the name of a contact person.

National Directory of Multicultural Arts Organizations, edited by Johanna L. Misey. National Assembly of State Arts Agencies, 1010 Vermont Avenue, NW, Suite 920, Washington, D.C. 20005, 1990. Contains more than twelve hundred entries, including listings for museums and galleries.

Organizing Artists, edited by Lane Relyea. National Association of Artists' Organizations, 918 F Street, NW, Washington, D.C. 20004, 1990. A critical examination of the evolution of artists' organizations and the artist-space movement, tracing the history of artist activism in the United States from 1905 to 1990.

Performing Arts Presenter Directory. Mid Atlantic Arts Foundation, 11 East Chase Street, Suite 2A, Baltimore, Maryland 21202-2524, revised annually. Profiles regional nonprofit presenters in the performing arts. Each profile includes details on organizational background, programming, scheduling, audience, and budget.

The Photograph Collectors' Resource Directory, edited by Peter Hastings Falk. The Consultant Press/The Photographic Arts Center, Limited, 163 Amsterdam Avenue, New York, New York 10023, revised 1992. More than seventeen hundred listings of galleries, museums, and dealers in the United States, Canada, and Europe.

The Photographer's Complete Guide to Exhibition and Sales Spaces by Peter Hastings Falk. The Consultant Press/The Photographic Arts Center, Limited, 163 Amsterdam Avenue, New York, New York 10023, revised 1992.

Photographer's Market, edited by Sam Marshall. Cincinnati: Writer's Digest Books, revised annually.

Photography in New York, 64 West 89th Street, #3F, New York, New York 10024. A comprehensive guide to photography galleries in New York City. Published bimonthly.

Public Hangings. The City Gallery, New York City Department of Cultural Affairs, 2 Columbus Circle, New York, New York 10019, updated annually. Lists more than eighty alternative spaces in New York City.

The Visual Arts Handbook. Visual Arts Ontario, 439 Wellington Street West, Toronto, Ontario, Canada M5V 1E7, revised 1991. A comprehensive guide to resources for artists, including galleries and exhibition space.

Washington Art: A Guide to Galleries, Art Consultants and Museums by Lorraine Arden, Carolyn Blakeslee, and Drew Steis. Art Calendar, P.O. Box 1040, Great Falls, Virginia 22066, 1988. Provides detailed profiles on commercial galleries, art consultants, art centers, alternative spaces, and museums in the Washington, D.C., area.

Wyoming Museum and Gallery Directory. Wyoming Arts Council, 2320 Capitol Avenue, Cheyenne, Wyoming 82002, revised 1991.

Exhibition Planning

PUBLICATIONS

The Art of Showing by James K. Reeve. The Consultant Press/The Photographic Arts Center, Limited, 163 Amsterdam Avenue, New York, New York 10023, 1987. Includes guidelines for protecting and displaying paintings, sculpture, and photographs, and information on display concepts, storage, records, and appraisals.

Art on the Move: A Directory of Fine Art Shippers, Packers and Warehouses. Gallery Association of New York, P.O. Box 345, Hamilton, New York 13346, 1988.

The Artist's Guide to Getting and Having a Successful Exhibition by Robert S. Persky. The Consultant Press/The Photographic Arts Center, Limited, 163 Amsterdam Avenue, New York, New York 10023, 1985.

Artist's Guide to Producing a Solo Show in New York by Gil Kerlin. Light Brown Press, 3384 Street Road, Doylestown, Pennsylvania 18901, 1986. Includes information on developing a mailing list, advertising, developing posters and invitations, managing sales, et cetera.

CARFAC Recommended Minimum Exhibition Fee Schedule. Canadian Artists' Representation Ontario (CARO), 183 Bathurst Street, Toronto, Ontario, Canada M5T 2R7, revised 1991.

Good Show! A Practical Guide for Temporary Exhibitions by Lothar P. Wittenborg. Smithsonian Institution Traveling Exhibition Service, Washington, D.C. 20506, 1981. Excellent how-to manual for developing temporary exhibitions.

On Opening an Art Gallery by Suzanne K. Vinmans, 2701 Commercial Avenue, Madison, Wisconsin 53704, 1990. Provides detailed information on organizing exhibitions.

The Photographer's Guide to Getting and Having a Successful Exhibition by Robert S. Persky. The Consultant Press/The Photographic Arts Center, Limited, 163 Amsterdam Avenue, New York, New York 10023, 1986.

Way to Go: Crating Artwork for Travel by Stephen A. Horne. Gallery Association of New York, Box 345, Hamilton, New York 13346, 1985. Provides information on how to crate two and three-dimensional work, how to pack three-dimensional objects, et cetera.

Also see "Artwork Care and Maintenance."

Gallery Relations

PUBLICATIONS

The Artists Survival Manual: A Complete Guide to Marketing Your Work by Toby Judith Klayman and Cobbett Steinberg. New York: Charles Scribner's Sons, revised 1987. See "Preparing to Negotiate with Dealers" and "Questions to Ask Your Gallery."

The Business of Art, edited by Lee Caplin. New York: Prentice Hall, revised 1991. See "Selling Art Under Contract" by Tennyson Schad and "The Integrity of the Artist, Dealer, and Gallery" by Tibor de Nagy.

The Right of Public Presentation: A Guide to Exhibition Right. Canadian Conference of the Arts, 189 Laurier Avenue East, Ottawa, Ontario, Canada K1N 6P1, 1990. Includes an overview of Exhibition Right guidelines, sample forms and contracts, and a list of options for typical situations.

General Arts References

PUBLICATIONS

American Art Directory. New York: R.R. Bowker, published triannually. A directory of arts organizations, art schools, museums, magazines, scholarships, and fellowships.

Directory of Artist Associations and Exhibition Spaces, Art Commissions, Museum Curators, and Art Critics. Directors Guild Publishers and The Consultant Press, P.O. Box 369, Renaissance, California 95962, 1990.

International Directory of the Arts. Wittenborn Art Books, Inc., 1018 Madison Avenue, New York, New York 10021-0163; revised biennially. Two-volume guide to museums, universities, associations, dealers, galleries, publishers, and others involved in the arts in Europe, the United States, Canada, South America, Asia, and Australia.

The Official Museum Directory. Wilmette, Illinois: National Register Publishing Company, 1990. Lists more than sixty-six hundred museums and galleries, and includes information on personnel, collections, and specialization.

The Photograph Collectors' Resource Directory, edited by Peter Hastings Falk. The Consultant Press/The Photographic Arts Center, Limited, 163 Amsterdam Avenue, New York, New York 10003, revised 1992. More than seventeen hundred listings of American, Canadian, and European galleries, private dealers, and exhibition spaces where photographic prints are sold, purchased, and exhibited.

The Visual Arts Handbook. Visual Arts Ontario, 439 Wellington Street West, Toronto, Ontario, Canada M5V 1E7, revised 1991. A comprehensive guide to resources for artists, including artists' associations, galleries, exhibition spaces, art colonies, and funding sources.

Who Does What. Canadian Conference of the Arts, 189 Laurier Avenue East, Ottawa, Ontario, Canada K1N 6P1, updated regularly. A guide to more than one hundred national Canadian associations, service organizations, and unions operating in most areas of the arts.

Whole Arts Directory, edited by Cynthia Navaretta. Midmarch Art Books, 300 Riverside Drive, New York, New York 10025, 1987. Lists organizations, periodicals, and support services for visual art, performance art, film, electronic, and print media, and craft artists.

Grants and Funding Resources

PUBLICATIONS

The Artist in Business: Basic Business Practices by Craig Dreesen. Arts Extension Service, Division of Continuing Education, University of Massachusetts, Amherst, Massachusetts 01003, 1988. Includes information on grants.

ArtistHelp: The Artist's Guide to Work-Related Human and Social Services, compiled by the Research Center for Arts and Culture, Columbia University. Neal-Schuman Publishers, 23 Leonard Street, New York, New York 10013, 1990. Systematic collection of information directly addressed to artists' work-related human and social service needs on a city, state, and national basis. Covers more than 120 cities in all fifty states and includes information on financial services.

Artlines 1991–1992: An Annotated Guide to Organizations and Publications Essential to Artists. National Network for Artist Placement, 935 West Avenue 37, Los Angeles, California 90065, revised 1990. Lists arts organizations lending support to artists, including those providing funding.

The Business of Art, edited by Lee Caplin. New York: Prentice Hall, revised 1991. See "Financial Resources for Artists—The Visual Arts Program at the Arts Endowment" by Jim Meichert and Michael Faubion and "Financial Resources for Artists—Grantsmanship" by Fred Eversly and Joanne Gigliotti.

Directory of Computer and High Technology Grants by Andrew J. Grant, Ph.D., Research Grant Guide, P.O. Box 1214, Loxahatchee, Florida 33470, 1991. Lists more than six hundred funding sources.

Directory of Financial Aids for Women. Reference Service Press, 1100 Industrial Road, Suite 9, San Carlos, California 94070, updated regularly. Identifies twelve hundred scholarships, fellowships, grants, awards, loans, and internships designed primarily or exclusively for women.

Directory of Grants in the Humanities. The Onyx Press, 4041 North Central, Suite 700, Phoenix, Arizona 85012-3397, revised regularly. More than four thousand listings of grants for humanities or art projects.

Directory of Private Funding. Association of Hispanic Arts, Inc., 173 East 116th Street, New York, New York 10029, revised 1985. Identifies foundations, corporations, and public agencies that fund arts organizations and individual artists.

Financial Aid for Research, Study, Travel and Other Activities Abroad by Gail A. Schlacter and R. David Weber. Reference Service Press, 1100

Industrial Road, Suite 9, San Carlos, California 94070, updated regularly. Provides information on sponsoring organizations; each listing includes address, phone number, purpose, eligibility, financial support, duration, special features and limitations, number of awards, and application deadlines.

Foundation Grants to Individuals. The Foundation Center, 79 Fifth Avenue, New York, New York 10003, revised 1991. Lists scholarships, educational loans, fellowships, residencies, internships, awards, and prizes available to individuals from private foundations. Also includes information on how to approach foundations.

Foundation News, 1828 L Street, NW, Suite 300, Washington, D.C. 20036. Published six times a year.

"Funding for Art Groups: NEA Art in Public Places Grants" by Drew Steis, *ArtCalendar*, P.O. Box 1040, Great Falls, Virginia 22066, November 1990.

Getting Funded: A Complete Guide to Proposal Writing by Mary Stewart Hall. Continuing Education Publications, Portland State University, P.O. Box 1491, Portland, Oregon 97207, 1988.

Grant Proposals That Have Succeeded by Virginia White. Plenum Press, 233 Spring Street, New York, New York 10012, 1983.

Grant Seekers Guide, edited by Jill R. Shellow. Mount Kisco, New York: Moyer Bell Limited, revised 1989.

Grants and Awards Available to American Writers. PEN American Center, 568 Broadway, New York, New York 10012, revised 1990. Lists American and international grant programs for writers. Includes deadlines, guidelines, and summaries of application procedures.

Grants Magazine: Journal of Sponsored Research and Other Programs. Plenum Press, 233 Spring Street, New York, New York 10012. Published four times a year.

Guide to Programs and Program Application Guidelines and Forms. Public Information Office, The National Endowment for the Arts, 1100 Pennsylvania Avenue, NW, Washington, D.C. 20506, revised regularly.

The Individual's Guide to Grants by Judith Margolin. Plenum Press, 233 Spring Street, New York, New York 10012, 1983.

"Interview with Charles C. Bergman, Executive Vice President, Pollack-Krasner Foundation" by Drew Steis, *ArtCalendar*, P.O. Box 1040, Great Falls, Virginia 22066, September 1990.

Money for Film and Video Artists, compiled by the American Council for the Arts. New York: American Council for the Arts and Allworth Press, 1991. Available from Allworth Press, 10 East 23rd Street, Suite 400, New York, New York 10010. Comprehensive resource guide to grants, fellowships, awards, and emergency assistance in the United States and in Canada.

Money for Performing Artists, edited by Suzanne Niemeyer. New York: American Council for the Arts and Allworth Press, 1991. Available from Allworth Press, 10 East 23rd Street, Suite 400, New York, New York 10010.

Money for Visual Artists, compiled by the American Council for the Arts. New York: American Council for the Arts and Allworth Press, 1991. Available from Allworth Press, 10 East 23rd Street, Suite 400, New York, New York 10010. Comprehensive resource guide to grants, fellowships, awards, and emergency assistance in the United States and Canada.

Money to Work: Grants for Visual Artists. Art Resources International, 5813 Nevada Avenue, NW, Washington, D.C. 20015, revised 1992. Provides information on fellowships and grants for visual artists working in the United States.

National Directory of Grants and Aid to Individuals in the Arts, P.O. Box 9005, Washington, D.C. 20003, published annually.

The National Guide to Funding in Arts and Culture. The Foundation Center, 79 Fifth Avenue, New York, New York 10003, 1992. Lists thousands of grants for arts and cultural programs from independent, corporate, and community foundations.

Standard and Poor's Rating Guide. New York: Standard and Poor's Corporation, revised annually.

Supporting Yourself as an Artist by Deborah A. Hoover. New York: Oxford University Press, revised 1989.

Washington International Arts Letter, P.O. Box 9005, Washington, D.C. 20003. Newsletter published ten times a year with information on grants and assistance by government and private foundations.

ORGANIZATIONS

Arts Resource Consortium Library, 1 East 53rd Street, New York, New York 10022. A national information and referral service for artists and arts managers. Sponsors the Visual Artist Information Hotline (800-232-2789), a toll-free information service that provides information on grants and funding sources.

Associated Grantmakers of Massachusetts, 294 Washington Street, #840, Boston, Massachusetts 02108. Offers services and resources for fund-raising.

The Foundation Center, 79 Fifth Avenue, New York, New York 10003. A national service organization that provides information on foundation funding. Services include disseminating information on foundations and publishing reference books on foundations and foundation grants.

The Foundation Center, Kent H. Smith Library, 1442 Hanna Building, 1422 Euclid Avenue, Cleveland, Ohio 44115.

The Foundation Center, 312 Sutter Street, San Francisco, California 94108.

The Foundation Center, 1001 Connecticut Avenue, NW, Suite 938, Washington, D.C. 20036

The Grantsmanship Center, P.O. Box 6210, Los Angeles, California 90014.

National Endowment for the Arts, 1100 Pennsylvania Avenue, NW, Washington, D.C. 20506.

National Endowment for the Humanities, 1100 Pennsylvania Avenue, NW, Washington, D.C. 20506.

Also see "Art Colonies and Artist-in-Residence Programs" and "International Connections."

Health Hazards

PUBLICATIONS

Acrylic Polymer Emulsion Paint Data File. The Ralph Mayer Center for Artists' Techniques, 303 Old College, University of Delaware, Newark, Delaware 19716.

Art Hazard News. Center for Safety in the Arts, 5 Beekman Street, Suite 1030, New York, New York 10038. Covers health hazards, precautions, legislation, government regulations, and lawsuits, and includes a calendar of related events. Published ten times a year.

The Artists Complete Health and Safety Guide by Monona Rossol. Allworth Press, 10 East 23rd Street, Suite 400, New York, New York 10010, 1990. A guide to using potentially toxic materials safely and ethically. Designed to help artists and teachers comply with applicable health and safety laws, including American and Canadian right-to-know laws and the new U.S. Art Materials Labeling Act.

Ceramics and Health by Monona Rossol. Compilation of articles published in *Ceramic Scope*, 1980–82. Available from the Center for Safety in the Arts, 5 Beekman Street, Suite 1030, New York, New York 10038.

Data Sheets. Center for Safety in the Arts, 5 Beekman Street, Suite 1030, New York, New York 10038. Data sheets available include: Air-Purifying Respirators; Art Painting; Asbestos Substitutes; Bibliography; Ceramic Glazes May Poison Food; Ceramics; Children's Art Supplies Can Be Toxic; Commercial Art Hazards; Dye Hazards and Precautions; Electric Kiln Emissions and Ventilation; Emergency Plans; Face and Eye Protection; Fiber Arts Hazards; Fire Prevention; Formaldehyde; Glove Selection; Hazards in the Arts; Health and Safety for Secondary School Arts/Industrial Arts; Health and Safety Program for Arts Organizations; Labels and Labeling; Lead Poisoning; Material Safety Data Sheets; Medical Surveillance Program for Art Schools; Organic Pigments; Paint Removers; Papier-Mâché; Photography; Plastics; Reproductive Hazards in Arts and Crafts; Respirators; Safety Rules for Power Tool Operation; Silica Hazards; Silk Screen Printing; Stained Glass; Storage and Disposal of Chemicals; Teaching Art Safety to the Disabled; Traditional Sculpture and Casting; Ventilation; Welding, Soldering and Brazing; Woodworking Hazard; Workers' Compensation for Artists; and Workshop Noise.

Health Hazards Manual for Artists by Michael McCann. Lyons and Burford, 31 West 21st Street, New York, New York 10010, revised 1985. Details harmful effects caused by art materials, and outlines procedures that can make working with these materials safer.

Overexposure: Health Hazards in Photography by Susan D. Shaw and Monona Rossol. New York: Allworth Press and the American Council for the Arts, revised 1991. Available from Allworth Press, 10 East 23rd Street, Suite 400, New York, New York 10010.

A Personal Risk Assessment for Craftsmen and Artists by Red Rickard and Ronald Angus. Center for Safety in the Arts, 5 Beekman Street, Suite 1030, New York, New York 10038, 1986.

Pigment Data File. The Ralph Mayer Center for Artists' Techniques, 303 Old College, University of Delaware, Newark, Delaware 19716.

Reproductive Hazards in the Arts and Crafts by Jean-Ann McGrane. Center for Safety in the Arts, 5 Beekman Street, Suite 1030, New York, New York 10038, revised 1987.

Safe Practices in the Arts and Crafts: A Studio Guide by Julian A. Waller, M.D. College Art Association of America, 275 Seventh Avenue, New York, New York 10001, revised 1985. Lists art processes alphabetically with ways of minimizing hazards.

Safety in the Art Room by Charles L. Qualley. Center for Safety in the Arts, 5 Beekman Street, Suite 1030, New York, New York 10038, 1986.

Studio Safety Checklist. Toronto: CARFAC, 1985. Available from CARO, 183 Bathurst Street, Toronto, Ontario, Canada M5T 2R7. Contains a checklist, information notes, and safety rules, and lists additional resources.

Ventilation by Nancy Clark, Thomas Cutter, and Jean-Ann McGrane.

Lyons and Burford, 31 West 21st Street, New York, New York 10010, 1988. Presents methods of properly ventilating a workshop or studio.

ORGANIZATIONS

Art and Craft Materials Institute, Inc., 715 Boylston Street, Boston, Massachusetts 02116. Certifies 90 percent of all art materials sold in the United States. Provides information on hazardous art products, and publishes a newsletter.

Artists Health Project, The Artists Foundation, Inc., 8 Park Plaza, Boston, Massachusetts 02116. A program that informs artists about hazardous art materials and alternatives for safe use.

Center for Safety in the Arts (formerly the Center for Occupational Hazards), 5 Beekman Street, Suite 1030, New York, New York 10038. National clearinghouse and information center for research and education on hazards in the visual arts, performing arts, educational facilities, and museums.

Insurance and Medical Plans

PUBLICATIONS

ArtistHelp: The Artist's Guide to Work-Related Human and Social Services, compiled by the Research Center for Arts and Culture, Columbia University. Neal-Schuman Publishers, 23 Leonard Street, New York, New York 10013, 1990. Identifies agencies offering health and human services to artists; provides addresses, phone numbers, names of contacts, and cost information.

The Business of Art, edited by Lee Caplin. New York: Prentice Hall, revised 1991. See "Insuring Artwork and the Artist" by Huntington T. Block.

"Health Insurance for Artists: The AIDS Stigma" by Daniel Grant, *American Artist,* July 1988.

Insurance by Hamish Buchanan. CARO, 183 Bathurst Street, Toronto, Ontario, Canada M5T 2R7, 1985. A basic introduction to insurance for artists, including studio and art work insurance, with examples of rates.

"Insurance for the Working Artist. Part I" by Peter Karlen, *ArtCalendar,* P.O. Box 1040, Great Falls, Virginia 22066, November 1989.

"Insurance for the Working Artist. Part II" by Peter Karlen, *ArtCalendar,* P.O. Box 1040, Great Falls, Virginia 22066, December 1989.

"Insurance for the Working Artist. Part III" by Peter Karlen, *Art-Calendar*, P.O. Box 1040, Great Falls, Virginia 22066, January 1990.

Insurance Project: Feasibility Study for a Nationwide Health Insurance Plan for Independent Artists. National Endowment for the Arts, 1100 Pennsylvania Avenue, NW, Washington, D.C. 20506, 1986.

"Liability Insurance for Artists" by Daniel Grant, *American Artist, Business Supplement*, July 1987.

ORGANIZATIONS

American Craft Council, 72 Spring Street, New York, New York 10012. Offers members group rates on insurance programs, including major medical, life insurance, and total studio protection.

American Institute of Graphic Arts, 1059 Third Avenue, New York, New York, 10021. Offers members group rates on medical insurance.

ArtsFund, 1101 rue Rachel est, suite 1105, Montreal, Quebec, Canada H2J 2J7 and P.O. Box 3129, Main Post Office, Vancouver, British Columbia, Canada V6B 3XX. Organization that makes affordable health, dental, and pension-plan programs available to individual artists and arts organizations throughout Canada.

Association of Independent Video and Filmmakers, Inc., 625 Broadway, 9th Floor, New York, New York 10012. Offers health insurance to members.

Boston Visual Artists Union, 33 Harrison Avenue, Seventh Floor, Boston, Massachusetts 02111. Offers health insurance to members.

Chicago Artists' Coalition, 5 West Grand, Chicago, Illinois 60610. Offers members group medical insurance.

College Art Association of America, 275 Seventh Avenue, New York, New York 10001. Offers members medical and life insurance at group rates.

Connell Howe Insurors, Inc., 119 West Pacific, Branson, Missouri 65616. Offers a Crafter Package Policy that covers general liability, products and completed operations liability, fire liability, medical payments, and the value of contents while work is on display.

Co-op of America, 2100 M Street, NW, Suite 403, Washington, D.C. 20036. Membership organization open to self-employed individuals. Offers health insurance to members.

Cultural Alliance of Greater Washington, 410 8th Street, NW, Suite 600, Washington, D.C. 20004. Offers members health and dental insurance.

Deaf Artists of America, Inc., 87 North Clinton Avenue, #408, Rochester, New York 14604. Offers members a health insurance plan.

Doctors for Artists, 123 West 79th Street, New York, New York 10024. A nonprofit referral service developed to aid performing and visual artists with health care at reduced rates.

Graphic Artists Guild, 11 West 20th Street, 8th Floor, New York, New York 10011. Offers members basic hospital and medical benefits, major medical, term life, and disability income insurance.

Huntington T. Block, 2101 L Street, NW, Washington, D.C. 20037-9973. Offers individual artists studio insurance and business package insurance.

International Sculpture Center, 1050 Potomac Street, NW, Washington, D.C. 20007. Offers members "all risk" fine art studio coverage and coverage while work is in transit.

National Artists Equity Association, P.O. Box 28068, Central Station, Washington D.C. 20038.

National Home Life Assurance Company of New York, 520 Columbia Drive, Johnson City, New York 13790.

New York Artists Equity Association, Inc., 498 Broome Street, New York, New York 10013. Offers members major medical, group indemnity, dental, and term life insurance.

PEN American Center, 568 Broadway, New York, New York 10012. Offers members medical insurance at group rates.

Small Business Service Bureau, 554 Main Street, P.O. Box 1441, Worcester, Massachusetts 01601. Membership organization open to self-employed individuals. Offers health insurance to members.

Support Services Alliance, P.O. Box 130, Schoharie, New York 12157. Membership organization open to self-employed individuals. Offers health insurance to members.

Also see "Pension Plans and Savings and Loan Programs."

Interior Design and Architecture

PUBLICATIONS

Architectural Design, 42 Leinster Gardens, London W2 3AN, England.

Architectural Digest, 5900 Wilshire Boulevard, Los Angeles, California 90036.

Architectural Record, 1221 Avenue of the Americas, New York, New York 10020.

Architectural Review, 9 Queen Anne's Gate, London SW1H 9BY, England.

Architecture d'Aujourd'hui, 67 avenue de Wagram, 75017 Paris, France.
Architecture Intérieure Créé, 106 boulevard Malesherbes, 75017 Paris, France.
Architektur Aktuell, Maxingstrasse 28A, A-1130, Vienna, Austria.
Architektur und Wohnen, Possmoorweg 5, 2000 Hamburg 60, Germany.
Arquitectura, Barquillo 12, 28004 Madrid, Spain.
Bauforum, Weimarer Strasse 91, Vienna 1190, Austria.
Baumeister, Verlag G.D.W. Callwey KG, Streitfeldstrasse 35, Postfach 800409, 8000 Munich 80, Germany.
Business Interiors, P.O. Box 2060, Red Bank, New Jersey 07701.
Canadian Architect. Southam Business Information, 1450 Don Mills Road, Don Mills, Ontario, Canada M3D 2X7.
Canadian Interiors. Maclean Hunter Limited, 777 Bay Street, #1000, Toronto, Ontario, Canada M5W 1A7.
Casabella, Via Trentacoste 7, 20134 Milan, Italy.
Contract, 1515 Broadway, New York, New York 10036.
Decor. Commerce Publishing Company, 408 Olive Street, St. Louis, Missouri 63102.
Designer Magazine, 328 Eighth Avenue, New York, New York 10001.
Designers West, 50 East 89th Street, New York, New York 10028.
Detail, Innere Cramer-Klett Strasse 6, 85 Nuremberg 1, Germany.
Domus, Via Grandi 5/7, 20089 Rozzano (MI), Italy.
The Guild. Kraus Sikes Inc., 228 State Street, Madison, Wisconsin 53703, published annually. A resource directory for architects and interior designers. Contains names, addresses, phone numbers, and photographs of American fine artists and crafts artists, as well as biographical information. Distributed free of charge to attendees of the American Society of Interior Designers and American Institute of Architects national conferences.
House Beautiful, 1700 Broadway, New York, New York 10019.
Interior Design, 249 West 17th Street, New York, New York 10017.
Interiors, 1515 Broadway, New York, New York 10036.
Japan Architect, 31-2 Yushima 2-chome, Bunkyo-ku, Tokyo 113, Japan.
Metropolis, 177 East 87th Street, New York, New York 10128.
Metropolitan Home, 750 Third Avenue, New York, New York 10017.
Process: Architecture, 3-1-3 Koishiakawa, Bunkyo-ku, Tokyo 112, Japan.
Progressive Architecture, 600 Summer Street, Stamford, Connecticut 06904.
Quadrens d' Arquitectura i Urbanismo, Placa Nova 5, Barcelona 08002, Spain.
Residential Interiors, 1515 Broadway, New York, New York 10036.

ORGANIZATIONS

American Institute of Architects, 1735 New York Avenue, NW, Washington, D.C. 20006.
American Society of Interior Designers, 1430 Broadway, New York, New York 10018.
Also see "Corporate Art."

International Connections

PUBLICATIONS

Amsterdam Art Guide, edited by Christian Reinwald. London: Art Guide Publications, 1985. Available from Talman Company, Inc., 150 Fifth Avenue, New York, New York 10011. Covers commercial galleries, museums, and print galleries in Amsterdam and neighboring cities.

Art & Auction International Directory. Art & Auction, 250 West 57th Street, New York, New York 10107, published annually. Includes the names, addresses, and phone numbers of art galleries in Europe, Canada, and the United States.

Art Diary: The World's Art Directory. Milan, Italy: Giancarlo Politi Editore, published annually. Available from *Flash Art* magazine, 799 Broadway, New York, New York 10003. Covers Europe, South America, the United States, and Japan, and lists galleries, museums, critics, organizations, agencies, and magazines.

The Artists Directory: A Handbook to the Contemporary British Art World by Heather Waddell and Richard Layzell. London: Art Guide Publications, revised 1988. Available from Talman Company, Inc., 150 Fifth Avenue, New York, New York 10011. Covers contemporary British galleries, offers exhibition advice, and provides information on regional resources, print studios, awards, competitions, taxes, law, and sponsorship of art in public places.

Artworld Europe. International Art Alliance, P.O. Box 1608, Largo, Florida 34649. Bimonthly newsletter that covers art and gallery-related news in Europe.

Australian Arts Guide, edited by Roslyn Kean. London: Art Guide Publications, revised 1989. Available from Talman Company, Inc., 150 Fifth Avenue, New York, New York 10011. Lists galleries, museums, and arts service organizations.

Berlin Arts Guide, edited by Irene Blumenfield. London: Art Guide Publications, 1987. Available from Talman Company, Inc., 150 Fifth

Avenue, New York, New York 10011. Covers museums; commercial, photography, and craft galleries; and cultural centers.

Directory of Sources for International Traveling Exhibitions. Washington, D.C.: International Council of Museums, revised regularly. Available from International Art Alliance, P.O. Box 1608, Largo, Florida 34649. Lists more than two hundred organizations in thirty-five countries that organize traveling exhibitions. Each entry includes name, address, name of contact person, and telephone number.

Financial Aid for Research, Study, Travel and Other Activities Abroad by Gail A. Schlacter and R. David Weber. Reference Service Press, 1100 Industrial Road, Suite 9, San Carlos, California 94070. Each financial aid program listing includes the program title, name of the sponsoring organization, address, phone number, purpose, eligibility requirements, amount of financial support, duration, special features, limitations, number of awards, and deadline date.

Glasgow Arts Guide, edited by Alice Bain. London: Art Guide Publications, 1989. Available from Talman Company, Inc., 150 Fifth Avenue, New York, New York 10011. Lists museums, galleries, and arts organizations.

Guide for Foreign Artists in New York. Consulate General of the Netherlands, 1 Rockefeller Plaza, New York, New York 10020-2094, 1991. Includes information on arts organizations, legal assistance, residency programs, and studio space.

International Directory of Corporate Art Collections. Copublished by the International Art Alliance and *ARTnews*, updated regularly. Available from the International Art Alliance, P.O. Box 1608, Largo, Florida 34649 and *ARTnews*, 48 West 38th Street, New York, New York 10018. Contains information on more than one thousand corporate art collections, including those in Japan and Europe.

International Directory of Resources for Artisans. The Crafts Center, 1001 Connecticut Avenue, NW, Washington D.C. 20036, revised biennially. Includes names and addresses of arts organizations, guilds, agencies, foundations, schools, and suppliers, arranged by region of the world.

International Directory of the Arts. Wittenborn Art Books, Inc., 1018 Madison Avenue, New York, New York 10021-0163, revised biennially. Two-volume guide to museums, universities, associations, dealers, galleries, publishers, and others involved in the arts in Europe, the United States, Canada, South America, Asia, and Australia.

London Art and Artists Guide, edited by Heather Waddell. London: Art Guide Publications, revised 1989. Available from Talman Company,

Inc., 150 Fifth Avenue, New York, New York 10011. Covers more than five hundred resources, including museums, galleries, national art centers, and alternative spaces.

Madrid Arts Guide, edited by Claudia Oliveira Cezar. London: Art Guide Publications, 1989. Available from Talman Company, Inc., 150 Fifth Avenue, New York, New York 10011. Lists galleries and museums, and includes interviews with art dealers.

Paris Art Guide, edited by Fiona Dunlop. London: Art Guide Publications, revised 1988. Available from Talman Company, Inc., 150 Fifth Avenue, New York, New York 10011. Provides details on galleries, museums, print studios, and arts organizations.

Performing Arts Yearbook for Europe, edited by Rod Fisher and Martin Huber. Arts Publishing International Limited, 1991. Available from the American Council for the Arts, 1 East 53rd Street, New York, New York 10022. Lists more than seventy-five hundred organizations in thirty countries, including ministries of culture, funding agencies, national organizations, networks, resource centers, arts centers, promoters, agents, festivals, and publications.

Photo Diary: The International Directory of Photography. Milan, Italy: Giancarlo Politi Editore, published annually. Available from *Flash Art* magazine, 799 Broadway, New York, New York 10003. Covers Europe, South America, the United States, and Japan, and lists photographic galleries, museums, critics, archives, agencies, important collections, and photographic magazines.

Resource Guide for Funding Sources for International Exchanges in the Arts. Arts International, 809 United Nations Plaza, New York, New York 10017, 1991.

The Visual Arts Handbook. Visual Arts Ontario, 439 Wellington Street West, Toronto, Ontario, Canada M5V 1E7, revised 1991. A comprehensive guide to resources for artists; lists artists' associations, galleries, exhibition space, art colonies, and funding sources.

World Crafts Council Directory/Europe. World Crafts Council, Secretariat, P.O. Box 2045, DK1012, Copenhagen K, Denmark, published annually. Covers twenty-five countries, with information on, and addresses of, government agencies concerned with crafts, institutions, schools, galleries, craft events, trade fairs, and publications.

ORGANIZATIONS

American Academy in Rome, 41 East 65th Street, New York, New York 10021-6508.

American Council on Germany, 14 East 60th Street, New York, New

York 10022. Awards thirty professional fellowships annually to promising young Germans and Americans in a wide variety of fields, including the arts.

The American Scandinavian Foundation, 127 East 73rd Street, New York, New York 10021. Awards fellowships and grants to professionals and scholars born in the United States or Scandinavian countries, including those in the creative and performing arts.

Arts Exchange, Massachusetts Council on the Arts and Humanities, 80 Boylston Street, 10th Floor, Boston, Massachusetts 02116. Funds international tours, exhibitions, and residencies.

Arts International, Institute of International Education, 809 United Nations Plaza, New York, New York 10017. Operates exchange and fellowship programs for individual artists and arts managers; arranges conferences on international cultural exchange; and publishes information on international arts activities, ranging from discussions of critical issues to practical data on touring and sources of support.

Bellagio Study Center, Rockefeller Foundation, 1133 Avenue of the Americas, New York, New York 10036.

German Academic Exchange Office (DAAD), Artists in Berlin Program, 950 Third Avenue, 19th Floor, New York, New York 10022. Selects young sculptors, painters, writers, composers, and filmmakers to spend twelve months in Berlin as artists-in-residence.

The Japan Foundation, 142 West 57th Street, New York, New York 10019. Awards fellowships to scholars, researchers, and artists in the United States to enable them to conduct research in Japan.

National Endowment for the Arts, Office of International Activities, 1100 Pennsylvania Avenue, NW, Washington, D.C. 20506. Offers international exchange fellowships for work and study in Japan and France to midcareer artists in various disciplines.

Partners of the Americas, 1424 K Street, NW, Washington, D.C. 20005. Arranges cultural exchange programs between the United States, Latin America, and Caribbean nations for visual, craft, and performing artists, including exhibitions and performances.

Studio Exchange International, 3625 East 12th Avenue, Denver, Colorado 80206. Provides information about exchanging studios on a temporary basis to artists throughout the world.

Two Continents Arts Exchange, 924 West End Avenue, New York, New York 10025. Provides advisory services to performing artists, arts organizations, and festivals in Europe and the United States, including arranging tours, handling bookings, providing referrals, and promoting exchange information.

Also see "General Arts References."

Law

PUBLICATIONS

"Advantages of Written Contracts" by Peter H. Karlen, *ArtCalendar*, P.O. Box 1040, Great Falls, Virginia 22066, February 1990.

An Artist's Guide to Small Claims Court. Volunteer Lawyers for the Arts, 1 East 53rd Street, New York, New York 10022, 1982. A step-by-step guide for preparing a case in New York City's small claims court.

Art and Law. Volunteer Lawyers for the Arts, 1 East 53rd Street, New York, New York 10022. Published quarterly.

Art Law: Rights and Liabilities of Creators and Collectors by Franklin Feldman and Stephen E. Weil. Boston: Little, Brown and Company, 1988.

The Art Law Primer by Linda F. Pinkerton and John T. Guardalabene. Lyons and Burford, 31 West 21st Street, New York, New York 10010, 1988. Briefs visual artists on the major legal issues that affect their work and business. Includes sections on copyright, contracts, leases, and artist/dealer relationships.

The Artist in Business: Basic Business Practices by Craig Dreesen. Arts Extension Service, Division of Continuing Education, University of Massachusetts, Amherst, Massachusetts 01003, 1988. Includes information on legal issues.

"Artist-Publisher Agreements" by Peter H. Karlen, *ArtCalendar*, P.O. Box 1040, Great Falls, Virginia 22066, June 1990.

ArtistHelp: The Artist's Guide to Work-Related Human and Social Services, compiled by the Research Center for Arts and Culture, Columbia University. Neal-Schuman Publishers, 23 Leonard Street, New York, New York 10013, 1990. Identifies agencies offering legal and other services to artists, with addresses, phone numbers, names of contacts, and cost information.

The Artist's Friendly Legal Guide by Floyd Conner, Roger Gilcrest, Peter Karlen, Jean Perwin, and David Spatt. Cincinnati: North Light Books, 1988. Includes questions and answers, checklists, sample contracts, invoices, purchase orders, and tax forms.

The Artists' Survival Manual: A Complete Guide to Marketing Your Work by Toby Judith Klayman and Cobbett Steinberg. New York: Charles Scribner's Sons, revised 1987. See sample contracts in appendix section.

Artlines 1991–1992: An Annotated Guide to Organizations and Publications Essential to Artists. National Network for Artist Placement, 935 West

Avenue 37, Los Angeles, California 90065, revised 1990. Lists arts organizations lending support to artists, including those offering legal advice.

Business Forms and Contracts (in Plain English) for Craftspeople by L. D. DuBoff. Madrona Publishers, P.O. Box 22667, Seattle, Washington 98122, 1986.

Business and Legal Forms for Fine Artists by Tad Crawford. Allworth Press, 10 East 23rd Street, Suite 400, New York, New York 10010, 1990. Includes sample contracts and instructions for a variety of situations, as well as a kit of tear-out contracts.

CARO-OAAG Artists-Public Gallery Agreement, CARO, 183 Bathurst Street, Toronto, Ontario, Canada M5T 2R7. Commentary for artists negotiating with galleries.

"Computers and Art" by Peter H. Karlen, *ArtCalendar*, P.O. Box 1040, Great Falls, Virginia 22066, June 1991.

"Contracts for Public Commissions, Part I" by Peter H. Karlen, *ArtCalendar*, P.O. Box 1040, Great Falls, Virginia 22066, May 1990.

"Copyright for Visual Artists," CARO Fact Sheet, Series #2.0. CARO, 183 Bathurst Street, Toronto, Ontario, Canada M5T 2R7, April 1990. Summarizes Canadian copyrights that commonly pertain to visual artists; discusses specific rights and examples of practical applications. Also includes amendments to the Canadian Copyright Act of 1988.

Copyright Information Kit. Copyright Office, Library of Congress, Washington, D.C. 20559. When ordering, specify that copyright is for visual art.

"The 'Droit de Suite' Revisited" by Peter Karlen, *ArtCalendar*, P.O. Box 1040, Great Falls, Virginia 22066, July/August 1991. Covers the pros and cons of resale royalties.

"Free Legal Services" by Daniel Grant, *American Artist*, 1515 Broadway, New York, New York 10036, February 1990.

"How to Negotiate Contracts" by Peter H. Karlen, *ArtCalendar*, P.O. Box 1040, Great Falls, Virginia 22066, November 1990.

The Law (in Plain English) for Craftspeople by L. D. DuBoff. Madrona Publishers, Inc. Box 22667, Seattle, Washington 98122, 1984. Discusses business skills and legal principles relating to the use of work.

"Legal Definitions: Their Importance" by Peter H. Karlen, *ArtCalendar*, P.O. Box 1040, Great Falls, Virginia 22066, September 1990.

Legal Guide for the Visual Artist by Tad Crawford. Allworth Press, 10 East 23rd Street, Suite 400, New York, New York 10010, revised 1989. Covers copyright and moral rights; sale of art by artist, gallery, or agent; sale of reproduction rights, including assignment confirmations, licensing, and book contracts; taxation and hobby loss challenges and the IRS; studios and leases; and estate planning. Model contracts are also included.

Licensing Art and Design by Caryn R. Leland. Allworth Press, 10 East 23rd Street, Suite 400, New York, New York 10010, 1990. A comprehensive guide to the mechanics of licensing images for use on apparel, ceramics, posters, stationery, and many other products.

"Minimum Artist-Dealer Agreement," National Artists Equity Association, P.O. Box 28068, Central Station, Washington, D.C. 20038. Sample contract available to National Artists Equity Association members that contains *basic* terms of an artist-gallery dealer relationship.

Model Agreements for Visual Artists: A Guide to Contracts in the Visual Arts by Paul Sanderson. CARO, 183 Bathurst Street, Toronto, Ontario, Canada M5T 2R7, 1982. An introduction to Canadian art law and professional business practices. Includes twenty-three model contracts and checklists, each accompanied by a commentary clarifying particular provisions.

Protecting Your Rights and Increasing Your Income: A Guide for Authors, Graphic Designers, Illustrators and Photographers by Tad Crawford. Allworth Press, 10 East 23rd Street, Suite 400, New York, New York 10010, 1991. Audiotape covering the basics of copyright law, how to handle contracts and negotiations, how to transfer limited rights, royalties, cancellation fees, advances, et cetera. Aimed at artists who sell reproduction rights and often work on assignment.

"The Protection of Ideas" by Peter H. Karlen, *ArtCalendar*, P.O. Box 1040, Great Falls, Virginia 22066, October 1990.

"Restrictions on Artistic Expression: Defamation" by Peter H. Karlen, *ArtCalendar*, P.O. Box 1040, Great Falls, Virginia 22066, March 1990.

"Restrictions on Artistic Expression: Obscenity Laws" by Peter H. Karlen, *ArtCalendar*, P.O. Box 1040, Great Falls, Virginia 22066, April 1990.

The Rights of Authors and Artists by Kenneth P. Norwick and Jerry Simon Chasen. American Civil Liberties Union, 1984. Available from Volunteer Lawyers for the Arts, 1 East 53rd Street, New York, New York 10022. Explains how authors and visual artists can protect themselves and their works under the present law; discusses copyright, libel, privacy, and obscenity laws; discusses contracts between writers and artists and their agents, collaborators, publishers, and galleries.

Trademarks and the Arts by William M. Borchard. New York: Columbia University School of Law, 1989. Available from the American Council for the Arts, 1 East 53rd Street, New York, New York 10022. Includes instructions on obtaining and retaining trademarks, information on protecting artistic elements as trademarks, and advice on shaping merchandising licensing agreements.

"The Visual Artists Rights Act of 1990" by Peter H. Karlen, *Art-Calendar*, P.O. Box 1040, Great Falls, Virginia 22066, February 1991.

VLA Guide to Copyright for the Performing Arts. Volunteer Lawyers for the Arts, 1 East 53rd Street, New York, New York 10022, 1987.

VLA Guide to Copyright for the Visual Arts. Volunteer Lawyers for the Arts, 1 East 53rd Street, New York, New York 10022, updated regularly.

VLA Membership Directory. Volunteer Lawyers for the Arts, 1 East 53rd Street, New York, New York 10022, updated regularly. Lists the names and addresses of New York state lawyers who are members of Volunteer Lawyers for the Arts.

VLA National Directory. Volunteer Lawyers for the Arts, 1 East 53rd Street, New York, New York 10022, updated regularly. Descriptions of VLA programs throughout the United States and Canada.

NATIONAL ORGANIZATIONS

National Resource Center for Consumer Legal Services, 1444 I Street, NW, 8th Floor, Washington, D.C. 20005.

Visual Artists and Galleries Association, 1 Rockefeller Plaza, Suite 2626, New York, New York 10020. Membership organization that reviews cases and helps artists determine whether they need professional legal assistance; in such instances, the organization provides attorney referrals.

ORGANIZATIONS BY STATE

ALABAMA

Alabama Lawyers for the Arts, 267 Chidester Avenue, Mobile, Alabama 36607.

CALIFORNIA

Artlaw Foundation, Suite C, 1295 Prospect Street, La Jolla, California 92037. Provides education about legal issues of concern to the arts community. Offers lectures, workshops, and educational materials.

California Lawyers for the Arts, 315 West 9th Street, Suite 1101, Los Angeles, California 90015.

California Lawyers for the Arts, Building C, Room 255, Fort Mason Center, San Francisco, California 94123.

San Diego Lawyers for the Arts, 1205 Prospect Street, Suite 400, La Jolla, California 92037.

COLORADO

Colorado Lawyers for the Arts, P.O. Box 300428, Denver, Colorado 80203.

CONNECTICUT

Connecticut Volunteer Lawyers for the Arts, 227 Lawrence Street, Hartford, Connecticut 06106.

DISTRICT OF COLUMBIA

District of Columbia Lawyers Committee for the Arts, Volunteer Lawyers for the Arts, D.C., 918 16th Street, NW, Suite 503, Washington, D.C. 20006.

Washington Area Lawyers for the Arts, 1325 G Street, NW, Lower Level, Washington, D.C. 20005.

FLORIDA

Business Volunteers for the Arts/Miami, Suite 2500, Museum Tower, 150 West Flagler Street, Miami, Florida 33130.

Volunteer Lawyers for the Arts/Broward Inc., 5900 North Andrews Avenue, Suite 907, Fort Lauderdale, Florida 33309.

GEORGIA

Georgia Volunteer Lawyers for the Arts, 34 Peachtree Street, NW, Atlanta, Georgia 30303.

ILLINOIS

Lawyers for the Creative Arts, 213 West Institute Place, Suite 411, Chicago, Illinois 60610.

KANSAS

Kansas Register of Lawyers for the Arts, c/o Susan J. Whitfield-Lungren, 400 North Woodlawn, East Building, Suite 212, Wichita, Kansas 67208.

KENTUCKY

Arts Council Services, 609 West Main Street, Louisville, Kentucky 40507.

Lexington Arts and Cultural Council, 161 North Mill Street, Lexington, Kentucky 40507.

LOUISIANA

Louisiana Volunteer Lawyers for the Arts, Arts Council of New Orleans, 821 Gravier Street, Suite 600, New Orleans, Louisiana 70112.

MAINE

Maine Volunteer Lawyers for the Arts Project, Maine Arts Commission, 55 Capitol Street, State House Station 25, Augusta, Maine 04333.

MARYLAND

Maryland Lawyers for the Arts, Belvedere Hotel, 1 East Chase Street, Suite 1118, Baltimore, Maryland 21201-2526.

MASSACHUSETTS

The Arts Extension Service, Division of Continuing Education, University of Massachusetts, Amherst, Massachusetts 01003.

Lawyers and Accountants for the Arts, The Artists Foundation, Inc., 8 Park Plaza, Boston, Massachusetts 02116.

MINNESOTA

Artlaw Referral Service, Resources and Counseling for the Arts, 429 Landmark Center, 75 West Fifth Street, Saint Paul, Minnesota 55102. A joint effort of Resources and Counseling for the Arts and the Art and Entertainment Law Committee of the Minnesota State Bar Association. Provides low-cost referrals for individual artists and nonprofit arts managers.

Minnesota Volunteer Lawyers for the Arts, c/o Fred Rosenblatt, 100 South 5th Street, Suite 1500, Minneapolis, Minnesota 55402.

MISSOURI

Kansas City Attorneys for the Arts, Gage and Tucker, 2345 Grand Avenue, Kansas City, Missouri 64141.

St. Louis Volunteer Lawyers and Accountants for the Arts, c/o St. Louis Regional Arts Commission, 3540 Washington, St. Louis, Missouri 63108.

MONTANA

Montana Volunteer Lawyers for the Arts, c/o Joan Jonkel, P.O. Box 8687, Missoula, Montana 59807.

NEW JERSEY

Volunteer Lawyers for the Arts of New Jersey, Center for Non-Profit Corporations, 15 Roszel Road, Princeton, New Jersey 08540.

NEW YORK

Arts Council in Buffalo and Erie County, 700 Main Street, Buffalo, New York 14202.

Huntington Arts Council, Inc., 213 Main Street, Huntington, New York 11743.

Volunteer Lawyers for the Arts, 1 East 53rd Street, New York, New York 10022.

Volunteer Lawyers for the Arts Program, Albany League of Arts, 19 Clinton Avenue, Albany, New York 12207.

NORTH CAROLINA

North Carolina Volunteer Lawyers for the Arts, P.O. Box 26484, Raleigh, North Carolina 27611-6484.

OHIO

Volunteer Lawyers and Accountants for the Arts Program, c/o Cleveland Bar Association, 113 St. Clair Avenue, Cleveland, Ohio 44114-1253.

Volunteer Lawyers for the Arts, Suite A, 421 North Michigan Street, Toledo, Ohio 43624.

OKLAHOMA

Oklahoma Accountants and Lawyers for the Arts, 3000 Pershing Boulevard, Oklahoma City, Oklahoma 73107.

PENNSYLVANIA

Philadelphia Volunteer Lawyers for the Arts, 251 South 18th Street, Philadelphia, Pennsylvania 19103.

PUERTO RICO

Volunteer Lawyers for the Arts, 563 Trigo Street, El Dorado Boulevard, Suite 5B, Miramar, Puerto Rico 00907.

RHODE ISLAND

Ocean State Lawyers for the Arts, P.O. Box 19, Saunderstown, Rhode Island 02874.

SOUTH CAROLINA

South Carolina Lawyers for the Arts, P.O. Box 8672, Greenville, South Carolina 29604.

TENNESSEE
Tennessee Arts Commission, 320 Sixth Avenue North, #100, Nashville, Tennessee 37219.

TEXAS
Austin Lawyers and Accountants for the Arts, P.O. Box 2577, Austin, Texas 78768.
Texas Accountants and Lawyers for the Arts, 5151 Belt Line Road, #1005, Dallas, Texas 75240.
Texas Accountants and Lawyers for the Arts, 1540 Sul Ross, Houston, Texas 77006.

UTAH
Utah Lawyers for the Arts, P.O. Box 652, Salt Lake City, Utah 84110-0652.

WASHINGTON
Washington Lawyers for the Arts, 1331 Third Avenue, Suite 512, Seattle, Washington 98101.

FOREIGN ORGANIZATIONS

Artists Legal Advice Services, 189 Laurier Avenue East, Ottawa, Ontario, Canada K1N 6P1.
Artists Legal Advice Services, Canadian Artists' Representation Ontario (CARO), 183 Bathurst Street, Toronto, Ontario, Canada M5T 2R7.
CARFAC Copyright Collective, 183 Bathurst Street, Toronto, Ontario, Canada M5T 2R7. Represents artists in the administration and protection of copyrights, and establishes exhibition fees.

Mailing Lists

ORGANIZATIONS

ArtNetwork (formerly Directors Guild Publishers), P.O. Box 369, Renaissance, California 95962. Offers arts-related mailing lists that includes addresses of publications, publishers, art consultants, U.S. and Canadian galleries, organizations, and critics.
Arts Extension Service, Division of Continuing Education, University of Massachusetts, Amherst, Massachusetts 01003. Provides mailing lists that include the names and addresses of individual artists, by discipline, in the visual and performing arts, and of arts councils,

craft organizations, and lawyers and other professionals who serve the arts.

Arts Information Exchange, Mid Atlantic Arts Foundation, 11 East Chase Street, #2A, Baltimore, Maryland 21202-2524. Sells computerized lists of arts-related organizations and individuals in the mid-Atlantic region.

Compuname, 411 Theodore Fremd Avenue, Rye, New York 10580-1497. Provides labels with names and addresses of all entries in the *Art in America Annual Guide to Galleries, Museums and Artists*, including museums, galleries, private dealers, art consultants, university galleries, and publishers.

Mailing List Labels, P.O. Box 661, Grand Central Station, New York, New York 10163-0661. Offers *The Percent for Art/Public Places Programs Mailing List*, which includes mailing labels and postcards requesting information about city, state, and national public art programs.

Media Distribution Co-op, 1745 Louisiana Street, Lawrence, Kansas 66044. Offers specialized lists for artists, photographers, filmmakers, musicians, and writers. In addition, offers a list of more than fifty mailing list brokers.

Caroll Michels, 491 Broadway, New York, New York 10012. Offers various arts-related mailing lists that include the names and addresses of curators, art consultants, critics, and press. Updated several times a year.

Unique Programs, Art Market Lists, P.O. Box 9910, Marina del Rey, California 90295.

Nonprofit Organizations

PUBLICATIONS

Application for Recognition of Exemption, IRS package 1023. Washington: Internal Revenue Service, revised 1990. Contact your local Internal Revenue Service office for a copy.

Beyond Profit: The Complete Guide to Managing the Nonprofit Organization by Fred Setterberg and Kary Schulman. New York: Harper & Row, 1985.

Financial Management Strategies for Arts Organizations by Frederick J. Turk and Robert P. Gallo. American Council for the Arts, 1 East 53rd Street, New York, New York 10022, 1986.

Governing Boards: Their Nature and Nurture by Cyril O. Houle. New

York: Jossey-Bass, 1989. Available from the American Council for the Arts, 1 East 53rd Street, New York, New York 10022, 1989.

Managing a Nonprofit Organization by Thomas Wolf. New York: Prentice Hall, 1984. Available from the American Council for the Arts, 1 East 53rd Street, New York, New York 10022. Explains the basics of financial management, organizing fund-raising drives, and assembling an effective board of directors.

Something Ventured, Something Gained: A Business Development Guide for Nonprofit Organizations by Laura Landy. American Council for the Arts, 1 East 53rd Street, New York, New York 10022, 1989.

This Way Up: Legal and Business Essentials for Nonprofits. Volunteer Lawyers for the Arts, 1 East 53rd Street, New York, New York 10022, 1988.

To Be or Not to Be: An Artist's Guide to Not-for-Profit Incorporation. Volunteer Lawyers for the Arts, 1 East 53rd Street, New York, New York 10022, revised 1986. Explains the pros and cons of not-for-profit corporate status, legal responsibilities and requirements, and alternatives to incorporation.

Organizing Paperwork

PUBLICATIONS

The Artist's Friendly Legal Guide by Floyd Conner, Roger Gilcrest, Peter H. Karlen, Jean Perwin, and David Spatt. Cincinnati: North Light Books, 1988. Includes invoices and purchase orders.

Business and Legal Forms for Fine Artists by Tad Crawford. Allworth Press, 10 East 23rd Street, Suite 400, New York, New York 10010, 1990.

Business and Legal Forms for Photographers by Tad Crawford. Allworth Press, 10 East 23rd Street, Suite 400, New York, New York 10010, 1991.

Business Forms and Contracts (in Plain English) for Craftspeople by L. D. DuBoff. Madrona Publishers, P.O. Box 22667, Seattle, Washington 98122, 1986.

COMPUTER SOFTWARE AND COMPANIES

Artstacks, 15 Millwide Lane, Mill Valley, California 94941. Designed for the Macintosh.

A Byte of Art. Software Creations, 5410 Wilshire Boulevard, #234, Los Angeles, California 90036. Designed for IBM-compatible equipment.

Shooting Star Software, Inc., P.O. Box 2878, Alameda, California 94501. Offers software for professional photographers, including Photo Star, StarTak, and The Assistant.

SoftArt. DBC Associates, 278 Court Street, Portsmouth, New Hampshire 03801.

Pension Plans and Savings and Loan Programs

PUBLICATIONS

The Artist's Tax Workbook by Carla Messman. Lyons and Burford, 31 West 21st Street, New York, New York 10010, revised annually. See "Retirement Plans."

Individual Retirement Arrangements (IRAs), IRS publication 590. Washington: Internal Revenue Service, revised annually. Contact your local Internal Revenue Service office.

Legal Guide for the Visual Artist by Tad Crawford. Allworth Press, 10 East 23rd Street, Suite 400, New York, New York 10010, revised 1989. See "Retirement Plans."

Self-Employed Retirement Plans, IRS publication 560. Washington: Internal Revenue Service, revised annually. Contact your local Internal Revenue Service office.

ORGANIZATIONS

The Artists Community Federal Credit Union, 5 Beekman Street, Room 600, New York, New York 10038. A federally insured credit union providing savings accounts, loans, and services to assist artists in establishing a credit rating. Open to out-of-state artists.

Chicago Artists' Coalition, 5 West Grand, Chicago, Illinois 60610. Offers members credit union services, including savings accounts, loans, and IRAs through the ATT Teletype Federal Credit Union.

Small Business Loan Programs. Contact your local Small Business Administration office. Provides a limited number of loans and loan guarantees to independently owned and operated profit-making small businesses, including culture-related businesses (teaching studios; performing arts schools; retail music, art, and crafts shops). Loans may be used to purchase real estate, buildings, machinery, equipment, and inventory, as well as to cover construction or expansion costs.

Also see "Insurance and Medical Plans."

Periodicals

Afterimage, 31 Prince Street, Rochester, New York 14607. For photographers and independent filmmakers and video artists. Published monthly except July through September.

Agenda. Visual Arts Ontario, 439 Wellington Street West, Toronto, Ontario, Canada M5V 1E7. Published quarterly.

American Ceramics, 9 East 45th Street, New York, New York 10017. Published quarterly.

American Craft. American Craft Council, 72 Spring Street, New York, New York 10012. Articles on all aspects of crafts, and information on grants, marketing, and exhibitions. Published bimonthly.

Art New England: A Resource for Visual Artists, 425 Washington Street, Brighton, Massachusetts 02135. Focuses on artists in New England. Published ten times a year.

Art Papers, P.O. Box 77348, Atlanta, Georgia 30357. Focuses on artists in the Southeast. Published bimonthly.

Art Washington. Cultural Alliance of Greater Washington, 410 8th Street, NW, Suite 600, Washington, D.C. 20004. Published monthly.

ArtCalendar, P.O. Box 1040, Great Falls, Virginia 22066. Comprehensive listing of professional opportunities for artists nationwide, including juried exhibitions, grants and awards, residencies, slide registries, public art programs, art consultants, internships, employment openings, and book reviews. Also features articles on marketing, career development, and legal issues. Published eleven times a year.

The Artists Magazine, 1507 Dana Avenue, Cincinnati, Ohio 45207. Published monthly.

Artlines 1991–1992: An Annotated Guide to Organizations and Publications Essential to Artists. National Network for Artist Placement, 935 West Avenue 37, Los Angeles, California 90065, revised 1990. Describes trade publications of interest to artists.

Artpaper. The Visual Arts Information Service, 119 North Fourth Street, #303, Minneapolis, Minnesota 55401. An artists' newspaper featuring articles, news, and information on national grants, competitions, and opportunities for artists in Minnesota and bordering states. Published ten times a year.

The Arts Journal, 324 Charlotte Street, Asheville, North Carolina 28801. Published monthly.

Artweek, 12 South First Street, Suite 520, San Jose, California 95113. Regional focus: the Northwest, the Southwest, Alaska, and Hawaii. Includes information on competitions, exhibitions, and festivals for visual and performance artists. Forty-four issues, published weekly September through May; biweekly June through August.

Association of Hispanic Arts Newsletter. Association of Hispanic Arts, Inc., 173 East 116th Street, New York, New York 10029. Published ten times a year.

Boston Visual Artists Union News, 33 Harrison Avenue, 7th Floor, Boston, Massachusetts 02111. Focuses on art news, events, and opportunities in the Boston area. Published monthly.

CARO Bulletin. Canadian Artists' Representation Ontario (CARO), 183 Bathurst Street, Toronto, Ontario, Canada M5T 2R7. Reports on programs and current events affecting the arts community. Discusses issues of concern to artists, financial opportunities, and other practical information. Published quarterly.

Chicago Artists' News. Chicago Artists' Coalition, 5 West Grand, Chicago, Illinois 60610. Published monthly.

For Your Information. New York Foundation for the Arts, 5 Beekman Street, New York, New York 10038. Published quarterly.

Godzilla. Asian American Arts Alliance, Inc., P.O. Box 879, Canal Street Station, New York, New York 10013-0864. Newsletter for Asian-American artists containing feature articles and information on exhibition opportunities and grants. Published quarterly.

Graphic Artists Guild Newsletter, 11 West 20th Street, 8th Floor, New York, New York 10011. Focuses on graphic-arts news throughout the country, and features legal and financial advice, book reviews, and conference reports. Published monthly.

New Art Examiner, 1225 South Wabash, 4th Floor, Chicago, Illinois 60605. Published monthly except July and August.

The Original Art Report, P.O. Box 1641, Chicago, Illinois 60690. A lively, highly opinionated newsletter covering a variety of arts-related issues. Published monthly.

Sculpture. International Sculpture Center, 1050 Potomac Street, NW, Washington, D.C. 20007. Published bimonthly.

Shuttle, Spindle and Dyepot. Handweavers Guild of America, 120 Mountain Avenue, #B101, Bloomfield, Connecticut 06002. International magazine of the Handweavers Guild of America. For weavers, spinners, and dyers. Contains technical and historical articles as well as marketing and business information. Published quarterly.

Ulrich's International Periodical Directory. New York: R. R. Bowker. Includes the names, addresses, and descriptions of periodicals published throughout the world. Revised annually.

Vantage Point. American Council for the Arts, 1 East 53rd Street, New

York, New York 10022. Includes articles about significant art events and problems, feature stories on major art developments, and arts-related news. Published bimonthly.

Views. Photographic Resource Center, 602 Commonwealth Avenue, Boston, Massachusetts 02215. Newsletter for photographers. Published monthly.

Westart, P.O. Box 6868, Auburn, California 95604. Provides an overview of the West Coast arts community. Published bimonthly.

Also see "Career Management, Business, and Marketing."

Pricing

PUBLICATIONS

The Artists' Survival Manual: A Complete Guide to Marketing Your Work by Toby Judith Klayman and Cobbett Steinberg. New York: Charles Scribner's Sons, revised 1987. See the chapter "Getting Ready: Pricing Your Work."

"Fair Market Value" by Peter H. Karlen, *ArtCalendar*, P.O. Box 1040, Great Falls, Virginia 22066, October 1989.

Graphic Artists Guild Handbook: Pricing and Ethical Guidelines. Graphic Artists Guild, 11 West 20th Street, 8th Floor, New York, New York 10011, revised biannually.

Prints and Printmaking

PUBLICATIONS

"An Artist for the Masses" by Clare Collins, *The New York Times*, 10 April 1988.

"Artist-Publisher Agreements" by Peter H. Karlen, *ArtCalendar*, P.O. Box 1040, Great Falls, Virginia 22066, June 1990.

"Botanical Prints: Collector's Primer" by Peter Carlsen, *The New York Times*, 10 November 1988.

Directory of Art Publishers, Book Publishers and Record Companies. Directors Guild Publishers and The Consultant Press, P.O. Box 369, Renaissance, California 95962, 1990. Includes information on areas of specialization, media and styles of interest, distribution possibilities, and review standards.

Guidelines for Printmakers, Report #14, ArtNetwork, P.O. Box 369, Renaissance, California 95962.

"Marketing Art Prints" by Marcia Saft, *The New York Times*, 12 July 1987.

Printnews. World Print Council, 230 Francisco Street, San Francisco, California 94133. Published bimonthly.

The Printworld Directory of Contemporary Prints and Prices. Printworld, Inc., P.O. Box 785, Bala Cynwyd, Pennsylvania 19004. Published annually.

Publishing Your Art as Cards and Posters by Harold Davis. The Consultant Press/The Photographic Arts Center, Limited, 163 Amsterdam Avenue, New York, New York 10023, 1990.

ORGANIZATIONS

Northwest Print Council, 800 NW 6th Street, #209, Portland, Oregon 97209. Juried membership organization for printmakers throughout the Northwest. Sponsors a newsletter and other programs.

World Print Council, 230 Francisco Street, San Francisco, California 94133. Sponsors an International Print Triennial and traveling exhibitions. Maintains a gallery in San Francisco with a slide referral service that includes the work of artists from around the world.

Public Art

PUBLICATIONS

Arts on the Line Handbook. Cambridge Arts Council, 57 Inman Street, Cambridge, Massachusetts 02139, 1988. A guide that offers advice and support to those participating in and/or embarking on a public art program. Documents the collaboration of the Massachusetts Bay Transit Authority and the Cambridge Arts Council in the Arts on the Line project. Documents the program's history, administration, and artist selection procedure, as well as the fabrication and installation of art and community involvement. Appendix includes sample budgets, contracts, and other documents.

The Business of Art, edited by Lee Caplin. New York: Prentice Hall, revised 1991. See "Financial Resources for Artists—Art in Public Places" by Patricia Fuller.

Competitions, P.O. Box 20445, Louisville, Kentucky 40250. Quarterly magazine devoted to articles on public art, architecture, and landscape architecture competitions in the United States and abroad.

Competitions Hotline, P.O. Box 20445, Louisville, Kentucky 40250.

Quarterly newsletter that lists public art, architecture, and landscape architecture competitions in the United States and abroad.

"Contracts for Public Commissions" by Peter H. Karlen, *ArtCalendar*, P.O. Box 1040, Great Falls, Virginia 22066, May 1990.

"Environmental Art" by Peter H. Karlen, *ArtCalendar*, P.O. Box 1040, Great Falls, Virginia 22066, December 1990.

"Funding for Art Groups: NEA Art in Public Places Grants" by Drew Steis, *ArtCalendar*, P.O. Box 1040, Great Falls, Virginia 22066, November 1990.

Going Public: A Field Guide to Developments in Art in Public Places. Arts Extension Service, Division of Continuing Education, University of Massachusetts, Amherst, Massachusetts 01003, 1988. Provides an overview of current issues, policies, and processes in the administration and preservation of public art. Appendices include information on two hundred ongoing public art programs.

Guidebook for Competitions and Commissions. Visual Arts Ontario, 439 Wellington Street West, Toronto, Ontario, Canada M5V 1E7, 1991. A guide to the process of commissioning art. Discusses methods for commissioning art, contexts and constraints, the role of the sponsor, and the role of the artist.

"Interview with Françoise Yohalem—Art Consultant" by Drew Steis, *ArtCalendar*, P.O. Box 1040, Great Falls, Virginia 22066, May 1990.

Public Art Programs. Arts Resource Consortium Library, 1 East 53rd Street, New York, New York 10022, revised regularly. List of thirty-four organizations in twenty-three states that sponsor public art programs.

Public Art, Public Controversy: The Tilted Arc on Trial by Dale Mc-Conathy, Barbara Hoffman, Judith Balfe, and Margaret Wyszomirski, 1987. Available from the American Council for the Arts, 1 East 53rd Street, New York, New York 10022.

ORGANIZATIONS

Association of Professional Art Advisors, Inc., 2150 West 29th Street, Denver, Colorado 80211. Provides planning and coordination assistance to the public and private sectors in areas of public art, art collecting, and program planning.

Creative Time, 131 West 24th Street, New York, New York 10011. Sponsors exhibitions and projects in public spaces throughout New York City.

Mailing List Labels, P.O. Box 661, Grand Central Station, New York,

New York 10163-0661. *Offers Percent for Art/Public Places Programs Mailing List,* which includes mailing labels and postcards for requesting information about city, state, and national public art programs.

Project for Public Spaces, Inc., 153 Waverly Place, New York, New York 10014. Specializes in public space planning, design, and management; assists city agencies, community groups, private developers, and planners in selecting and placing art in public spaces. Maintains a slide registry and offers workshops and conferences on public space planning.

Public Art Fund, Inc., 1 East 53rd Street, New York, New York 10022. Promotes the integration of art into the urban landscape, sponsors art installations in public spaces throughout New York City, and provides educational and informational services.

Social and Public Art Resource Center (SPARC), 685 Venice Boulevard, Venice, California 90291. A multicultural arts center that produces, exhibits, distributes, and preserves public artwork. Sponsors exhibitions, workshops, and mural production.

Urban Arts, P.O. Box 1658, Boston, Massachusetts 02205. A public arts agency that accepts contracts to place art in public places. Houses a nationwide slide registry of artists in all disciplines.

NATIONAL PERCENT FOR ART PROGRAMS
(† slide registry)

Art-in-Architecture Program, Veterans Administration, 110 Vermont Avenue, NW, Washington, D.C. 20420.†

Art in Public Places, Visual Arts Program, National Endowment for the Arts, 1100 Pennsylvania Avenue, NW, Washington, D.C. 20506.

Percent for Art Program, Art-in-Architecture Program, General Services Administration, 19th & F Streets, NW, Washington, D.C. 20405.†

STATE AND MUNICIPAL PUBLIC ART PROGRAMS
(*Open to out-of-state residents; † slide registry)

ALASKA
*Percent for Art Program, Alaska State Council on the Arts, 411 West 4th Avenue, Suite 1E, Anchorage, Alaska 99501-2343.†

Percent for Art Program, Municipality of Anchorage, Capital Projects Office—POB 196650, Anchorage, Alaska 99519-6650.

ARIZONA
Art in Public Places, Casa Grande Arts and Humanities Commission, 300 East 4th Street, Casa Grande, Arizona 85222.

*Art in Public Places Program, Artscape, c/o Scottsdale Cultural Council, 7383 Mall, Scottsdale, Arizona 85251.†

*Art in Public Places Program, City of Sierra Vista, 2400 East Tacoma Street, Sierra Vista, Arizona 85635.

*Art in Public Places Program, Oscar Yram Community Center, 3020 East Tacoma Street, Sierra Vista, Arizona 85635.

*Art in Public Places Program, Tempe Arts Commission, Library Building, 3500 South Rural Road, Tempe, Arizona 85282.†

*Art in Public Places Program and Education in the Arts Program, Sedona Department of Arts and Culture, P.O. Box 3002, Sedona, Arizona 86336.†

*Percent for Art Program, Center for the Arts, City of Chandler, 125 East Commonwealth, Chandler, Arizona 85225.

*Percent for Art Program, Glendale Arts Commission, 5850 West Glendale Avenue, Glendale, Arizona 85301.

*Percent for Art Program, Peoria Arts Commission, P.O.B. C-4038, Peoria, Arizona 85345.

*Percent for Art Program, Phoenix Arts Commission, 323 West Roosevelt, Suite A-100, Phoenix, Arizona 85003.†

*Public Art Program, Tucson/Pima Arts Council, P.O. Box 27210, Tucson, Arizona 95701.†

COLORADO
*Art in Public Places Program, City of Loveland, 503 North Lincoln, Loveland, Colorado 80537.†

*Percent for Art Program, Commission on Cultural Affairs, 303 West Colfax, Suite 1600, Denver, Colorado 80204.†

CONNECTICUT
*Percent for Art Program, City of Stamford, 888 Washington Boulevard, Stamford, Connecticut 06954-2152.†

*Percent for Art Program, Connecticut Commission on the Arts, 227 Lawrence Street, Hartford, Connecticut 06106.†

*Percent for Art Program, Department of Cultural Affairs, City of New Haven, 770 Chapel Street, New Haven, Connecticut 06510.†

DELAWARE
*Wilmington Arts Commission, City-County Building, 800 North French Street, Wilmington, Delaware 19801.

DISTRICT OF COLUMBIA
*Art in Public Places Program, District of Columbia Commission on the Arts, 410 8th Street, NW, Fifth Floor, Washington, D.C. 20004.

FLORIDA

*Art in Public Places Board, Lee County, Department of Community Services, P.O. Box 398, Fort Myers, Florida 33902.

*Art in Public Places Program, Broward County, Office of Cultural Affairs, 100 South Andrews Avenue, Fort Lauderdale, Florida 33301.†

*Art in Public Places Program, City of Miami, Planning, Building and Zoning Department, 275 Northwest Second Street, Miami, Florida 33128.

*Art in State Buildings, Florida Arts Council, Division of Cultural Affairs, Florida Department of State, The Capitol, Tallahassee, Florida 32399-0250.†

*Metro-Dade Art in Public Places Program, 111 Northwest First Street, Suite 610, Miami, Florida 33218.†

*Percent for Art Program, Bass Museum of Art, 2121 Park Avenue, Miami Beach, Florida 33119.

*Percent for Art Program, Orlando Public Art Board, City of Orlando, 400 South Orange Avenue, Orlando, Florida 32801.†

*Public Art Program, City of Tampa, 1420 North Tampa Street, Tampa, Florida 33602.†

GEORGIA

Art in Public Places Program, Georgia Council for the Arts, 2082 East Exchange Place, Suite 100, Tucker, Georgia 30084.

Georgia Art Acquisition Program, Georgia Council for the Arts, 2082 East Exchange Place, Suite 100, Tucker, Georgia 30084.

*Percent for Art Program, City of Atlanta, Department of Cultural Affairs, 236 Forsyth Street, SW, Suite 402, Atlanta, Georgia 30303.†

*Public Art Collection, Clarke County Cultural Services Division, Department of Parks, 325 East Washington Street, Athens, Georgia 30603.

GUAM

*Percent for Art Program, Insular Arts Council of Guam, P.O. Box 2950, Agana, Guam 96910.

HAWAII

*Art in City Buildings Program, Mayor's Cultural and Arts Office, City Hall, Room 404, Honolulu, Hawaii 96813.

*Art in Public Places Program, State Foundation on Culture and the Arts, 335 Merchant Street, Room 202, Honolulu, Hawaii 96813.†

ILLINOIS

Percent for Art Program, Capitol Development Board, State of Illinois, 401 South Spring Street, Springfield, Illinois 62706.

*Percent for Art Program, Department of Cultural Affairs, The Cultural Center, 78 East Washington Street, Chicago, Illinois 60602.†

IOWA

*Art in State Buildings Program, Iowa Arts Council, Department of Cultural Affairs, Capitol Complex—1223 East Court, Des Moines, Iowa 50319.†

*Iowa Town Squares Program, Iowa Arts Council, Department of Cultural Affairs, Capitol Complex—1223 East Court, Des Moines, Iowa 50319.†

LOUISIANA

*Percent for Art Program, Arts Council of New Orleans, 821 Gravier Street, #600, New Orleans, Louisiana 70112.†

MAINE

*Percent for Art Program, Maine Commission on the Arts, 55 Capitol Street, State House Station 25, Augusta, Maine 04333.†

MARYLAND

*Art in Public Architecture, Montgomery County Planning Department, 110 North Washington Street, 3rd Floor, Rockville, Maryland 20850.

*Art in Public Architecture Program, The Maryland–National Capital Park and Planning Commission, 9500 Brunett Avenue, Silver Spring, Maryland 20902.†

*Art in Public Places Program, 34 Market Place, Suite 325, Baltimore, Maryland 21202.†

*Percent for Art Program, City of Baltimore, Civic Design Commission, 1105 Abel Wolman Municipal Building, Baltimore, Maryland 21202.†

*Percent for Art Program, City of Rockville, Recreation and Park Department, Maryland Avenue at Vinson Street, Rockville, Maryland 20850.

MASSACHUSETTS

*Art in Public Places Program, Massachusetts Cultural Council, 80 Boylston Street, 10th Floor, Boston, Massachusetts 02116.†

*Boston Art Commission, 1 City Hall Square, Room 805, Boston, Massachusetts 02201.

Percent for Art Program, Cambridge Arts Council, 57 Inman Street, Cambridge, Massachusetts 02139.†

*Public Art Task Force, Office of the Arts and Humanities, Boston City Hall, #802, Boston, Massachusetts 02201.

MICHIGAN

Art in Public Places Program, City of Southfield, Department of Parks and Recreation, 26000 Evergreen, Southfield, Michigan 48037.†

*Percent for Art Program, Commission on Art in Public Places, 1200 Sixth Avenue, P-120, Detroit, Michigan 48226.†

MINNESOTA

*Percent for Art Program, Duluth Public Arts Commission, City Hall, Room 322, Duluth, Minnesota 55802-1196.

*Percent for Art Program, Minnesota State Arts Board, 432 Summit Avenue, Saint Paul, Minnesota 55102.†

MISSOURI

*Percent for Art Program, Kansas City Municipal Arts Commission, City Architect's Office, City Hall, 17th Floor, 414 East 12th Street, Kansas City, Missouri 64106.

*Percent for Art Program, Regional Arts Commission, 3540 Washington Street, St. Louis, Missouri 63103.

MONTANA

*Percent for Art Program, State of Montana, Montana Arts Council, 48 North Last Chance Gulch, Helena, Montana 59620.

*Public Art Program, Missoula Public Art Committee, Office of Community Development, 435 Ryman, Missoula, Montana 59802.†

NEBRASKA

*Percent for Art Program, Nebraska Arts Council, 1313 Farnam-on-the-Mall, Omaha, Nebraska 68102-1873.

NEVADA

*Art in Public Places Program, City of Las Vegas Arts Commission, 749 Veterans Memorial Drive, Las Vegas, Nevada 89101.†

*Art in Public Places Program, Nevada State Council for the Arts, 329 Flint Street, Reno, Nevada 89501.

NEW HAMPSHIRE

Percent for Art Program, New Hampshire State Council on the Arts, 40 North Main Street, Concord, New Hampshire 03301.† Open only to Northeast artists.

NEW JERSEY

*Arts Inclusion Program, Cape May County Cultural and Heritage Commission, DN-101, Library Office Building, Cape May Court House, Cape May, New Jersey 08210-3050.†

*Arts Inclusion Program, New Jersey State Council on the Arts, 4 North Broad Street, CN306, Trenton, New Jersey 08625-0306.†

*Percent for Art Program, Office of Cultural Affairs and Heritage, 1333 Atlantic Avenue, 7th Floor, Atlantic City, New Jersey 08401.

NEW MEXICO

*Art in Public Places Program, Los Alamos County, P.O. Box 30, Los Alamos, New Mexico 87544.†

*Percent for Art Program, City of Santa Fe, Capital Improvement Department, P.O. Box 909, Santa Fe, New Mexico 97504-0909.†

*Percent for Art Program, c/o Kimo Theatre, City of Albuquerque, 423 Central Avenue, NW, Albuquerque, New Mexico 87102.†

*Percent for Art Program, New Mexico Arts Division, 224 East Palace Avenue, Santa Fe, New Mexico 87501.

NEW YORK

*City Arts Workshop, 625 Broadway, New York, New York 10012.†

*Percent for Art Program, Art in Public Places Committee, The Arts Council of Rockland County, 22 South Madison Avenue, Spring Valley, New York 10977.†

*Percent for Art Program, New York City Department of Cultural Affairs, 2 Columbus Circle, New York, New York 10019.†

*Public Art Program, Battery Park Redevelopment Authority, One World Financial Center, 18th Floor, New York, New York 10281-1097.

NORTH CAROLINA

*Percent for Art Program, Charlotte-Mecklenburg Art Commission, Charlotte-Mecklenburg Planning Commission, 600 East 4th Street, Charlotte, North Carolina 28202-2853.

*Percent for Art Program, North Carolina Arts Council, Department of Cultural Resources, Raleigh, North Carolina 27601-2807.

OHIO

*Art in Public Places Program, Arts Commission of Greater Toledo, 618 North Michigan Street, Toledo, Ohio 43624.†

*Art in Public Places Program, Ohio Arts Council, 727 East Main Street, Columbus, Ohio 43205-1796.†

OKLAHOMA

*Percent for Art Program, Arts and Humanities Council of the City of Tulsa, 2210 South Main Street, Tulsa, Oklahoma 74114.

*Percent for Art Program, Park and Recreation Department, Oklahoma City Arts Commission, 201 Channing Square, Oklahoma City, Oklahoma 73102.

OREGON

*Percent for Art Program, Beaverton Arts Commission, P.O. Box 4755, Beaverton, Oregon 97076.†

*Percent for Art Program, City of Eugene, Department of Facilities Development, One Eugene Center, Eugene, Oregon 97401.

*Percent for Art Program, Metropolitan Arts Commission, 1120 SW Fifth Avenue, Room 1023, Portland, Oregon 97204.

*Percent for Art Program, Oregon Arts Commission, 835 Summer Street, NE, Salem, Oregon 97301.†

PENNSYLVANIA

*Percent for Art Program, Arts Commission, City of Pittsburgh, City County Building, #301, 419 Grant Street, Pittsburgh, Pennsylvania 15219.

*Percent for Art Program, Office of Arts and Culture, City of Philadelphia, 1680 Municipal Services Building, Philadelphia, Pennsylvania 19102-1684.†

*Percent for Art Program, Redevelopment Authority of Philadelphia, 1234 Market Street, Philadelphia, Pennsylvania 19107.†

RHODE ISLAND

*Art in Public Places Program, Rhode Island State Council on the Arts, 95 Cedar Street, Suite 103, Providence, Rhode Island 02903.†

SOUTH CAROLINA

*Art in Public Places Program, South Carolina Arts Commission, 1800 Gervais Street, Columbia, South Carolina 29201.†

TENNESSEE
*Public Art Program, Tennessee Arts Commission, 320 6th Avenue, Suite 600, Nashville, Tennessee 37219.†

TEXAS
*Art in Public Places Program, City of Austin, Parks and Recreation Department, P.O. Box 1088, Austin, Texas 78767.†
*Art in Public Places Program, Municipal Arts Commission, City of Corpus Christi, P.O. Box 9277, Corpus Christi, Texas 78469-9277.†
*Percent for Art Program, Houston Municipal Art Commission, Office of the Mayor, P.O. Box 1562, Houston, Texas 77251.†
*Percent for Art Program, Office of Cultural Affairs, Majestic Theatre, Suite 500, 1925 Elm Street, Dallas, Texas 75021.†
Public Exhibition Program, Arts Council of Brazos Valley, 111 University, Suite 217, College Station, Texas 77840.†

UTAH
*Percent for Art Program, Salt Lake City Art Design Board, Salt Lake City Arts Council, 54 Finch Lane, Salt Lake City, Utah 84101.†
*Percent for Art Program, Utah Arts Council, 617 East South Temple, Salt Lake City, Utah 84102.†

VERMONT
*Art in State Buildings, Vermont Council on the Arts, 136 State Street, Montpelier, Vermont 05602.†

VIRGINIA
*Civic Arts Program, Portsmouth Museums, P.O. Box 850, Portsmouth, Virginia 23705.†
*Percent for Art Program, Arts and Humanities Commission, City of Virginia Beach, Room 340, Virginia Beach, Virginia 23456.†

WASHINGTON
*Art in Public Places Program, Kent Arts Commission, 220 4th Avenue South, Kent, Washington 98032.
*Art in Public Places Program, Pierce County Arts Commission, 3711 Center Street, Tacoma, Washington 98409.
*Art in Public Places Program, Winslow Arts Advisory Committee, 40 Winslow City Hall, 625 Winslow Way East, Bainbridge Island, Washington 98110.

*Municipal Arts Program, Everett Cultural Commission, 3002 Westmore Avenue, Everett, Washington 98201-4073.

*Percent for Art Program, Bellevue Arts Commission, P.O. Box 90012, Bellevue, Washington 98009-9013.

*Percent for Art Program, Edmonds Arts Commission, 700 Main Street, Edmonds, Washington 98020-3032.

*Percent for Art Program, King County Arts Commission, 506 Second Avenue, 1115 Smith Tower, Seattle, Washington 98104-2323.

*Percent for Art Program, Mountlake Terrace Arts Commission, 5303 228th Street, SW, Mountlake Terrace, Washington 98043.

*Percent for Art Program, Renton Municipal Arts Commission, 200 Mill Avenue, S.—City Hall, Renton, Washington 98055.

*Percent for Art Program, Spokane Arts Commission, West 808 Spokane Falls Boulevard, Spokane, Washington 98201-3333.

*Percent for Art Program, Washington State Arts Commission, Mail Stop GH-11, 110 Ninth and Columbia Building, Olympia, Washington 98504-4111.†

*Percent for Art Program, Wenatchee Arts Commission, c/o Wenatchee City Hall, 129 South Chelan Street, Wenatchee, Washington 98801.

*Public Art Program, Seattle Arts Commission, 305 Harrison Street, Seattle, Washington 98109-4695.

WEST VIRGINIA

*Art in Public Places Program, Division of Arts and Humanities, Department of Education and the Arts, Cultural Center, Capitol Complex, Charleston, West Virginia 25305.

WISCONSIN

*Art in Public Places Program, Madison Parks Department, P.O. Box 2987, 215 Martin Luther King Boulevard, Madison, Wisconsin 53701.†

*Percent for Art Program, Milwaukee Arts Commission, 809 North Broadway, Milwaukee, Wisconsin 53202.†

*Percent for Art Program, Wisconsin Arts Board, 131 West Wilson Street, #301, Madison, Wisconsin 53702.†

CANADIAN PUBLIC ART PROGRAM

Visual Arts Program, Archive, Department of the City Clerk, City of Ottawa, 111 Sussex Drive, Ottawa, Canada K1N 5A1.

MASS TRANSIT AND AIRPORT PUBLIC ART PROGRAMS
(*Open to out-of-state residents; † slide registry)

Art for Rail Transit, Los Angeles County Transportation Commission, 818 West 7th Street, Suite 1100, Los Angeles, California 90017.†

*Art in Public Places Program, Sky Harbor International Airport, Phoenix Arts Commission, 3400 Sky Harbor Boulevard, Phoenix, Arizona 85034.

Art in Public Places Program, Tucson Airport Authority, Tucson International Airport, Tucson, Arizona 85706.

*Arts for Transit, Metropolitan Transportation Authority, 347 Madison Avenue, New York, New York 10017.

*Arts in Transit Program, Bi-State Development Agency, 707 North First Street, St. Louis, Missouri 63102.†

*Arts on the Line, Cambridge Arts Council, 57 Inman Street, Cambridge, Massachusetts 02139.†

*Exhibitions and Acquisitions Program, Seattle-Tacoma International Airport, Port of Seattle, P.O. Box 68727, Room 301, Seattle, Washington 98168.

*Percent for Art Program, Metro Arts Program, MS 130, 821 2nd Avenue, Seattle, Washington 98104.

*Percent for Art Program, Port Authority of New York and New Jersey, One World Trade Center, Room 82W, New York, New York 10048.†

*Visual Arts Program, Santa Cruz Metropolitan Transit District, 230 Walnut Avenue, Santa Cruz, California 95060.

Public Relations/Press Relations

PUBLICATIONS

Developing the Press Packet. Media Distribution Co-op, 1745 Louisiana Street, Lawrence, Kansas 66044. Provides information on compiling a press packet, including press releases, photographs, and follow-through. Includes sample forms and a bibliography of public-relations directories.

Editor and Publisher Syndicate Directory. Editor and Publisher Company, 11 West 19th Street, New York, New York 10011. Lists syndicates serving newspapers in the United States and abroad with news and feature articles.

Encyclopedia of Associations, edited by Katherine Gruber. Detroit: Gale Research Company, revised regularly. Indexed by title and subject. Each entry includes address, purpose, programs, and publications.

Fine Art Publicity: The Complete Guide for Galleries and Artists by Susan Abbott and Barbara Webb. Art Business News, P.O. Box 3837, Stamford, Connecticut 06905, 1990. Provides information on effective methods and procedures for obtaining publicity and attracting the attention of the art-buying public. Also includes information on press releases and getting exposure on radio and television.

"Getting into Print: News Releases" by Carolyn Blakeslee, *ArtCalendar*, P.O. Box 1040, Great Falls, Virginia 22066, June 1991.

Internal Publications Directory. National Research Bureau, 225 West Wacker Drive, Suite 2275, Chicago, Illinois 60604. Provides detailed information on internal and external house organs of more than thirty-five hundred U.S. and Canadian companies, government agencies, clubs, and other groups.

Magazine Industry Market Place. New York: R. R. Bowker, revised annually. Lists thirty-five hundred publications, indexed by subject.

Media Personnel Directory. Detroit: Gale Research Company, updated regularly. Lists editors, publishers, columnists, correspondents, and bureau chiefs of more than seven hundred magazines and periodicals in the United States.

National Radio Publicity Directory. Peter Glenn Publications, Limited, 17 East 48th Street, New York, New York 10017, updated regularly. Lists more than thirty-five hundred network, syndicated, and local talk shows in the nation's two hundred major markets and more than forty-five hundred local and college radio stations.

Professional's Guide to Publicity by Richard Winer. Public Relations Publishing Company, Inc., 888 7th Avenue, New York, New York 10106, updated periodically.

Talk Show Directory for Radio and Television. National Research Bureau, 225 West Wacker Drive, Suite 2275, Chicago, Illinois 60604, revised regularly.

Talk Show Guest Directory by Mitchell P. Davis. Broadcast Interview Source, 2233 Wisconsin Avenue, NW, Washington, D.C. 20007, revised regularly. Used by radio and television producers to locate talk-show guests.

Talk Shows. Media Distribution Co-op, 1745 Louisiana Street, Lawrence, Kansas 66044. Bibliography of talk-show directories and placement organizations, and tips on how to get your project publicized.

Writer's Market, edited by Glenda Tennant Neff. Cincinnati: Writer's Digest Books, published annually.

Slide Registries

ORGANIZATIONS

American Craft Council Library, 72 Spring Street, New York, New York 10012. Operates a slide registry on American craft artists in all media.

Art Information Center, 280 Broadway, New York, New York 10007. Operates two registries: Unaffiliated Artists, an open file of slides and résumés of artists unaffiliated with commercial galleries, and Affiliated Artists, a file designed to help artists, dealers, museum personnel, the press, collectors, and the public locate the work of living artists.

Art League of Houston, 1953 Montrose Boulevard, Houston, Texas 77066. Maintains slide registry of Texas or Texas-born artists.

Artists Book Works, 1422 West Irving Park Road, Chicago, Illinois 60613. Slide registry of book artists used by curators, collectors, educators, and museum personnel.

Artists Space, 223 West Broadway, New York, New York 10013. Sponsors a computerized slide registry of New York State artists who are not represented by commercial or co-op galleries.

Boston Visual Artists Union, 33 Harrison Avenue, 7th Floor, Boston, Massachusetts 02111.

Chicago Artists' Coalition, 5 West Grand, Chicago, Illinois 60610.

The Drawing Center, 35 Wooster Street, New York, New York 10012. Exhibition, research, and study center for contemporary drawings.

Empire State Crafts Alliance, 511 Broadway, Saratoga Springs, New York 12866. Maintains a registry of craft professionals.

Florida Center for Contemporary Art/Artists Alliance, Inc., P.O. Box 75184, Tampa, Florida 33605. Registry is open to artists in the Southeast region.

Georgia Artists Registry, Atlanta College of Art Library, Woodruff Arts Center, 1280 Peachtree Street, NE, Atlanta, Georgia 30309. Open to artists living in Georgia.

Houston Center for Photography, 1441 West Alabama, Houston, Texas 77006. Slide registry is open to all photographers.

International Sculpture Center, 1050 Potomac Avenue, NW, Washington, D.C. 20007. Sponsors Sculpture Source, a computerized slide registry for sculptors.

Museum of Contemporary Hispanic Art (MOCHA), 584 Broadway, New York, New York 10012. Maintains a slide registry for Hispanic artists.

Nassau County Museum of Fine Art, P.O. Box 346, Roslyn, New York

11576. Slide registry is open to visual artists and craftspersons in Long Island, New York.

National Center on Arts and the Aging, 409 Third Street, SW, 2nd Floor, Washington, D.C. 20024. Sponsors a slide registry for artists over sixty-five years of age.

New Organization for the Visual Arts (NOVA), 4614 Prospect Avenue, #410, Cleveland, Ohio 44103. Maintains a slide registry for Northeast Ohio artists.

Organization of Independent Artists, 19 Hudson Street, #402, New York, New York 10013. Registry is open to professional artists.

Resources for Artists with Disabilities, 77 Seventh Avenue South, Suite PHG, New York, New York 10011-6645.

Visual Arts Ontario, 439 Wellington Street West, Toronto, Ontario, Canada M5V 1E7.

World Print Council, 230 Francisco Street, San Francisco, California 94133. Maintains a slide referral service for work by print artists from around the world.

Also see "Public Art."

Surplus-Material Programs

PUBLICATIONS

Materials for the Arts: A Handbook. New York City Department of Cultural Affairs, 2 Columbus Circle, New York, New York 10019, undated.

ORGANIZATIONS

Emergency Materials Fund, Artists Space, 223 West Broadway, New York, New York 10013.

Materials for the Arts, New York City Department of Cultural Affairs, 2 Columbus Circle, New York, New York 10019.

Notes

1. Tom Wolfe, *The Painted Word* (New York: Farrar, Straus & Giroux, 1980), 14.
2. Betty Chamberlain, *The Artist's Guide to the Art Market* (New York: Watson-Guptill, 1983), 18.
3. Ralph Charell, *How to Make Things Go Your Way* (New York: Simon and Schuster, 1979), 149.
4. Ronald H. Silverman, "Art Career Education: The Third Imperative," *School Arts*, volume 79, number 6, February 1980, 42.
5. Ibid.
6. Comment by Barbara Price, academic dean and vice-president for academic affairs, Maryland Institute, College of Art, Baltimore, reprinted with permission from the American Council for the Arts from "Support for Artists by Institutions: Comment and Discussion," in *The Modern Muse: The Support and Condition of Artists*, edited by C. Richard Swaim (New York: American Council for the Arts, 1989), 126.
7. From *Has Modernism Failed?* by Suzi Gablik. Copyright © 1984 Thames and Hudson (p. 68). Reprinted by permission of the publisher.
8. Judith Appelbaum and Nancy Evans, *How to Get Happily Published* (New York: Harper & Row, 1978), 12.

9. Tad Crawford, *Legal Guide for the Visual Artist* (New York: Allworth Press, 1989), 1.

10. Ibid., 163.

11. Ibid.

12. Richard Hyman, *The Professional Artist's Manual* (New York: Van Nostrand Reinhold/Simon and Schuster, 1980), 76. Copyright © by Litton Educational Publishing, Inc. Reprinted by permission of the publisher.

13. Ibid.

14. Artist statement by Anne Raymond, New York City.

15. Artist statement by David Camilleri, New York City.

16. Artist statement by Ann Lowe, San Lorenzo, New Mexico.

17. David Camilleri, op. cit.

18. Telephone interview with Dick Termes.

19. *Artists Gallery Guide for Chicago and the Illinois Region*, Chicago Artists' Coalition, 1990.

20. Ibid.

21. From a press release issued by Laura Foreman and John Watts for *Wallwork*, New York City, 1 May 1981.

22. Ibid.

23. Jack Anderson, " 'Sold Out' Performances That Never Actually Took Place," *The New York Times*, 12 July 1981, 13. Copyright © 1981 by The New York Times Company. Reprinted by permission.

24. Daniel Grant, "The Publicity of Art and the Art of Publicity," *Artworkers News*, March 1981, 1.

25. From a press release issued by the Integral Consciousness Institute for "Synthesis," an exhibition at the Soho Center for Visual Artists, New York City, June 1979.

26. From a press release issued by the Rotunda Gallery, Brooklyn, New York, for the exhibition "Sculptor's Drawings," 17 February 1983.

27. From a press release issued by Adelphi University, Garden City, Long Island, New York, for a one-person exhibition by Francine Fels, "Happy Birthday, Rev—A Dancework in 50 Paintings," 31 May 1988.

28. From a press release issued by Lydia Afia for a one-person exhibition, "Behind Glass," at Tiffany & Company, New York City, January 1988.

29. "Barbara Rose," interview by Eva Cockcroft, *Artworkers News*, April 1980, 13.

30. Interview with Nina Pratt, New York City, 1990.

31. "John Perrault," interview by Walter Weissman, *Artworkers News*, April 1980, 19.

32. Edith DeAk and Walter Robinson, "Alternative Periodicals," in *The New Artspace: A Summary of Alternative Visual Arts Organizations*, prepared in conjunction with a conference held on 26–29 April 1978 (Los Angeles: Los Angeles Institute of Contemporary Art, 1978), 38.

33. Suzanne K. Vinmans, *On Opening an Art Gallery* (Madison, Wisconsin: Suzanne K. Vinmans, 1990), 30–31.

34. Lisa Gubernick, "I Was an Artist for *The Village Voice*," *The Village Voice*, 7–13 October 1981, 71.

35. *Recommended Guidelines for Juried Exhibitions* (Washington, D.C.: National Artists Equity Association, 1991).

36. Carolyn Blakeslee, "Entry Fees," *ArtCalendar*, June 1991, 3.

37. Ellen Baum, "The Whitney: Acquisitions Policies and Attitude Toward Living Artists," *Artworkers News*, December 1980, 13.

38. Ibid.

39. Brenda B. Harris, "The Benefits of Working with Art Advisors," *ArtCalendar*, April 1990, 5.

40. Drew Steis, "Interview with Françoise Yohalem—Art Consultant," *ArtCalendar*, May 1990, 4.

41. Carolyn Blakeslee, "Buying Ad Space in Artists' Sourcebooks," *ArtCalendar*, July/August 1991, 12.

42. Ibid.

43. From a press release for an exhibition entitled "A, E, Eye, O, U, and Sometimes Why," organized by the Organization of Independent Artists, curated by Deborah Gardner and Karen Loftus, 15 May–20 June 1980.

44. An exhibition held at Ronald Feldman Fine Arts, New York City, March 1981.

45. From a press release issued by Ronald Feldman Fine Arts, New York City, for an exhibition entitled "Top Secret: Inquiries into the Biomirror," March 1981.

46. Nina Pratt, *How to Sell Art: A Guide for Galleries, Art Dealers, Consultants, and Agents* (New York: Succotash Press, 1992), 6.

47. Ibid., 26.

48. Ibid.

49. Ivan C. Karp, "The Artist and the Dealer: A Curious Relationship," *Art in America*, March 1989, 51.

50. Ibid., 53.

51. Interview with Nancy Hoffman, "How to Succeed (By Really Trying)," by Paul Gardner, *ARTnews*, February 1990, 134.

52. Edward Feit, "Securing Gallery Representation," *American Artist*, Business Supplement, June 1989, 69.

53. Jana Jevnikar, "An Incredible Journey: The Search for a Gallery," *American Artist*, September 1983, 103.

54. Interview with Walter Wickiser, "Artists' Career Development," by Daniel Grant, *American Artist*, September 1989, 12.

55. Interview with Louise Bourgeois, "How to Succeed (By Really Trying)," by Paul Gardner, *ARTnews*, February 1990, 134.

56. Interview with Judy Levy in *Artists Observed*, edited and photographed by Harvey Stein (New York: Harry N. Abrams, Inc., 1986), 61.

57. Interview with Tony Delap in ibid., 70.

58. Interview with Nina Pratt, New York City, 1990.

59. Ibid.

60. Ibid.

61. Ibid.

62. Ibid.

63. Interview with André Emmerich in *The Art Dealers* by Laura de Coppet and Alan Jones (New York: Clarkson Potter, 1984), 62.

64. Grace Glueck, "Gallery Etiquette: A Duel of Dealers and Browsers," *The New York Times*, 8 March 1991, C1.

65. *Artists Gallery Guide for Chicago and the Illinois Region*, Chicago Artists' Coalition, 1990.

66. Hilton Kramer, "The Case Against Price Tags," *The New York Times*, 20 March 1988, Section II, 33.

67. Letter to the editor by Alvin S. Lane, *The New York Times*, 24 April 1988, Section II, 15.

68. Letter to the editor by Roy Bohon, *The New York Times*, 24 April 1988, Section II, 15.

69. Prepared by the Task Force on Discrimination in Art, a CETA Title VI project, sponsored by the Foundation for the Community of Artists in conjunction with Women in the Arts, 1979.

70. Nancy Jervis and Maureen Shild, "Survey of NYC Galleries Finds Discrimination," *Artworkers News*, April 1979, A7.

71. Ibid., A7–A8.

72. Ibid., A8.

73. Reprinted from *The Art Biz: The Covert World of Collectors, Dealers, Auction Houses, Museums, and Critics* by Alice Goldfarb Marquis, © 1991 (pp. 3–4). Used with permission of Contemporary Books, Inc., Chicago.

74. "Richard Lerner," interview by Jean E. Breitbart, *Artworkers News*, March 1981, 29.

75. "Lucy Lippard," interview by David Troy, *Artworkers News*, April 1980, 16.
76. Peter H. Karlen, "The 'Droit de Suite' Revisited," *ArtCalendar*, July/August 1991, 11.
77. Jane C. Hartwig, "Betting on Foundations," in *Foundation Grants to Individuals*, edited by C. M. Kurzig, J. B. Steinhoff, and A. Bonavoglia (New York: The Foundation Center, 1979), xiii.
78. Funding guidelines of the John F. and Anna Lee-Stacey Scholarship Fund.
79. Hartwig, op. cit.
80. Bruce M. Holly, "Choices," *ArtCalendar*, May 1990, 7.
81. Jane Madson, *The Artist's and Critic's Forum* 1, 1 (1982).
82. Billy Curmano, "Rejecting Rejection," *Artworkers News*, January 1981, 34.
83. Ibid.
84. Ibid.

Index

257